CLASSROOM SECOND LANGUAGE DEVELOPMENT

A study of classroom interaction and language acquisition

ROD ELLIS

Ealing College of Higher Education, Ealing, London

PERGAMON PRESS

Oxford · New York · Toronto · Sydney · Paris · Frankfurt

U.K.	Pergamon Press Ltd., Headington Hill Hall, Oxford OX3 0BW, England
U.S.A.	Pergamon Press Inc., Maxwell House, Fairview Park, Elmsford, New York 10523, U.S.A.
CANADA	Pergamon Press Canada Ltd., Suite 104, 150 Consumers Road, Willowdale, Ontario M2J 1P9, Canada
AUSTRALIA	Pergamon Press (Aust.) Pty. Ltd., P.O. Box 544, Potts Point, N.S.W. 2011, Australia
FRANCE	Pergamon Press SARL, 24 rue des Ecoles, 75240 Paris, Cedex 05, France
FEDERAL REPUBLIC OF GERMANY	Pergamon Press GmbH, Hammerweg 6, D-6242 Kronberg-Taunus, Federal Republic of Germany

First Edition 1984

Library of Congress Cataloging in Publication Data
Ellis, Rod.
Classroom second language development.
(Language teaching methodology series)
1. Language and languages—Study and teaching.
2. Language acquisition.
3. Communicative competence. I. Title. II. Series.
P53.E43   1984   418'.007'1   84–445

British Library Cataloguing in Publication Data
Ellis, Rod
Classroom second language development. —
(Language teaching methodology)
1.   Language and languages—Study and teaching
I. Title   II. Series
418'.007'1   P51
ISBN 0–08–031516–X

Printed in Great Britain by A. Wheaton & Co. Ltd., Exeter

To Goretti

Preface

LIKE so many second language (L2) acquisition researchers, I began life as a teacher of English as a second language. Like other language teachers in the 1960s and early 1970s, I was preoccupied with the techniques I could use to transmit a correct knowledge of English to my students. Although it was apparent to me that my students tended to reproduce certain types of error irrespective of the teaching I provided, I stuck to my teacher-centred view of things and went on providing more of the same. I assumed that if only I could get the teaching right, the students would learn. And learning meant avoiding the stigma of error.

My first awareness that 'good' audiolingual teaching might not be the best answer came from reading 'Error Analysis' edited by Jack Richards in 1974. This made me aware that the learner had his own way of doing things which could not easily be subverted by teaching. Recognising the importance of the learner's psycholinguistic processes, however, did not affect how I taught (or recommended others to teach). I still conceived of teaching as the transmission of linguistic knowledge. I think this was because, interesting though the learner's mental processes were, it was not clear to me how the teacher was to take account of them. In a way the 'mentalist' view of language learning presented in 'Error Analysis' did not seem to hold out much for the teacher, whose job it was to look after the 'input'.

At the end of the 70s I was engaged in some empirical research into the role that mothers' speech played in L1 acquisition. This was the single most important factor in changing my attitude about language teaching. It was clear that mothers were not trying to *teach* their children the language but merely trying to *communicate* with them as best they could. Somehow by communicating the children got to discover the rules of the language. It did not seem too far fetched to imagine that this happens in L2 acquisition as well and subsequent reading about L2 learners who picked up a knowledge of a L2 naturally gave support to such a view.

The question that I then asked myself was the obvious one: Could classroom learners of a L2 also 'pick up' a knowledge of a L2 if they were given the chance to communicate in it? And related to this question was a second: Was communicating in a L2 a more effective way for learners to master the L2 rule system than teaching it? I began to scour the published literature to try to discover answers to these questions. To my surprise I could find no studies of classroom L2 acquisition comparable to those of natural acquisition. There were various suggested answers to the questions but they were all speculative. Nobody had actually bothered to find out what classroom L2 acquisition was like.

This, then, was the starting point of three years of research that led to a doctoral thesis. This book is an attempt to make available in (what I hope is) an accessible form what I have found out about second language development in a classroom.

I would like to acknowledge the assistance and support of the following: the pupils and staff at Isleworth Language Unit (in particular Manny Velasquez), John Norris, students at St Mary's College who have reacted to and helped me to form many of my ideas and, most important, my family for their unwavering support.

Ealing College of Higher Education   ROD ELLIS

Contents

Chapter 1

Introduction:
Investigating Classroom
Second Language Development

What is 'classroom second language development'?

The focus of this book is the process of classroom second language development (SLD), as this is manifested in the discourse that occurs when language lessons are being taught. It needs to be emphasised from the beginning that this is *not* a book about language teaching, although many issues important for teaching a second language (L2) will be considered. It is a book about how learners come to know a L2 through participating in language lessons of one sort or another. As such, it seeks to bring together what is known about second language acquisition on the one hand and classroom interaction on the other. By so doing it is hoped that insight can be gained into the *process* of development.

It has been pointed out by Cook (1981) that there are potentially an indeterminate number of types of SLD as a result of the variety that exists in both learners and learning contexts. It is, however, both practically and theoretically desirable to identify a number of 'structural' types which can guide and shape enquiry. Wode (1980a) attempts just this. His list of 'acquisitional types' includes four which relate to SLD:

(1) Bilingualism or trilingualism, i.e. the concurrent acquisition of two or more languages.
(2) Naturalistic L2 acquisition, i.e. the non-simultaneous acquisition of a L2 without any formal instruction.

1

(3) Foreign language teaching, i.e. the L2 acquisition that occurs in the contexts providing formal instruction.
(4) Relearning a L2.

The principal distinction is between 'naturalistic' and 'classroom' development. However, as much SLD occurs in contexts that afford both natural and classroom exposure this distinction is often a blurred one. There is a continuum of types between the poles of 'naturalistic' and 'classroom'. The continuum cuts across the distinction traditionally made between 'foreign' and 'second' language teaching. 'Foreign' refers to environments where language study occurs as part of a wider curriculum and 'second' to language study that is complemented by some exposure to the target language (TL) outside the curriculum (Ellis and Tomlinson, 1980). The 'foreign/second' distinction, however, is not a useful one. Many learners studying the TL as a 'foreign' language may also come into outside contact with it at some time or another (if only by radio) while 'second' language learners may have almost no contact with communities for whom the TL is a language of wider communication (Swain, 1981). A better distinction, therefore is between 'pure' classroom SLD (where the learner is totally dependent on instruction) and 'impure' classroom SLD (where instruction is supplemented by varying degrees of general exposure). Most of the available studies of SLD are either of 'pure naturalistic' SLD or of 'impure classroom' SLD. But, as Felix (1981), has observed, to separate out the effects of natural mechanisms and formal language instruction, it is necessary to study naturalistic and classroom SLD in their 'pure' forms as far as possible.

The problem of identifying the precise nature of classroom SLD is compounded by the problem of determining the relevant data of this SLD type. Classroom learners are able to utilise different strategies for producing utterances in the TL. Wode (1980b) observes that they can memorise or imitate fairly long sequences of speech material, they can produce TL tokens for (or from) a rule that has been explicitly presented and they can also produce spontaneous speech in much the same way as occurs in naturalistic SLD. The problem is twofold; how can the data that result from one kind of strategy be distinguished from those which result from another and what is the relationship, if any, between the knowledge that underlies the use of these different strategies?

It would seem necessary to distinguish two basic kinds of data; 'modelled' data consisting of utterance tokens where the focus is on form and where the learner treats the target language as an object of study rather than as a means of communication and 'communicative' data consisting of utterance tokens where the focus is on meaning and where the language is being used to realise behavioral goals important to the learner. It is also possible to identify sub-categories of each type. 'Modelled' data can contain both 'rote-learned' utterances (i.e. where the learner has access to an utterance from short-term memory or as a 'gestalt' from long-term memory) and 'rule-constructed' utterances (i.e. where the learner makes use of an explicit rule to construct an utterance). 'Communicative' data can consist of 'rule-derived' utterances (i.e. where the learner utilises implicit rules from his 'creative' rule system) or 'improvised utterances' (i.e. where the learner employs compensatory communicative strategies to express a proposition for which he lacks creative rules).[1]* This categorisation of classroom language data is not easy to apply, however. Consider the following utterances, all produced by classroom learners in a classroom context:

(1) My name is John.
(2) These are snowmens.
(3) A bicycle no pedals.
(4) Foots no front walk.
(5) I don't know.

To which category does each utterance belong? There is nothing intrinsic in the form of each utterance to enable the researcher to make a decision. Only by inspecting both the situational context in which each utterance is produced and the other utterances produced by the same learners at this stage in their development is it possible to account for these utterances. Thus (1), which occurred in a drill-like sequence in which several pupils had already used the frame 'My name is _____' and (2), which occurred in a language drill practising utterances of the

---

*Superscript numbers refer to Notes at end of chapters.

form 'These + are + N (plural)' are probably examples of 'modelled' data, (1) being 'rote-learned' and (2) 'rule-constructed'. (3) occurred when the learner was describing a picture of a bicycle without any pedals and at a stage when many of the learner's spontaneous utterances omitted the verb 'have'. (4) also occurred when the learner was describing a picture, but differs from (3) in that it is entirely idiosyncratic in form. There are no other utterances like it in his corpus. (3) and (4), therefore, might be considered examples of 'communicative' data, (3) being 'rule-derived' and (4) 'improvised'. (5), however, is less easy to classify. The learner was clearly focused on meaning but the utterance was distinct in that other utterances at this stage did not contain either the auxiliary 'do' or the negator 'not'. Formulaic speech such as 'I don't know' seems to fall halfway between 'modelled' and 'communicative' speech. It is not easy to identify.

There is also the theoretical problem of deciding which types of data should serve as the basis for description and explanation in classroom SLD. The central question is this: What is the relationship between 'modelled' and 'communicative' data? Because a learner can correctly produce a grammatical feature in 'modelled' speech it does not follow that he will be able to do so in 'communicative' speech. What constitutes mastery of this feature? This is a vital theoretical and methodological issue in classroom SLD. The answer will determine whether *all* the available data or only certain kinds of data are used in accounts of development. The position adopted in this study of classroom SLD is that 'communicative' data are primary. This is partly because the learner reveals the state of his creative rule system most systematically in 'communicative' speech (Tarone, 1982), but there is a much more important reason. Language teaching typically seeks to equip the student with TL knowledge through 'modelled' speech so that this can be used in 'communicative' speech. The assumption is that by systematically planning the input of TL data, the learner will be helped to participate in everyday conversation. The test of the validity of this assumption requires an examination of 'communicative' data, therefore. This is not tantamount to assuming that classroom SLD is identical to naturalistic SLD, as the 'communicative' speech produced by classroom learners may or may not be the same as that produced by 'street' learners in naturalistic SLD. If 'communicative' data are deemed primary, classroom SLD research faces the problem of how to obtain sufficient data. Corder (1976) has elegantly expressed the compounded theoretical and methodological problem:

> . . . learners do not use their interlanguage very often in the classroom for what we call 'normal' or authentic communicative purposes. The greater part of interlanguage data in the classroom is produced as a result of formal exercises and bears the same relation to spontaneous communicative use of language as the practising of tennis strokes to playing tennis. (p. 68)

Whether or not 'classroom' SLD is distinct from 'naturalistic' SLD is an open question. There are a number of possible positions that will be examined. The first is that 'classroom' SLD is a particular kind of development constrained by the special nature of the interactions that take place in the classroom. If this proves the case then the *route* through which learners pass will be different in the two acquisitional types. The second position is that 'classroom' and 'naturalistic' SLD are more-or-less similar as the result of a socio-cognitive predisposition to process TL input in fixed ways. Evidence for this second position would be found if it could be shown that there was a 'natural order' of development which occurred in both acquisitional types. If this second position is adopted there are still potential differences between the types with regard to *rate* of development. 'Classroom' SLD may be either slower or faster than 'naturalistic' SLD. As will be seen in Chapter 7 many existing theories of SLD are *not* open to these various possibilities. They either ignore classroom SLD altogether or assume that it is identical to naturalistic SLD.

The neglect of classroom SLD

It may seem surprising to read that very little is known about how learners develop a knowledge of a L2 in the classroom. There are, however, a number of reasons why it is true.

The first reason is that classroom SLD has always been treated as an issue amenable to a logical rather than an empirical approach. Language development has been seen as the product of *what* is taught. It occurs most successfully and rapidly when the best description of the teaching content, optimally ordered and optimally taught, is used. There has been a continuing debate about how best the teaching content can be stated. This is reflected in the various discussions concerning the organisation of a language teaching syllabus, in particular whether to follow a notional or structural model (see Applied Linguistics, 2, 1981, for example). This 'curriculum-centred' approach (Altman, 1980) precludes any consideration of how SLD takes place in the classroom. It emphasises instead the importance of making the facts known to the learner. It is an approach that holds many attractions. In particular it enables the focus to be placed on the information about language made available by linguistics. One reason why classroom SLD has been neglected, then, is because of the importance attached to what linguistics has to offer as a basis for specifying *what* teachers should teach.

The second major reason why classroom SLD has been neglected concerns the recent history of language acquisition theory and research. The overriding commitment to a behaviourist account of language development in America and Western Europe up to the 1960s led to the conviction that language development was the product of stimulus–response links that were developed through imitation, practice and reinforcement.[2] Classroom SLD was treated as a known factor, despite the fact that there had been hardly any empirical study of language development in classrooms. Theorists were happy to extrapolate from general learning theory based on laboratory experiments with animals. The conviction that teaching and learning a second language in the classroom was a straightforward affair with no mystery is reflected in Rivers' (1964) comment:

A clear-cut viewpoint on the teaching of foreign languages has emerged and is being increasingly adopted in schools. The time has now come for a critical appraisal of this method in the light of the recent conclusions on the learning process. (p. v)

The 'clear-cut viewpoint' referred to by Rivers soon disappeared, however, largely as a result of the re-evaluation of behaviourist accounts of language development that followed Chomsky's (1959) critique of Skinner's 'Verbal Behaviour'. The theory that replaced it emphasised the learner's 'universal grammar' or 'language acquisition device' in first language development (FLD) and the 'built-in-syllabus' or 'interlanguage' in SLD[3]. There followed extensive empirical research in FLD, and following in its wake, SLD. In both cases the principal target of the research was to identify and describe the 'built-in-syllabus'. It might have been expected that the paradigm shift from behaviourist to mentalist, with the concurrent growth in concern for describing and explaining the course of language development would have led to a substantial interest in *classroom* SLD. This did not occur, however.

Chomsky's assertion that experience of language was very much the minor partner in the nature-nurture interaction determining the 'steady state' that eventually evolved was initially accepted. As a result, SLD was treated as a uniform phenomenon, relatively undifferentiated even by the effects of the learner's first language (L1). Thus, although the 1970s saw a growing body of empirical studies of SLD, this largely consisted of non-classroom SLD, even when the applied focus of the research was language teaching. Both mentalist and behaviourist paradigms resulted in a neglect of classroom SLD as a distinct acquisitional type.

This position is now undergoing revision, mainly as the result of a reappraisal of the role of experience in language development. Again FLD research led the way by demonstrating that the speech addressed to young children is not 'degenerate' as claimed by Chomsky but remarkably well-formed and, furthermore finely-tuned to the child's stage of development. An interest in the role 'motherese' played in FLD has led to a similar interest with 'foreigner-talk', and, where the classroom is involved, with 'teacher-talk'. This preparedness to recognise the role played by the linguistic environment has led to a differentiation of types of SLD. So the climate has been set for the detailed study of classroom SLD without any preconceptions regarding its similarity to or difference from other types.

Sources for classroom SLD research

Before the various sources that may provide information about classroom SLD are considered, it is important to look at a number of methodological problems. Although these are present in all types of SLD research they exist in a heightened form in classroom SLD.

Data-collection procedures are particularly problematic in a class-room context. As the above discussion of data types should have made clear, both information relating to the context of situation of each utterance and to the stage of development in which the utterance occurred is required in order to determine the data type to which each utterance belongs. Such information is more likely to become available in longitudinal case studies of individual learners than in cross-sectional studies, although the latter have predominated in classroom language research. Hatch (1978a) spells out the practical difficulties of case study research; observations need to be frequent because SLD can take place so rapidly, learners may opt for a listening strategy in the early stages so little actual language is produced and also the data is limited by the contexts that are investigated. These difficulties are greater in classroom SLD than in naturalistic SLD, of which Hatch writes. It is not easy to conduct a case study of an individual learner when this learner is immersed in a class of twenty or more such learners. Also the classroom learner typically produces little and what little he does produce is not easy to record as a result of the 'noise' problems attendant in any context involving groups of people. The data obtained is likely to be sparse and messy. It is perhaps not surprising, therefore, that, as Allwright (1977) has observed, 'the case study approach . . . has not typically been thought sensible for learners in class' (p. 1). The alternative to using naturally-occurring data produced in authentic classroom situations is to employ various elicitation devices. This has its own problems, the most serious of which is the representativeness of the data. There is ample evidence (Burmeister and Ufert, 1980; Chun, 1979; Larsen-Freeman, 1976; Lococo, 1976) to point to the existence of differential language processing systems which are reflected in different kinds of tasks used to elicit language. Despite the increasing evidence for variability as a product of task, there has been, as Tarone (1982) claims, an assumption that different kinds of data can provide access to the same 'built-in-syllabus'. It would seem essential that classroom SLD studies, like naturalistic studies, must at least complement experimental research utilising elicited data with longitudinal studies that collect authentic classroom data of various kinds.

Also problematic are data-processing procedures. Statistical procedures which seek to tabulate the frequencies with which different kinds of categories (grammatical, semantic, functional) occur in the data and then to interpret the frequencies in terms of whether each category can be said to have been mastered are difficult to apply to all SLD data. Again the problems of variability in the data, common to all SLD research, and of a paucity of 'communicative' data, acute in classroom SLD, are the source of difficulty. The lack of an index of development (Larsen-Freeman, 1978) serves to inhibit reliable comparisons between learners. Statistical procedures that rely on quantification of data are widely used in SLD research but cannot easily cope with the interactionist perspective (Cook, 1981) that is now recommended as a means of accounting for learner variability. Descriptive procedures, which seek to examine actual protocols of learner language in order to discover the pattern of development, may be more informative, at least in the initial stages of classroom SLD. They are open, however, to the criticisms that the observations provided are speculative and not generalisable. Nevertheless, much of the illustrative material offered in this book will be presented in this form.

The existing sources of information about SLD reflect the methodological difficulties discussed above. The informational lacuna is the result of both neglect of classroom SLD and the methodological problems that are heightened in this acquisitional type. In particular, because there have been few longitudinal studies, there is no detailed picture available of the development profile of classroom learners. Nevertheless there are a number of useful sources—three that offer direct information about classroom SLD and three others that offer information that may be of indirect value.

(1) *Error analysis*

Svartvik (1973) suggests the use of the term 'error analysis' to refer to the performance of language learners in pedagogic settings.

Typically this involves the collection of samples of classroom learner-language (usually written and usually discrete, decontextualised utterances), the classification of errors according to the different levels of language description, the explanation of errors by reference to various learning processes and the evaluation of errors for the purposes of assessment or remediation (see Corder, 1974, for a detailed account of this procedure). Error analyses that have followed this procedure offer lists of errors that groups of pupils are likely to produce (e.g. Richards, 1974). These lists, however, represent the *products* of the pupils' language development. Because they are collected out of context and at a single point in time, they throw little light on the *process* of development, which is the stated focus of this book.

(2) *Bilingual education research*

Bilingual education was advanced in Canada and the United States as an alternative to education programmes which submerge the L2 learner in classrooms where the TL was used as a native language. Cohen and Swain (1976) contrast the characteristics of submersion and immersion (i.e. bilingual) programmes, concluding that the latter have been more successful in promoting SLD. Cummins (1981) also argues that bilingual programmes result in faster SLD than submersion programmes, even when such programmes are supplemented with ESL. The nature of the research methods employed in the various studies of bilingual education, however, has precluded any investigation of the classroom interactions that occurred in the two kinds of programmes.[4] It is only possible to surmise, as does Krashen (1982), that immersion programmes provide more 'comprehensible input' than submersion programmes and so speed up to the process of development. Precisely *how* immersion programmes provide this facilitative input cannot be specified from the available resources.

(3) *Acquisitional studies of classroom SLD*

Studies that directly explore the nature of classroom SLD by looking at the developmental profile of learners are few and far between. They can be divided into two types—those that seek to discover what role, if any, formal instruction plays in SLD (e.g. Perkins and Larsen-Freeman, 1976) and those that compare classroom SLD with naturalistic SLD (e.g. Felix, 1981). Both are important issues for this book. Sources relating to both types will be dealt with in full in Chapters 2 and 6. The limitation of both types is that they fail to examine the actual discourse that classroom participants construct. As a result there is little in the way of explication of how and why SLD takes place.

(4) *Experimental method studies*

Experimental methods studies have typically attempted to compare the effects of different 'treatments' on proficiency levels achieved by different groups of pupils. Examples of such studies are Scherer and Wertheimer (1964) and Politzer and Weiss (undated). In the experimental design a pre-test was administered and then followed by separate methodological 'treatments' to a number of different groups of pupils. After a fixed period of time a post-test was given. The effects of the different pedagogic techniques were measured in terms of the differences on the pre- and post-tests. As Long (1980) has pointed out, it was characteristic of this kind of research that no attempt to investigate the events that took place in the classroom in the name of different 'treatments' was ever made. Typically, no observations of what went on in the classroom as part of the teaching provided were made. Thus with few exceptions (e.g. Smith, 1970) the possibility of variables derived from the quality and quantity of different kinds of interactions between teacher and pupils influencing the outcome that was measured was discounted.

(5) *Studies of 'naturalistic' language acquisition*

As explained earlier, the 1960s saw a growing volume of research into FLD and the 1970s a corresponding burgeoning of research into SLD, mainly the naturalistic and mixed types. This research has provided considerable insight into how both L1 and L2 learners develop the ability to produce correctly both a range of morphemes and the features of such sub-systems as negatives and interrogatives, and into the strategies that the learner employs. There still remains, of course, work to be done in plotting the developmental profile of complex syntactical structures but this is also under way (e.g. Schumann's, 1980, study of relative clause acquisition). Rather more neglected is semantic development (but see Ellis, 1982a). It is, of course, uncertain whether classroom and naturalistic SLD are the same or different, but until the latter is convincingly demonstrated the research referred to above must continue to serve as an important source of information about language development processes. This research provides a point of reference for classroom SLD studies.

(6) *Studies of language-learner discourse*

The reawakening of interest in the contribution of the linguistic environment to language development has led to input-studies of both the language addressed to L1 and L2 learners (e.g. Snow, 1976; Arthur *et al.* 1980) and interactional-studies that investigate the discourse that mature speakers and learners jointly construct (e.g. Scarcella and Higa, 1981; Wells *et al.*, (1979). There have also been some studies investigating the nature of input in the classroom (Henzl, 1979) and of classroom discourse (McTear, 1975). Ellis (1981a) has compared sample interactions between mother and child on the one hand and pupil and teacher on the other to show that they need not be so very different. If the net is widened further to consider source material that treats the nature of classroom interaction in general (Sinclair and Brazil, 1982) and the relationship between classroom interaction and learning of content subject material (Barnes *et al.*, 1969) there is a wealth of literature now available. All these studies are considered of central importance for the indirect light they shed on how classroom SLD might take place.

This discussion of the various sources available for studying classroom SLD suggests that for a book that intends to focus on explicating the *process* of development the more relevant sources are (3), (5) and (6). In contrast (1), (2) and (4) have little to say about what goes on in the classroom itself and how this contributes to development over time.

Classroom SLD as a process

The purpose of this book is the exploration of classroom SLD as a *process*. In what sense, then, can SLD be thought of as a 'process'? There are, in fact, three rather different senses in which the term 'process' can be usefully applied to SLD. These are considered separately below.

(1) *The developmental process*

When SLD is referred to as a process, recognition is given to the continuous pattern of development that occurs over time. This contrasts with viewing SLD as a 'product', which occurs when isolated learner utterances are examined without reference to the developmental state to which they belong. It is, of course, obvious that in order to describe the process of SLD it is necessary to look at the 'product' i.e. the utterances that learners actually produce. The important point, however, is that the products are treated as relative rather than absolute phenomena. It is the changes that occur from one point to the next that are important not the characteristics of utterances produced at a single point in time. In this sense, then, treating SLD as a process involves a diachronic rather than synchronic perspective. Thus from a process-orientation it is not possible to talk of 'errors', for each utterance produced is a 'correct' reflection of the learner's existing interlanguage system (or systems). Only from a product-orientation can overt comparisons between the utterances learners produce and the target language system be made and the resulting 'errors' described.

Longitudinal case-studies are typically process-oriented, whereas cross-sectional studies that seek to interpret the 'accuracy' order of selected grammatical morphemes that occur in utterances produced at a single point in time as an 'acquisition' order are product-oriented.[5] Error analyses are also product-oriented, as commented on earlier.

(2) *Process as interaction*

Language development is the result of an interaction between the learner's existing state of knowledge (linguistic and conceptual) and the linguistic environment to which he is exposed. There are many forms of possible exposure, but the most natural is conversation. This is a feature of both naturalistic and classroom SLD. It is by negotiating the exchange of meaning through conversation that the learner typically obtains information about the target language which enables him to revise his existing interlanguage system. Thus both the negotiation of conversation itself and the way in which this contributes to development must be seen in terms of 'process'. In this sense, an understanding of how discourse involving the learner is constructed is central to an understanding of SLD.

As an example of how the process of interaction influences SLD, consider the following extract from a classroom conversation between a teacher and a 10-year-old learner in the early stages of SLD.

(*Teacher and pupil are looking at and talking about pictures*)

T. Take a look at the next picture.

P. Box.

T. A box, yes.

P. A box banana.

The pupil's final utterance ('A box banana') is one of the first recorded examples of two-part utterances in his 'communicative' speech. This utterance appears to be the result of collaboration between teacher and pupil. The teacher begins by announcing a new picture, the pupil labels one of the referents in the picture using N, this is expanded into 'Det. + N' by the teacher's confirmation of the label, and finally the utterance is further expanded by the pupil himself into 'Det. + N + N'. The pupil's final utterance, therefore, is a 'vertical' construction, made possible by the process of building the discourse.

(3) *Process as mental operations*

By focusing on discourse involving the learner it is possible to identify in fairly precise terms how the linguistic environment contributes to development. This, however, is not the whole picture. There is still the need for explanation of the hidden, mental processes that operate.

Traditionally, a distinction is made between two kinds of mental processes in SLD. First, there are those involved in the internalisation of new linguistic knowledge. Faerch and Kaspar (1980) refer to these as 'processes of IL (interlanguage) formation'. They account for both how the learner constructs hypotheses about the IL system and also how he tests them out. Second, there are those involved in L2 performance, referred to by Faerch and Kaspar as 'realisation processes'. These account for how the learner utilises his available L2 knowledge in receiving and producing messages in the target language. They operate by enabling the learner to meet a particular goal by setting up a plan on the basis of his linguistic system and his assessment of the situation before selecting items and rules to go into the plan. All these processes are only open to study by inspecting the language the learner produces in communication. Mental processes, then, can only be inferred from the interpersonal processes referred to in (2).

Ultimately, a full account of classroom SLD will require both a description of the developmental process, (1), and an explanation of this in terms of interactional and mental processes, (2) and (3). What are the stages of development through which classroom learners pass? In what ways do interactions in the classroom contribute to development? What mental processes are involved in discourse participation and how do these guide development? It is these questions that the subsequent chapters try to answer.

An outline of the rest of the book

The account of classroom SLD provided by this book draws extensively on the case studies of three classroom learners (Ellis, 1982b) learning English as a L2 in a special withdrawal unit for ESL secondary school pupils in a London borough. The purpose of the book, however, is not to report exclusively on these case studies. It is to build up a picture of what is currently known about classroom SLD and its relationship to naturalistic SLD by examining relevant qualitative research, as discussed on p. 12. It must be emphasised, however, that because there is little direct information about classroom SLD, this book is to be seen as an initial exploration of the nature of classroom SLD. The tremendous variety of environmental conditions to be found in language classrooms and the differences in the kinds of learners that learn a L2 in the classroom means that any generalisations must inevitably be tentative.

The following three chapters examine how classroom learners develop a competence in L2 English. The chapter after this looks at the different kinds of interactions that take place in a language classroom and their possible relationship to SLD. Together these chapters provide the basis for considering the role of instruction in classroom SLD, developing an initial theory of classroom SLD and examining the implications for teaching.

Chapter 2 looks at the development of grammatical competence in classroom learners. Three areas of grammar are considered—negation, interrogation and verb morphology. The acquisition of each of these areas is described and compared to the order of acquisition reported for naturalistic learners. In general, the orders are the same, suggesting that the processes responsible for acquisition inside the classroom are similar to those outside.

Chapter 3 considers a neglected area of SLD research—semantic development. It illustrates the way in which three classroom learners reduce the propositional content of their communicative speech by omitting case categories such as agent and dative. This eases the processing burden and enables them to communicate messages that are beyond their actual linguistic competence. It is suggested that this kind of 'semantic simplification' is a universal phenomenon, as it occurs in the speech of L1 learners of naturalistic L2 learners and in pidgins as well as in the language of at least some classroom learners. It constitutes further evidence that classroom SLD involves universal learning processes.

Chapter 4 looks at formulaic speech (i.e. utterances learnt and used as wholes rather than derived from a set of creative rules), as this is used in an ESL classroom. Case studies of naturalistic L2 learners have demonstrated that formulaic speech plays an important part in early SLD. This chapter shows that in ESL classrooms where there is the opportunity or need to use language communicatively, formulaic speech is also prevalent.

In Chapter 5 the classroom is viewed as a special type of language learning situation in which different types of interaction involving the pupils and the teacher take place. A framework is provided for describing these various interactions, and an attempt made to suggest which types are more likely to promote SLD. It is argued that although naturalistic and classroom settings are very different they share certain key interactional features which may be important for SLD.

Chapter 6 addresses the role that formal instruction plays in SLD. A range of research relevant to this issue is reviewed. However, because of the complexity of the issue—'instruction' can vary in an indefinite number of ways, while learners also differ on a host of individual learner variables—it is difficult to reach a firm conclusion. The available evidence indicates that formal instruction does not strongly influence the route of SLD. Whether it influences the rate is also not clear, but seems more likely.

Chapter 7 attempts to draw together the various threads of the argument in the form of a set of hypotheses about classroom SLD. The basis of the theory is the distinction between 'planned' and 'unplanned discourse'. It is argued that participation in these two types of discourse involves different discourse processes. Learner performance is variable as a result of the discourse processes utilised to take part in different types of discourse. Mastery of the processes involved in 'planned discourse' does not directly help the classroom learner participate in 'unplanned discourse'. The learner needs to experience the natural communicative uses of language in order to develop the processes associated with 'unplanned discourse'. Because 'unplanned discourse' is seen as primary it is the discourse process linked to this type of communication which needs to be developed. It is argued that the distinction between 'planned' and 'unplanned discourse' can account for the available data more convincingly than other theories of SLD, in particular Krashen's Monitor Model.

In the final chapter the implications for teaching of the view of classroom SLD developed throughout the book are considered. These implications are traced with regard to policy, approach, syllabus design and material production and also with regard to the actual practice of classroom teaching. The main argument is that L2 teaching needs to place greater emphasis on ensuring that the learners have the opportunity to take part in 'unplanned discourse', although it is also important to continue to cater for 'planned discourse' as this may help the learner to store up knowledge which can later be activated in spontaneous communication.

Summary

Classroom SLD is a particular type of SLD. It is likely to be characterised by 'modelled data' where the learner is focused on form and 'communicative data' where he is focused on meaning. In examining how learners develop a knowledge of a L2 in the classroom it is important to separate the two kinds of data. 'Communicative data' are to be considered as primary because they represent the kind of performance that occurs in everyday speech.

Classroom SLD has been neglected. In particular there are few studies of the *process* of learning. Most of the research involving classroom learners has been quantitative, consisting of error analyses of the products of language use or correlational studies involving measures of L2 proficiency. The focus of this book is firmly on the qualitative study of how classroom learners acquire a L2 by participating in classroom discourse.

A full account of classroom SLD is not possible at the moment. This book represents a start. It seeks to compare the pattern of development observed in some classroom learners with that observed in naturalistic language learning (both first and second), to analyse how classroom interaction might contribute to development and to posit an initial theory of classroom SLD. Finally, implications for teaching are considered.

Notes

1. Selinker (1972) refers to communicative strategies as one of the processes responsible for interlanguage. A number of typologies have since been developed (e.g. Faerch and Kaspar, 1980; Tarone *et al.*, 1976). Examples of compensatory communicative strategies are 'lexical paraphrase', 'circumlocution' and 'request for assistance'.
2. See for instance Lado (1964) and Brooks (1960). The behaviourist view of SLD was reflected in the Contrastive Analysis Hypothesis, which in its strong form (Wardhaugh (1970) stated that all learner errors derived from the transfer of L1 patterns into the L2).

3. Chomsky argued that the child comes equipped with a set of very ge
which can be found in all natural languages, and a set of discovery rules
out how the innate universal rules are realised in the language he is tryin
Together these constitute his 'language acquisition device'. Chomsky's
language acquisition were applied to SLD, where the term 'interlanguage' was
coined (Selinker, 1972) to refer to the transitional systems which characterise the
learner's progress towards the target language. The term 'built-in-syllabus' was used
by Corder (1967) to refer to the hypothetical immutable order of development
through which L2 learners pass.

4. The procedure used in this research consisted of obtaining measures of the learners'
proficiency in the L2 by means of tests or teacher grades and then establishing
statistically what relationship there is between these measures and independent
variables such as aptitude, motivation and age. In this kind of research, therefore,
the classroom remains a 'black box' (Long, 1980) as no attempt is made to examine
what happens inside it.

5. In order to determine 'accuracy orders' the following procedure is followed. (1) A
list of the formal features to be investigated is drawn up; (2) the corpus of learner
utterances is inspected to isolate all the 'obligatory occasions' for each formal
feature (i.e. those contexts that require the use of each formal feature); (3) the
percentage of occasions on which each formal feature is correctly used is calculated;
(4) the formal features are ranked according to how accurately they were used. This
order is then equated with an 'acquisitional order' (see Burt and Dulay, 1980, for
a full account of the methodology).

Chapter 2
Developing Grammatical Competence in the Classroom

THIS chapter is the first of three that seeks to describe classroom second language development. It will focus on the development of grammatical competence, or, more specifically, the development of a small set of grammatical sub-systems, which have been selected to facilitate comparison between naturalistic and classroom SLD. All three sub-systems have been extensively investigated in naturalistic SLD. The main aim of the chapter is, therefore, to consider in what ways, if any, classroom SLD differs from naturalistic SLD.

Different general theories of SLD give rise to different predictions regarding the relationship between structured and unstructured language learning. These predictions can be divided into two groups: (1) those that claim that SLD is a universal process which reflects innate properties of the human mind (i.e. those that take up a 'similarity' position) and (2) those that potentially, at least, distinguish SLD types on the basis of the learner's adaptations to different linguistic environments (i.e. those that take up a 'difference' position). An example of a theory that supports a similarity position is the 'creative construction' model of SLD proposed by Dulay and Burt (1978). This emphasises the learner-internal factors which contribute to learning and argues that the process of acquisition is the result of innate mechanisms which operate more-or-less independently of input factors. SLD is seen as a 'natural' process which is not influenced by the linguistic environment. An example of a theory that supports a difference position is the discourse model of SLD proposed by Hatch (1978b). According to this theory the order of grammatical development is the result of the types of conversations which learners

21

typically take part in. These are constrained by the learner's limited L2 resources. The input provided by the native-speaker under these conditions is restricted, with the result that certain grammatical forms are used more frequently than others. It is the frequency of forms in the input which governs the order of grammatical development. Although the discourse model has been propounded with regard to naturalistic SLD only, it follows that where the natural frequency of input forms is disturbed, as is likely to be the case in classroom discourse, a different order of development will emerge.

It is an implicit assumption of much language teaching that formal instruction can influence both the route and rate of SLD by manipulating the linguistic environment. It is, therefore, of central interest to discover whether the kinds of linguistic environments found in classrooms do or do not influence the pattern of development.

The effect that the classroom has on SLD has been examined chiefly by means of correlational studies of the amount of classroom exposure different learners have received and their level of TL proficiency. Examples of such studies have been reviewed by Krashen (1982b). Brière (1978) found that attendance at a village school was one of the best predictors of the acquisition of Spanish as a L2 by Mexican children, aged 4 to 12 years. Fathman (1975), however, found that children enrolled in English-medium schools in Washington, did not appear to benefit from ESL classes, a finding also supported by Hale and Brudar's (1970) study of immigrant adolescents in Hawaiian junior high schools. Krashen explains the different results that these studies report in terms of the availability of naturalistic exposure to the TL. When learners have access to comprehensible input outside the classroom (i.e. either in the wider school community or outside the school), the classroom has little effect on their development. But when the only source of input is the classroom itself, instruction can play a part. However different interpretations of the research Krashen considered are possible. Long (1983) re-examines all the studies closely in an attempt to show that even in those studies which claimed that teaching had no effect, it is in fact possible to show that formal instruction aided development. Long concludes:

For SLD theory and SL educators alike, on the basis of currently available studies, an answer to the question 'Does SL instruction make a difference?' is a not-so-tentative 'Yes'. (p. 380)

Differences in opinion such as those between Krashen and Long are perhaps to be expected in interpreting quantitative studies.

Correlational studies like the ones referred to above are useful for investigating the relationship between formal instruction and SLD. They can shed no light on whether the *process* of SLD is substantially affected by the linguistic environment. The issue that Krashen examines—what role formal instruction plays in SLD—is theoretically separate from the primary issue of whether classroom SLD is to be treated as a separate acquisitional type. The two issues need to be ordered; first, *what* is classroom SLD? and second, *why* is it like it is? If it can be demonstrated that classroom SLD does constitute a discrete type, the answer can then by sought in the nature of classroom interactions, particularly those derived from formal instruction. On the other hand, if it can be shown that classroom SLD is essentially identical to naturalistic SLD, any consideration of the role of formal instruction will be restricted to how it influences the *rate* of development. The primary need is for a sound descriptive base about the *route* through which classroom learners pass. Without this, the relationship between teaching and learning will remain a matter of speculation.

A thorough search of the literature reveals very few studies of classroom learners that examine the *process* of development. In fact, there are only three which provide longitudinal evidence (Ellis, 1982b; Felix, 1981; and Lightbown, 1983). Despite the reasons for the neglect of classroom SLD (see Chapter 1), it remains surprising that there have been so few longitudinal studies of the route that classroom learners follow. Inevitably with so small a corpus of research to draw upon, this chapter can do more than suggest an answer to the central question that has been posed.

The procedure that will be followed will be first to describe the subjects and the data-base of the three studies. This will be followed by an account of the developmental profile of the classroom learners on each of the three grammatical sub-systems to be investigated. This profile will be compared with that reported for naturalistic SLD. A number of tentative conclusions will then be drawn and some questions posed to direct future enquiry.

Subjects and data

(1) *Felix's study*

Felix's study is part of the Kiel Project on Language Acquisition which has as its main object the comparative analysis of different types of SLD. It seeks to discover how different learning situations influence the processes of development.

Felix (1981) reports on an eight month study of 34 (19 female and 15 male) L2 learners of English in a first-year class of a German high school. The pupils were aged 10 to 11 years. The pupils received one 45 minute period of English teaching for five days a week. All the lessons were audio-recorded.

Apart from in the classroom, the pupils did not receive any notable exposure to English (pop music excepted). Felix emphasises that the learning situation is 'totally dissimilar to what is usually reported by most other L2 studies' (p. 90). The nature of the linguistic environment provided by the classroom is described as follows:

> There was hardly any room for spontaneous utterances; in their (i.e. the pupils') verbal productions students were expected to strictly conform to the type of pattern presented by the teacher. Errors were immediately and consistently corrected, and any spontaneous verbal attempts which deviated from the intended pattern were immediately blocked by the teacher. (p. 90)

The linguistic environment provided by this classroom, therefore, can be thought of as a fairly traditional one.

In analysing the data Felix apparently makes no attempt to distinguish different types of speech. Indeed, judging from his account of the kind of teaching that took place, there could have been hardly any 'communicative' data (see Chapter 1). For negatives, Felix notes that there were only two spontaneous utterances in the first three weeks. Felix's study, therefore, examines predominantly 'modelled' data.

(2) *Ellis's study*

Ellis' study was undertaken as part of the research for a doctoral thesis that sought to investigate the nature of classroom discourse processes and their role in SLD.

Ellis examined three L2 learners of English in Britain. They were aged 10–13 years and at the beginning of the study were all complete beginners. One of the pupils (a boy) spoke Portuguese as his L1, the other two (a boy and girl) spoke Punjabi. The Portuguese boy was literate in his L1 and to a more limited extent so was the girl in Urdu. The Punjabi-speaking boy, however, was not only illiterate but had had very little prior experience of classrooms before coming to Britain. Examples of the speech they produced in classroom contexts were collected over a two-year period, principally by a paper-and-pencil method, although there were also some audio recordings.

It is not possible to claim that these pupils did not receive any exposure to English outside the classroom. The Portuguese boy almost certainly did from an early date. He may best be considered a 'mixed' learner, therefore. However, the two Punjabi-speaking children were firmly enclosed in their own community (i.e. experienced acute 'social distance') and so were almost entirely reliant on the classroom for exposure to English, particularly in the early stages.

The three children all attended a Language Unit in southwest London. This catered for full and part-time withdrawal of L2 pupils from local secondary schools. The linguistic environment constituted by the Unit is obviously very different to that reported in Felix's study. First, English was not only taught as a subject but also used as a medium of instruction both inside the classroom and in the wider school framework. English functioned as a lingua-franca among pupils with different L1s. In the case of the Punjabi-speaking children, however, there was little evidence of any use of English in non-classroom situations, as they spent all their time within a social group that used Punjabi exclusively for communication. Second, the approach to language teaching was less traditional than in Felix's study; although there were plenty of examples of formal language instruction there were also opportunities for using English more spontaneously in activity sessions involving physical education, cooking and handicraft. Later, there were attempts to use English to teach other school subjects, in particular maths. As a result, the data include plenty of examples of 'communicative' as well as 'modelled' speech.

(3) *Lightbown's study*

The study by Lightbown was part of a larger research project involving both cross-sectional and longitudinal approaches used to trace the development of English by French-speaking students in Quebec. Lightbown emphasises that with few exceptions the students had few contacts with English outside the clsssroom. In all there were 75 students studied in Grade 6 but only 36 were followed through Grades 7 and 8. They were aged 11–14 years and they had all started English in Grade 4.

The students appear to have been exposed to teaching that was fairly formal. They had 80–120 minutes of English per week in Grades 4, 5 and 6, when they used 'Look, Listen and Learn' (Alexander and Dugas, 1972–3) and approximately 200 minutes per week in Grade 7, when they used Book 1 of the Lado English Series. Lightbown does not describe all the teachers, but observes that the Grade 6 teacher used French during the English lessons.

Unlike Felix and Ellis, Lightbown collected speech data outside the classroom by recording an oral communication game played between individual students and an interviewer. Each student played the game three times—once in Grade 6 (April) and twice in Grade 7 (December and May). The principal aim of the game was to elicit spontaneous speech. The data can be considered 'communicative', therefore.

A comparison of the subjects and data used in the three studies reveals some similarities and some differences. In all three studies the subjects are in the 10 + age range. The type of teaching the students were exposed to in the Felix and Lightbown studies appears to have been predominantly audio-lingual in style, but although the students in Ellis's study were also taught in this way they were also exposed to teaching where the focus was on meaning rather than form. The students in Felix's and Lightbown's studies shared a common language—German or French respectively—but those in Ellis's study needed to use the L2 as a lingua franca in the classroom and school. In terms of the distinction between 'pure' and 'impure' classroom (see Chapter 1) Felix's classroom was 'pure', Lightbown's more-or-less 'pure' but Ellis's somewhat less so. Ellis and Felix collected data from within the classroom; Lightbown collected it outside. However, despite the differences, these three studies provide a picture of how classroom learners develop grammatical competence. In all three studies the focus is on the qualitative study of classroom language development.

In the following account of grammatical development, the Ellis and Felix studies will be used to report on transitional constructions (i.e. negatives and interrogatives) and the Ellis and Lightbown studies to examine verb morphology.[1]

Transitional constructions

The first two-grammatical sub-systems were investigated by Ellis and Felix. They are examples of what have been called 'transitional constructions', defined by Dulay, Burt and Krashen (1982) as 'language forms learners use while they are still learning the grammar of a language' (p. 121). As the label suggests, transitional constructions reveal information about the progress learners make in internalising the rule system of a L2. For this reason they are well-suited to the task of describing the *process* of classroom SLD. It should be pointed out, however, that as existing studies of naturalistic language development point to striking similarities in FLD and SLD in transitional structures, there may be strong *a priori* reasons for predicting that this aspect of grammatical competence is not very sensitive to environmental differences. The two types of transitional structures that were investigated are negatives and interrogatives. These are considered separately below.

(1) *Negatives*

Studies of negative acquisition in naturalistic SLD have found a very similar profile to that reported for FLD by Klima and Bellugi (1966). Learners typically begin by using external negation in Stage I (i.e. the negative operator is attached either to the beginning or end of the utterance). They then progress to internal negation in Stage II, often first in copula sentences and later in main verb sentences (Wode, 1980b) and finally to internal negation involving a full range of auxiliary verbs that are correctly inflected for number and tense in Stage III. There is also a developmental pattern in the use of negative particles; 'no' first, then 'not' and finally unanalysed 'don't'.

There is little evidence of L1 transfer in the naturalistic acquisition of negatives. Milon (1974) reports almost none. However, Wode (1976) and Ravem (1968) identify a stage where German and Norwegian children learning English place the negative particle after the main verb (i.e. 'John go not to school') by analogy with the pattern in their L1s. Also Cazden et al. (1975) suggest that their Spanish subjects start by transferring the common negative pattern in Spanish (i.e. 'no + V') but their examples for Stage I have exact parallels in both studies on non-Spanish (L1) learners and in FLD.

Nearly all the naturalistic studies report tremendous variability in learner performance. Thus the stages referred to above do not comprise discrete developmental stages but points on a developmental continuum. Cazden et al. (1975) devised a procedure for coping with the descriptive problems posed by this variability. They catalogued the various negative devices used by their subjects and then calculated the proportion of each type in each subject's corpus at the separate data collection points. The developmental profile they report, therefore, consists of a shifting pattern of the dominance of the various devices from sample to sample. It should be emphasised, however, that despite variability there is almost total agreement that all naturalistic learners gradually progress through the three stages described above.

It is not so easy to plot the profile of development of negatives in classroom SLD because of the different types of data that are to be found (see Chapter 1). There are two possible approaches. One is to examine the data to see whether there are any utterances that resemble those produced by naturalistic learners for each of the three stages. The other is to examine only the learners 'communicative' speech in order to determine the characteristics of those negative utterances which the learner produces, when he is not focusing on form. Because of the nature of their respective data, Felix concentrated on the first of these approaches and Ellis on the second.

Table 1 shows that both Felix's German learners of English as a foreign language and Ellis's learners of English as a second language produced utterances that correspond to the three stages identified by Klima and Bellugi. Felix reports that the first negative particle to be taught was 'no' in elliptic sentences (e.g. no, it isn't). The pupils had no difficulty in using 'no' as an external negator but were unable to use affirmative or negative elliptic sentences until the third month, despite extensive drilling. Main verb sentence negation was taught in the second half of the school year. Despite lengthy explanation of the grammatical principles of tense and number marking, 48% of the utterances that the pupils produced under drill conditions were not well-formed. A typical incorrect utterance involved the random use of 'don't' or 'doesn't' placed in sentence initial position (i.e. as in external negation) in the statements the children produced as answers to the teacher's questions. Felix suggests that the children were unable to simultaneously handle the placement and inflection rules and frequently resorted to the same strategy evident in external negation in naturalistic SLD. He also suggests that the pupils treated 'don't' or 'doesn't' as monomorphemic variants of 'not' and 'no'.

Felix's analysis shows that even in 'modelled' classroom speech, learners frequently fail to produce well-formed negative utterances and instead resort to utterances that are identical in form to those produced by naturalistic learners. Although Felix does not draw attention to the fact, there are some features of his reported data that suggest that classroom SLD may differ from naturalistic SLD. The most obvious is that the majority of the pupils' utterances were in fact well-formed. This is in stark contrast to the data provided by Wode (1976), Milon (1974) and Cazden et al. (1975). Another feature is that as early as the third month the classroom learners appear to have reached a high level of accuracy in elliptic sentences, although, as Felix notes, this is generally one of the last aspects of negatives to be acquired naturalistically. It could be argued, therefore, that Felix's data provided evidence that in classroom SLD there are two kinds of processes at work—those also observed in naturalistic SLD and others, which are

TABLE 1
A Comparison of Negative Utterances Produced by Naturalistic and Classroom L2 Learners

Stage (Klima and Bellugi)	Naturalistic SLD (Wode, 1976)	Classroom SLD Felix (1981)	Ellis (1982)
Stage I Negative particle occurs external to rest of the sentence	no no, you no play baseball	no, I can no, it isn't doesn't she eat apples don't I like cake	no red, no no very good no sir finish
Stage II Negative particle occurs internal to rest of sentence, but is limited to 'no', 'not', 'don't'.	that's no good John go not to the school lunch is no ready	it's no my comb Britta no this .. no have .. this You doesn't[a] drink a cup of tea	here's no colour I'm no drawing chu??? You don't play is not pull it out somebody not driving with this
Stage III Negative particle now realised with full range of correctly formed auxiliaries.	I cannot hit the ball I didn't can close it Don't tell nobody.	(Pupils reported to have produced examples but none given)	this man can't read (= single example in 1st year; produced by Portuguese speaker)

[a]At this stage 'don't' and 'doesn't' were used in free variation.

the result of attending to form. However, because Felix's pupils produced almost no 'communicative' speech, it is impossible to tell whether the 'natural' developmental profile was influenced by practising negative utterances that would normally only be produced in Stage III. The two 'spontaneous' utterances Felix quotes (see Stage II in Table 1) suggest that this is not the case.

Ellis's study focused entirely on the 'communicative' negative utterances produced by the three learners. Figure 5 shows the development of the two Punjabi-speaking pupils' (R = the boy; T = the girl)[2] negative utterances over the first year of the study (divided into 7 equal periods). Three aspects of development were analysed. The first was the use of a verb in negative utterances. This was investigated because many of the children's early negative utterances were verbless. Before the children could progress into Stage II and III they needed to be able to incorporate verbs into their utterances. The second aspect was internal negation. The third was the use of the negative operator 'not' (i.e. rather than 'no').

The developmental profile that emerges for these two children is more-or-less identical to that observed in naturalistic SLD, despite the fact that negative patterns (including elliptic sentences) were formally taught at various points during the year. Initially negative utterances consist of anaphoric negation (i.e. 'no' by itself or 'no' + a separate statement). This is followed by a stage where there is external negation, first in verbless utterances and later in utterances containing a verb. As utterances containing a verb become more common, so too does internal negation. Also there is a gradual change from the use of 'no' to 'not'. It is evident that these children relied entirely on the same processes that characterise the development of negatives in naturalistic SLD. The only noticeable difference may lie in the use of the negative operator, as neither of the children made more than occasional use of 'don't'.

Figure 1 shows that the development of negatives by the two children is very slow. Neither of the children has begun Stage III by the end of the first school year. Indeed, it was not until period 6 that a majority of the boy's utterances displayed internal negation and not until period 7 that the girl's did so. Thus in one school year the children had only barely reached Stage II.

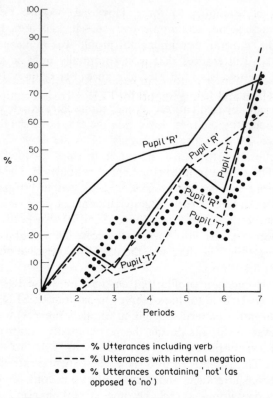

% Utterances including verb
---- % Utterances with internal negation
•••• % Utterances containing 'not' (as opposed to 'no')

FIG. 1. The classroom development of negatives by two pupils.

(2) *Interrogatives*

Interrogatives have been almost as well researched in FLD and naturalistic SLD as negatives. Once again Klima and Bellugi's (1966) study has served as a reference point. They identify three developmental stages in FLD. In Stage I children use intonation questions (i.e. declarative word order spoken with a rising intonation) and a number of WH routines (e.g. What(s) this?). In Stage II intonation questions continue but have a fuller sentence structure and WH questions become productive, usually for 'what' and 'where' first. Stage III is concurrent with considerable grammatical development; inversion appears in yes/no questions but not in WH questions. Later developments involve inversion in WH questions and embedded WH questions (e.g. He asked what my name was?).

It is also possible to identify a fairly reliable sequence for the development of interrogatives in naturalistic SLD. This is very similar to what Klima and Bellugi report for FLD. Here is a composite picture of naturalistic SLD for interrogatives based on a number of different studies:

(1) There may be an early non-communicative stage, when the learner simply repeats the question that someone has asked him (Huang and Hatch, 1978).

(2) Intonation questions are the first communicative use of interrogatives (Adams, 1978; Butterworth and Hatch, 1978; Huang and Hatch, 1978). Initially these may be memorised wholes derived from (1). The first creative questions of this type are likely to be telegraphic and propositionally reduced.

(3) At approximately the same time as (2) or slightly later WH questions appear as formulae (Cazden et al., 1975; Huang and Hatch, 1973).

(4) WH pronouns are used productively with a declarative nucleus (Adams, 1978; Ravem, 1974). More-or-less concurrently, inversion occurs in yes/no questions with modals but this may also be formulaic. 'Can' questions do not go through a non-inverted stage (Huang and Hatch, 1978).

(5) Inversion now occurs in both yes/no and WH questions. There are examples of main verb inversion (e.g. Know you?) in some studies (e.g. Wode, 1978) but in others this is absent (e.g. Adams, 1978). The copula is inverted more regularly in WH questions. In yes/no questions it is often omitted altogether (Adams, 1978). 'Be' inversion precedes 'do' inversion.

(6) Embedded questions begin to appear, often with inversion initially.

Felix found evidence of utterances that belong to the early stages of development in the corpus of the German classroom learners. During the first two weeks 21% of yes/no questions were declaratives with rising intonation:

e.g. This is flag?
    It's big shoe?

Felix notes that during the same period the teacher did not once use an intonation question himself, suggesting that the learners were applying natural processing strategies. Intonation questions continued for about two months, but then ceased to appear. The first WH questions produced by the children also lacked inversion:

e.g. What they are picking?
    How many turkeys she is feeding?

In a two-and-a-half-week period 43% of WH questions were uninverted.

The same points can be made about Felix's study of interrogatives as were made about his study of negatives. There is clear evidence of the kind of processing that occurs in naturalistic SLD. Equally, there is evidence that the children can produce questions which more closely resemble the TL forms by using alternative strategies. Felix draws attention to these in his observation that for a period of five to six weeks the students did not always distinguish yes/no and WH questions in their answers, a phenomenon that occurs in FLD (e.g. Felix, 1980) but is not reported on in naturalistic SLD. In general, however, it is difficult to establish a clear developmental profile because of Felix's failure to separate 'communicative' and 'modelled' data.

Ellis again sets out to identify the developmental route through which the three children in his study passed by considering only their 'communicative' utterances. Again only the results relating to the two Punjabi-speaking children will be reported. Figure 2 shows their development of interrogative utterances over their first four terms at the Language Unit (divided into 10 equal periods). The three aspects of development which were analysed were: (1) the use of declarative utterances with rising intonation (i.e. intonation questions); (2) the presence or absence of the main verb in an interrogative utterance; and (3) inversion of subject and verb in all interrogative utterances.

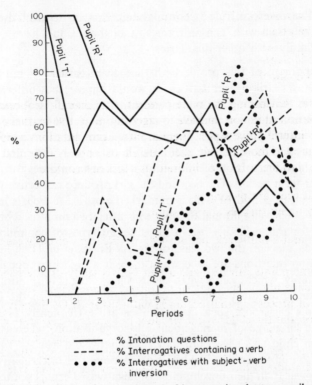

% Intonation questions
% Interrogatives containing a verb
% Interrogatives with subject - verb inversion

FIG. 2. The classroom development of interrogatives by two pupils.

A fairly clear pattern of development emerges. This can be summarised as follows:

(1) Imitation (i.e. the pupil repeats the teacher's question).
(2) Intonation questions only—these are initially verbless.
(3) Routines—both WH questions (e.g. What's this?) and yes/no questions (e.g. Can I have . . .?) occur.
(4) Creative WH and yes/no questions—both types occur more-or-less simultaneously, although there are very few of the latter. WH questions appear first as single words (e.g. Where?), then as uninverted but more fully-formed questions and then, as previous routines are analysed, as inverted questions.

(5) The inversion rule is consolidated, first in interrogatives with 'be', then with 'can' in frames other than 'Can I have . . .?' and finally with other auxiliaries.

A comparison of this profile with that given earlier for naturalistic SLD shows striking similarities. It would appear that differences in linguistic environment do not affect the overall sequence. The differences that do appear have to do with the relative frequency of the various interrogative types. There are few examples of inverted yes/no questions and those that do occur are almost entirely restricted to 'be'. Also a high proportion of intonation questions continues throughout the four-term period. The boy and the girl produce respectively 34.8% and 36.4% in period 10. This is in marked contrast to Felix's learners, who stopped using intonation questions after two months. The explanation for this probably lies in the different types of communication that took place in the two classrooms. As Brook *et al.* (1980) observe intonation questions are used when there is a high presupposition of a 'yes' reply, which occurs when the user is seeking confirmation about something previously stated or contextually implied. In the Punjabi children's classroom such opportunities arose frequently as English was the language of management and organisation, whereas in the German children's classroom they presumably did not.

The Punjabi-speaking children's development of interrogatives was even slower than their development of negatives. There is not the rapid spread of 'new' forms across a range of syntactic types that is one of the recorded characteristics of naturalistic SLD. Thus, for instance, whereas the gap between 'be' and 'do' inversion is not usually a large one in naturalistic development, it is considerable for these learners. Their slowness may be the product of an environment where the intonation question is a communicative requisite. The absence of any need to use information-seeking questions, which was apparent in the two children, may explain why they are in no hurry to incorporate the more complex characteristics of interrogatives into their interlanguages.

Verb morphology

Verb morphology was investigated by Ellis and Lightbown. An analysis is included here in order to make a partial comparison with the results of the morpheme studies in naturalistic SLA (e.g. Bailey *et al.*, 1974; Dulay and Burt, 1972; Krashen *et al.*, 1978). These studies were all cross-sectional but by equating 'accuracy order' with 'acquisitional order' (see Chapter 1, note 5) a developmental profile was provided.

In Ellis's study the verb morphemes that were analysed were the copula, the auxiliary 'be' and the past tense. The same method was used as in the naturalistic studies, namely the context of occurrence of a specific item was treated as 'a kind of test item' (Brown, 1973) which was passed or failed according to whether the required morpheme is supplied. In this way, the percentage of correct occurrences of each feature was calculated in relation to the total number of obligatory contexts. In cross-sectional studies this procedure has led to an 'accuracy order' by ranking the scores obtained on each morpheme; in longitudinal studies the point of 'acquisition' has been defined as the month when the learner reaches a 90% criterion of correctness for the third consecutive month. Table 2 compares the results of three naturalistic studies (one longitudinal and two cross-sectional) and of Ellis's study of the four morphemes. The development of the verb phrase, therefore, appears to follow the same route in naturalistic and classroom SLD. The basic principle seems to be that bound morphemes (e.g. past tense) are developed later than free morphemes (e.g. copula and aux-be) as Wode (1980b) has observed.

TABLE 2
A Comparison of the SLD of Four Verb Morphemes in Naturalistic and Classroom SLD

Dulay and Burt (1974)— mixed cross-sectional	Hakuta (1974)— naturalistic longitudinal	Rosansky (1976)— naturalistic longitudinal	Ellis (1982b)— classroom longitudinal
Copula	Copula	Copula	Copula
Aux—Be	Aux—Be	Aux—Be	Aux—Be
Past Reg.[3]	Past Irreg.[3]	Past Irreg. ⎫[3]	Past Reg.[3]
Past Irreg.	Past Reg.	Past Reg. ⎭	Past Irreg.

In Ellis's study only the Portuguese boy reached 90% criterion level on the copula after four terms. The Punjabi-speaking boy reached 76%

and the girl 71%. For aux-be the Portuguese boy reached 81%, the Punjabi-speaking boy 59% and the girl 69%. The scores for both regular and irregular past tense were very low—in the case of the two Punjabi-speaking pupils only a few, mainly regular forms were evident. It was not until several months had passed that any of the children even made an attempt to refer to a past event, i.e. initially no obligatory occasions occurred. It may be that the kinds of communicative contexts calling for spontaneous, creative speech in the ESL classroom do not typically involve reference to past events. This, combined with the inherent complexity of past tense morphology in English may account for the quite remarkable slowness of development.

The verb morphemes investigated by Lightbown were the copula, auxiliary-be, -ing and 3rd person singular. Lightbown found that the overall accuracy order of these morphemes was different from that reported in the naturalistic morpheme studies. Figure 3 compares Krashen's (1977) proposed 'natural' order for these morphemes with Lightbown's order. This difference was the result of a far lower accuracy with regard to -ing in the French-speaking classroom learners. When Lightbown investigated the use of -ing longitudinally she found that there was a sharp decrease in both the accuracy and frequency of use from Grade 6 to Grade 7. Whereas the Grade 6 students preferred the -ing form (e.g. 'He's taking a cake'), the Grade 7 students preferred an uninflected verb form (e.g. 'He's take a cake').

Lightbown argues that in a natural setting learners might be expected to use the uninflected verb form in the earliest stage of

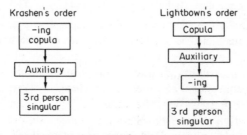

FIG. 3. Comparison of Krashen's proposed natural order for four verb morphemes with Lightbown's order.

development and then add grammatical markers such as -ing gradually. In the classroom, however, this pattern may be disturbed if a later form (such as -*ing*) is 'overlearned'. Although Lightbown can find no evidence of any relationship between the frequency of -ing in the input made available to the students in the classroom and the accuracy/frequency of -ing in the students' speech in Grade 6, she observes that the preference for -ing shown by the Grade 6 students may have been the result of frequent exposure to it in Grade 5. In other words the effect of the input is a delayed one. The decline in frequency and corresponding rise in the frequency of the uninflected form in Standard 7 may have been the result of a similar pattern in the input language in Grade 6. If Lightbown is right, then some aspects of grammatical competence may be susceptible to influence by the linguistic environment of the classroom. However, Lightbown believes that the 'natural' order will eventually reassert itself (i.e. 'overlearning' will have to be overcome).

Some conclusions

This chapter has sought to investigate whether the classroom situation influences the developmental route through which L2 learners pass. It is conceivable that it might do so in two ways. First, formal instruction in grammatical structures that are normally acquired late on in naturalistic SLD might lead to these structures being mastered much earlier. Second, the type of interactions that occur in the classroom may differ, if not in absolute terms, at least relatively and this might also affect the order of development, perhaps by altering the frequency of specific grammatical items in the input made available to the learners. Implicit in the first possibility is the assumption that those processes responsible for naturalistic SLD are not the only processes that can be used to develop grammatical competence in a L2. Implicit in the second possibility is the assumption that a single set of processing mechanisms will operate differently when fed different information. An alternative to the 'difference' position, however, is the 'similarity' position. Classroom SLD may follow a more-or-less identical route to naturalistic SLD either because there are universal processes of language learning that operate irrespective of differences in the linguistic environment or because classroom discourse provides similar opportunities for language development to naturalistic discourse.

The results of three studies of classroom SLD (Ellis, 1982b; Felix, 1981; Lightbown, 1983) have been summarised to show the effects of a structured setting on different groups of 10–13 year old students. It must be emphasised that these studies do not provide sufficient evidence to reach a firm conclusion regarding the similarity or difference between classroom and naturalistic SLD, even for the particular age group investigated. However, two tentative conclusions can be ventured. The first is that in language classrooms where there is little opportunity for spontaneous speech in the L2 (as was the case in the classrooms of Felix's and Lightbown's studies), children aged 10+ years appear to fall back on natural processes, when asked to produce structures that appear late in naturalistic SLD. As a result they produce utterances that are identical in form to these produced by 'street' learners. The second conclusion is that teaching may have a very limited effect on the order of development of at least some grammatical features. This may be more likely in classrooms where the overall orientation is towards the form of the L2. Ellis found that his learners followed an almost identical developmental route in their 'communicative' speech to that reported for naturalistic SLD for both transitional constructions and verb morphology, despite the fact that they received formal instruction in these areas. However, Lightbown found that French-speaking ESL students may have been influenced by the special linguistic environment of the classroom; one verb morpheme (-ing) was learnt earlier than would be expected in naturalistic SLD because of the 'overlearning' which resulted from frequent exposure to this form. However, the effects of this 'overlearning' were short-lived and the 'natural' form reasserted itself in the learners' L2 system. The main difference between Ellis's and Lightbown's study is that in the former there may have been more many more opportunities for normal patterns of communication (see Chapter 5). In general, the picture which emerges from these three studies is that learners rely on natural processing mechanisms, which in the long run cannot be short-circuited by manipulating the linguistic environment of the classroom.

It has been pointed out in Chapter 1 that classroom learners produce both 'modelled' and 'communicative' speech in differing degrees depending on the nature of the linguistic environment provided. What is the relationship between these two types of speech? Where the *route* of SLD is concerned it does not appear that what learners do in their modelled speech carries over into their communicative speech. Classroom learners do not find it any easier to handle late-appearing structures than do other kinds of learners. Felix suggests that when they are asked to do so in modelled speech they are likely to fall back on two basic strategies; they either resort to a random selection of any one structure from a repertoire that has been memorised but not incorporated into the interlanguage system or to the processes involved in naturalistic acquisition. The first strategy leads to utterances that are unique to classroom SLD (e.g. Doesn't she eat apples.) and the second to utterances which will also be found in naturalistic SLD. It would seem, therefore, that far from the processes responsible for modelled data intruding on those responsible for communicative data, the reverse is more likely. However, where particular forms are concerned—such as the -ing verb form—constant use in modelled speech may have an effect on communicative speech, although the natural order will ultimately reimpose itself (i.e. the form derived from modelled speech will fall out of use until it reappears in its natural position). It is also possible that other forms found in naturalistic SLD (e.g. 'don't' used as a monomorphemic marker of negation) may not appear in classroom SLD as a result of differences in the input. In general, however, the communicative data produced by classroom learners do not differ from those produced by naturalistic learners, suggesting that similar processes are involved in both acquisitional types and that these processes cannot be supplanted except in relatively minor ways by those processes involved in modelled data.

It is still possible, however, that availability of modelled data facilitates the *rate* of classroom SLD, perhaps by sensitising learners to language forms, which can then be more easily processed at a later date. The fact that Felix's children succeeded in mastering elliptic sentences by the third month—remarkably early in terms of naturalistic SLD—might be taken as evidence of this. However, Felix's children presumably learnt to control production of elliptic sentences in modelled speech and there is no data available to demonstrate whether this mastery stretched to their communicative speech. Ellis's children were slow learners, particularly the two Punjabi speaking children. One explanation for this could be that because they were socially distanced (Schumann, 1978) they did not seek input and were not open to that which was provided. Another explanation is that the nature of classroom communication restricts the kinds of processes required to develop grammatical competence and so slows down development. The very late development of past tense morphemes—apparent even in the Portuguese boy—may be a reflection of the fact that much classroom interaction is rooted in the here-and-now and so does not require past time reference. Similarly the predominance of intonation questions may be the result of the importance of procedural functions (which typically are realised by means of intonation questions) in classroom interaction. The evidence from the three studies considered in this chapter, however, does not make it clear whether rate of development is favourably or adversely affected by classroom settings.

Before a clear picture of classroom SLD can be drawn it is necessary to conduct a series of studies such as those by Felix, Ellis and Lightbown, involving detailed investigation of both whole classes and also individual classroom learners. There are a number of variables whose effects need to be investigated:

—age; children vs adolescents vs adults;
—type of grammatical structure (it is possible, for instance that the effects of overlearning are only felt on a limited range of linguistic forms such as -ing;
—type of classroom environment; communicative vs structured;
—individual variables; motivation, personality, cognitive style etc.

Not until information is available about different grammatical structures produced by different learners under different classroom conditions will it be possible to draw up a profile of the classroom learner as has been done for the naturalistic learner.

Notes

1. Felix investigated two other grammatical features; sentence types and pronouns. During the first three weeks the pupils were confronted with three distinct sentence types (NP + be + NP/PP; There + be + NP; Pronoun + can + V + NP), which they confused in 24% of their answers, producing errors peculiar to classroom SLD. 63% of all pronouns the pupils used were incorrectly chosen, despite the possibility of transferring L1 German knowledge. When left to their own devices, the pupils avoided pronouns as much as possible, otherwise they followed the teacher's model (i.e. used a pronoun if the teacher did so). Lightbown also investigated noun morphology. She found that the students' plural accuracy was lower than in other morpheme studies and suggested that this could be explained by the fact that in L1 French the s is silent in pronunciation. She also found that the students avoided the inflected possessive in favour of the periphrastic possessive (e.g. 'the dress of the girl' was preferred to 'the girl's dress'). This can also be explained in terms of L1 transfer.

2. The Portuguese boy was excluded from this analysis on the grounds that he was more of a 'mixed' than a 'pure' classroom learner. In fact his profile of development was broadly similar to that of the Punjabi-speaking children with the exception of 'don't', which the Portuguese boy made more extensive use of. Also he produced utterances with internal negative (e.g. 'Me no ruler') from the first weeks.

3. Reported differences in the order of past regular and past irregular may not amount to much. Some learners initially make use of only a limited number of highly frequent irregular verbs and thus are computed to have developed the past irregular first. Other learners employ a fuller range of verbs and are computed to have developed the past regular first. Which form of the past tense is developed first, therefore, may simply reflect which verbs are used.

Chapter 3
Semantic Development in the Classroom

SLD research has focused almost exclusively on the acquisition of grammar. This is in marked contrast to FLD research, which, taking its lead from the work of Lois Bloom (1970) and Roger Brown (1973), has increasingly recognised the importance of studying semantic development in order to account for the whole process of acquisition. Roger Brown writes:

> ... the semantic approaches have made salient the continuities of development which the Chomsky approach made it easy for all of us to overlook. (p. 243)

In particular, the early 'telegraphic' stages of FLD appear to be most convincingly explained in semantic terms.

The difficulty for SLD research lies in the assumption that because semantic relations such as 'agent', 'object' and 'locative' are thought to be universal, there is no need for the learner to rediscover them when learning a L2. He already has access to them in his L1 and so merely needs to find out how they are realised in the L2. From this perspective the difference between FLD and SLD lies in the greater cognitive maturity of the L2 learner (see Rosansky, 1975, for a detailed discussion of this difference). As a result, where SLD research has considered semantic features, it has concerned itself predominantly with the acquisition of the language specific meanings associated with various lexical and morphological systems (e.g. Strick, 1980, investigated the development of the meanings associated with address terms; Heilenmann, 1981, looked at the meanings of a number of

45

inflectional items in SLD). There have been few studies of how universal semantic roles are developed in SLD.

In fact, the assumed difference between FLD and SLD may not exist. Cognitive psychologists of the Piagetian school have suggested that language arises out of the child's sensorimotor schema. Sinclair de Zwart (1973), for instance, proposes that the child 'brings to the task of acquiring his mother tongue a set of universal cognitive strategies, which have been built up during the first year of life' (p. 11). He illustrates how early language behaviour draws on the child's existing motor knowledge of how people and objects are related. Similar statements have been made by Wells (1974) and Bates (1976). It would appear, therefore, that the child also has prior access to semantic relations, which he represents through actions or perceptual systems. It would seem learning the L1 does not entail the simultaneous acquisition of semantic roles, as these have already been developed and are available to the learner in other forms of representation. FLD involves recognising how the enactive and iconic systems of representation can be recoded linguistically. The L2 learner is potentially in exactly the same position as the L1 learner in so far that it is possible they both have to discover how actions and objects in the real world can be represented linguistically. Two distinct hypotheses present themselves:

(1) SLD commences, like FLD, with the learner discovering how objects, states and events, their interrelationships and their predicates, which he already knows non-linguistically, are represented in the target language.

(2) SLD commences with the learner transferring his knowledge of how to represent semantic roles and relations from his L1 to the L2.

This chapter will examine the evidence for the first of these hypotheses. It will begin by looking at how the process of semantic development works in FLD and naturalistic SLD. Then it will try to show that the same process can also operate in classroom SLD by considering the early speech of the two Punjabi-speaking children referred to in the previous chapter. A final section considers the role of semantic simplification in SLD.

Early semantic development in FLD

The basis of early developmental progression is cognitive. It can best be understood in terms of Fillmore's (1968) case grammar which draws a distinction between the propositional and modality components of a grammar.[1] Whereas the propositional meanings are seen as conceptual (i.e. rooted in general cognitive abilities), the modality meanings (e.g. past and present time, definite and indefinite reference, necessity, possibility, alienable and inalienable possession) are both language specific and language determined. Thus it is possible to treat Fillmore's propositional case categories as amodal, capable of coding not only sentences but the action sequences to which the sentences refer.

FLD is characterised by an initial stage where propositional development takes place. During this stage the child 'operates . . . as if grammatical morphemes were optional' (Roger Brown, 1973, p. 245), and his utterances typically consist of strings of words, which have no 'grammar' but are simply linguistic realisations of semantic propositions. Here is a list of utterances taken from the speech of a 2-year-old child (see Ellis, 1982b) which are indicative of the kind of 'raw' propositions that children produce at this stage:

Utterance	Context
Lie down Lwindi	She was about to lie down.
Want pussy Lwindi	She was chasing the cat.
Milk	She was moving towards a cup of milk she wanted.
Lwindi pullover on	She was trying to put a pullover on.
Lwindi crying.	She had stopped crying a few minutes ago.
Daddy write	Her father was writing down what she was saying.
Giving doggy bone	She was looking at a picture of a butcher giving a dog a bone.
Cutting meat	Her mother was fetching a knife to cut up the meat on her plate.
Daddy down.	She wanted her daddy to put her down.
Falling down	She had nearly fallen off her chair but had just stopped herself.

The child makes no attempt to mark these utterances for tense, aspect or mood or even to modify the propositions adverbially. She also produces utterances that do not conform to the grammatical order in adult speech (e.g. lie down Lwindi). This lack of a defined word order in early L1 speech has also been commented on by Felix (1978). Apparently the child is encoding the elements of action sequences in the order in which she perceives them.

The cognitive basis of FLD has been most fully described by Greenfield and Smith (1976):

> Children might use the context of real-world events as a structured framework which could gradually be filled in with verbal forms. (p. 30)

They conducted an analysis of two children's single word utterances. They suggest that these utterances consist of two major components; an 'event', which can be represented wholly or in part by non-verbal elements and is realised as a number of entities, and a 'modality' which can also be represented non-verbally (e.g. by pointing) and which reflects the child's relation to the event. Children interpret situational events in terms of entities (i.e. point-at-able objects) and relations (i.e. the actions, operations, states that an entity can undergo). Language development in the first place is the steady accretion of semantic elements that the child is able to encode.

The various semantic rules and relations that Greenfield and Smith were able to identify appear in a definite order. To begin with the children's utterances were 'performatives' (i.e. the action was performed in the act of uttering). Next utterances with an indicative function appeared followed by utterances with a volitional function.[2] The children also referred to their own actions before they referred to those of other agents, but they expressed other people as agents before themselves. With regard to actions (i.e. verbs), those involving a change of state (action-processes) were encoded before those involving a constant state (state-processes). Relationships involving possession and habitual location were late to appear.

Brown (1973) carried out a similar analysis of children's two word utterances. Below is the frequency order of semantic relations in the two-word utterances produced by three children acquiring English as a mother tongue (based on Table 22 on p. 174). In fact, the first three

Two-term relations	Example	Frequency ranking for 3 children
Action and object	Hear horn	1
Possessor and possessed	Adam belt	2
Agent action	Adam write	3
Entity and attribute	Big dog	4
Demonstrative and entity	This dog	5
Agent and object	Eve lunch	6
Entity and locative	Pictures in there	7
Action and locative	Write paper	8

relations (action-object, possessor-possessed, and agent-action) accounted for the vast majority of utterances that the children produced.

In the early stages of development, when the child is restricted to one-, two- or three-term relations, it is obvious that he is not able to encode in language all the roles present in a situational event. It is necessary, therefore, for him to select which one(s) to encode. Greenfield and Smith suggest that the child chooses one particular semantic element (in one-word utterances) to stand in relation to the other non-verbalised semantic roles on the basis of the principle of informativeness. The element that is encoded is that which contains the greatest uncertainty from the child-speaker's point of view. They suggest that this procedure is analogous to the procedures that the adult uses in producing single word responses to WH questions; only the 'new' information is provided. It may be wrong to overemphasise the regularity of the principle of informativeness, however. Brown observes that the child's omissions in the two and three word stages are not always 'lawful'. He notes that the child seems to expect to be understood if he produces any appropriate word at all.

The process of propositional reduction is a very powerful and a very useful one. It is powerful because it enables the child to communicate propositions of far greater complexity than he can produce. Imagine a situational event consisting of the following elements:

(daddy) (eat) (porridge) (spoon)

which an adult might realise as:

Daddy is eating his porridge with a spoon.

The child might be able to communicate the fact that he is thinking about this event by encoding any one of the semantic roles that constitute it, although he is more likely to succeed if he chooses (spoon) or (porridge) than (daddy), which might be taken as realising a simple indicative intent. The child's message is the product not just of the word(s) he speaks but of the other situated elements that are implied by the use of language in context. The process is a useful one because it may help the child to increase his linguistic competence. This can happen in two possible ways. First, the production of propositionally-reduced utterances slowly enables the child to automatise increasingly long utterances and so frees his channel capacity to attend to 'modality' elements. Second, his propositionally reduced utterances are frequently expanded by a caring adult. Roger Brown (p. 105) gives these examples:

Child utterance	Mother's expansions
Mommy sandwich	Mommy'll have a sandwich.
Throw Daddy	Throw it to Daddy.
Eve lunch	Eve is having lunch.
Pick glove	Pick the glove up.

There is increasing evidence that parental utterances that extend discourse in this way may facilitate rapid development (Cross, 1977; Ellis and Wells, 1980).

Semantic development in naturalistic SLD

There are only two studies that examine early semantic development in the speech of L2 learners. Otherwise, as has been already noted, interest in semantic development is restricted to language specific features associated with the modality component of grammar.

Hernandez-Chavez (1977) investigated a three year old Spanish boy's acquisition of English in an English-speaking day care centre. He noticed that the basic semantic relations were learnt before various markers of modality. Equational sentences types appeared first, followed by imperative and indicative types in that order. Early equational sentences consisted of a subject together with a verbless predicate. The first verbs appear in imperatives, as did objects and locatives. The first subject–verb combinations appeared in indicative utterances. Hernandez-Chavez emphasises that although a particular category (e.g. noun phrase) might be available to a child it was not immediately distributed over the full range of semantic relations under his control. In other words, the development of syntax and semantic relations did not go hand in hand.

Hernandez-Chavez argues that the child does not make use of the semantic structure of his L1 in developing English but instead systematically develops the relations of the L2 from scratch. He suggests the L2 learners 'must learn which (semantic) functions the second language expresses before they can learn *how* to express them' (p. 143; his emphasis). Such a view implies that linguistic propositional meaning is separate from the nonlinguistic conceptual system. Thus Hernandez-Chavez does not give consideration to the possibility that the L2 learner has immediate access to the underlying semantic relations of the target language through his knowledge of how situational events are structured.

In the second study of semantic development Pienemann (1980)[3] investigated three eight-year-old Italian girls' acquisition of German in Germany. One of the girls acquired the L2 very slowly making it possible to describe the early stages in some detail. For several weeks this girl's speech consisted entirely of one-constituent utterances. However, Pienemann argues that this one-word stage is not analogous with FLD, as it reflected a communication strategy; the child used its knowledge of 'dialogue' rules to give elliptical answers to questions by omitting those constituents that occurred in the preceding utterance. Subsequent development involved the successive emergence of subject + verb, subject + verb + locative and subject + verb + object. Many of the utterances quoted by Pienemann display the same kind of propositional reduction found in the speech of L1 learners:

ich italienier   (I am Italian)
ein junge ball weg   (A boy threw the ball away)
ein mädchen bier   (A girl brought some beer)
zwei kinder   (There are two children)

The children's sentences followed an almost invariable order:

NP + V (NP) (PP) (PP)

Pienemann suggests that this order may reflect the natural structure for speech perception and production and that it serves as the basis for the development of syntax. This is in contrast to FLD, where, as has been observed earlier, the ordering of elements is variable.

These studies give grounds for thinking that the early stages of naturalistic SLD may not be so different from FLD. Both acquisitional types are characterised by propositional reduction and by the steady accretion of semantic roles in multi-constituent utterances. There are, however, differences between SLD and FLD. L2 learners adhere to a fixed word order (an observation also made by Felix, 1978) and the initial one-word stage may be the result of a discourse strategy. Accurate comparisons between SLD and FLD are difficult to make, however, because neither of the two studies reported above makes use of the 'rich' categorisation made possible by case-grammar approach such as that undertaken by Brown and Greenfield and Smith. Ellis (1982a), however, has attempted to apply Fillmore's case categories to the speech produced by a 10-year-old Portuguese boy learning English. This 'mixed' learner (i.e. part naturalistic, part classroom) produced utterances that were very 'telegraphic'. They included few modality elements in the first few months and were also propositionally reduced. They could be described very effectively using case-grammar catego-ries. Ellis suggests that the process of 'semantic simplification', which this learner uses, is an outstanding characteristic of early SLD. This process is considered in detail in the final section.

Semantic development in classroom SLD

In this section the early speech of the two Punjabi-speaking pupils described in the previous chapter will be examined in order to establish to what extent the types of semantic development evident in FLD and less certainly in naturalistic SLD can also be found in classroom SLD. Only the children's 'communicative' speech which was freely 'created' will be considered. Thus both 'modelled' speech and formulaic speech is excluded on the grounds that they exploit alternative processes of production. There is a marked difference between early 'creative' speech and speech that is derived either as a 'gestalt' or from the application of some explicit rule. Consider the following examples taken from Ellis (1982a):

'Creative' speech:
    me no blue   (I don't have a blue crayon)
    you milkman   (Do you need a milkman?)
    me breaktime   (I'm leaving because it's breaktime)

'Modelled' or 'formulaic' speech
    my name is John
    you all leave it please
    I don't know

Whereas this learner's 'creative' utterances were spontaneously produced and are subject to substantial propositional reduction, his 'modelled' and 'formulaic' utterances occurred in response to a frequently-observed situation or to a specific demand by the teacher to produce a particular kind of utterance.

In order to analyse the propositional structure of the two Punjabi-speaking children's utterances, the following framework (slightly adapted from that of Greenfield and Dent, 1980) was used:

A. Arguments

(1) Agent (Ag): animate instigator of an action-process
(2) Object (O): inanimate entity affected by the action-process
(3) Dative (D): animate entity affected by the action process or state process. This can refer to a recipient, beneficiary, possessor or experiencer of a perception.
(4) Locative (L): location or spatial orientation of the action or state process.

B. Predicates

(5) Action-Process (AP): the action which is performed by the agent and affects an object.

(6) State-Process (SP): the static or dynamic condition influencing an object or dative.
(7) Property of Object (PO): state or condition of the object.
(8) Locative State (LS): state of object which results from locative action or state process.

As an example of the descriptive power of this system consider the following example:

(1) Phoc has a toy gun and is pointing it at R, who has put his hands up into the air. The teacher asks R why he has just put his hands up. R points at Phoc and says 'Gun'.

The proposition which R constructs by means of his one-word utterance, his gesture and the situational elements can be represented in the form of a tree diagram, where Ø represents elements that are situationally available but not verbally encoded, M refers to the 'mime' used by R and 'gun' his actual utterance:

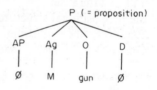

The complete proposition represented by the diagram is 'Phoc is pointing a gun at me'.

Table 3 shows the utterances and the weeks in which each of the above semantic roles first appears in the creative speech of the boy (R) and the girl (T). There is a high degree of similarity in the developmental profiles of the two children. For the first two weeks there were no spontaneous, creative utterances. The two children either kept silent or occasionally repeated a word from the utterance addressed to them, using a discourse strategy similar to that noticed by Pienemann (1980). The first semantic roles to appear in the children's creative speech were Action-Process and Property of Object. This is probably a reflection of the communicative values of these two roles in the

TABLE 3

First Occurrences of Semantic Functions in the Creative Utterances of Two Classroom L2 Learners.

Semantic function	R Utterance	Context	Week	T Utterance	Context	Week
Agent	You writing	Describing action of another pupil	8	Finish Baljit?	Asking if her friend had finished her work	6
Object	Sir sir pencil	Teacher had taken his pencil	3	A small square	Requesting a shape from the teacher	3
Dative	Show me ruler on the board	Asking the teacher to identify word on blackboard	7	Lakbir blue	Describing colour of a girl's dress	6
Locative	You here	Telling a pupil where to sit	7	Me house	Telling the teacher she lived in a house	6
Action-Process	Sir, kick	Telling the teacher a boy had just kicked him	3	Sir, writing?	Wanting to know if she needed to write	3
State-Process	I have no pen	The teacher had told him to get his pen	8	Cold	Teacher had asked what was wrong with another pupil	6
Property of Object	Small circle	Requesting shape from teacher	3	A small square	Requesting a shape from the teacher	3
Locative state	Ruler on the board	Telling another pupil where word was	7	Eating at school	Another pupil has said she never ate meat	10

classroom, where it is more important to identify the action than, say, the agent (which is situationally self-evident) and some attribute of an object which will enable the hearer to distinguish it from other, similar objects that are contiguous. The Object role also occurs early, however;

one of the main functions of classroom communication is to obtain the necessary tools to perform an activity the teacher has nominated (i.e. pencils, rubbers, rulers, crayons etc.). Later occurring roles include both Agent and Dative, which in surface grammar typically occupy the subject position in sentences. These roles are potentially less important for 'survival' communication in the classroom. The State-Process role also occurs late; this is most frequently realised by the copula ('be') and is often deleted in various types of simplified speech (see Ferguson, 1971), probably because it conveys little propositional information. Locative State is realised initially by 'here' in R's speech and only later by more complex forms such as prepositional phrases, when he is able to process three-constituent utterances:

Two children sitting on the floor.
Girl sitting on the settee.
Track (= traffic) is on the road.
(Week 11).

The general order of semantic development evident in the two children's creative speech is broadly similar to that reported by Greenfield and Smith for FLD. This is also true for some of the details e.g. Agents are first used to refer to other people rather than the speaker himself.

A few examples will help to illustrate the way in which the two learners exploit the context of interaction to supplement their meagre lexical resources in the first few months:

(2) The pupil sitting next to R has just kicked him. R attracts the teacher's attention, points to the pupil and says, 'Sir, kick'.

In this instance it is the Action-Process that is encoded as the event referred to took place in the past; because the Agent and the Dative of the event are still physically present, the greatest uncertainty is in the Action-Process itself.

(3) The teacher is discussing the eating of meat. The pupil sitting next to T explains that T doesn't eat any meat. T, dissenting, says, 'No, eating at school'.

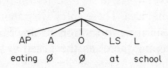

This example differs from the previous two in that the 'given' information derives from the verbal rather than the situational context. The two elements T chooses not to encode are just those present in the preceding utterance.

The process of propositional reduction is evident in the vast majority of the two learner's early creative utterances. It is an extremely powerful process, as it allows the learners to construct relatively elaborate propositions with limited linguistic resources and poorly developed production capacity. This is, perhaps, most clearly illustrated by the way that once a given role is mastered it rapidly spreads across utterance types as the learner seeks to maximise its communicative potential. For instance, in week 10 R uses 'here' to express the Locative role in a marvellously condensed utterance:

(4) The teacher is operating a tape-recorder. R points at the girl sitting next to him and then at the tape-recorder and says 'You here'. The teacher took this as a suggestion that he should tape-record the girl.

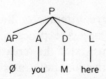

Slightly later in the same lesson the following message occurs:

(5) The pupils are in the process of getting seated. R looks at the pupil next to him and points at a chair. He says, 'You here'.

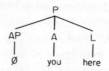

A little later he adjusts the proposition to describe where he himself is going to sit by keeping 'here' as the Locative and introducing an Object role:

(6) As he sits down R says, 'My seat here'.

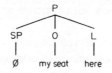

There then ensues a sequence where the teacher is trying to establish why R has not got a pencil. R cannot explain. But shortly afterwards T comes into the room.

(7) R suddenly stands up and points at T. He shouts out 'My pencil here'.

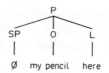

This sequence of Locative utterances illustrates what Widdowson (1979a) has called 'the language processing ability of the learner' (p. 249). Initially this consists of the 'creative construction' of utterances in context through the manipulation of configurations of semantic roles in conjunction with situational information. In the space of a lesson R demonstrates his ability to use 'here' in a range of utterances and contexts. It appears with various other case roles and finally (i.e. (7)) is used as an alternative to the possessor function which R has not yet developed.

It is apparent from these examples that it is the principle of informativeness that guides the learners in the choice of which roles to encode. This is also evident in an analysis of the frequency with which the various semantic roles were encoded in the children's speech. Table 4 gives the proportions of five of the semantic roles that R and T encoded and left unencoded in their creative utterances produced during their first 12 weeks in the classroom. The analysis is restricted to five roles because for the others it was not possible to establish 'obligatory occasions'. Those semantic cases that appeared early in the speech of the two children are also those that are frequently encoded, while those cases that appeared late are often left unencoded.

TABLE 4
Proportions of Coded and Unencoded Semantic Roles in Two Children's Creative Speech.

| Semantic | R | | T | |
function	Coded	Not coded	Coded	Not coded
Agent	31.6	69.4	36.4	63.6
Dative	47.6	53.4	444.4	55.6
Object	76.7	23.3	68.8	31.2
Action-Process	63.6	36.4	66.6	33.3
State-Process	20.8	79.2	9.1	91.9

Semantic simplification

The early stages of language development may best be described in terms of semantic development. There is now plenty of evidence to support such a statement for FLD. There is, however, very little evidence for SLD, whether naturalistic or classroom, as semantic development has not been investigated sufficiently. From the evidence that is available it would appear that child L2 learners, at least, produce utterances that display the same 'telegraphese' qualities that have been observed in the speech of L1 learners. Even children who are dependent on the classroom for an input in the target language and who have few opportunities for 'creative' speech produce utterances that are not only devoid of modality markings such as number, tense and mood but are also severely propositionally reduced. Krashen (1982b) has suggested that in the early stages the 'natural' thing for learners to do is to keep silent, 'acquiring' through listening. In many learning situations this is not possible—and may not be desirable—so learners need strategies for encoding messages that communicate maximum information with minimum linguistic resources. The strategy that they use is one of 'semantic simplification'.

The notion of 'simplification' as an explanatory process in interlanguage has attracted many commentators. However, as Faerch and Kaspar (1980) point out 'simplification' makes little sense from the learner's perspective because to begin with the learner lacks a knowledge of the target language rule system to simplify. Thus claims such as Widdowson's (1975) that L2 learner errors are the result of the attempt to derive 'context rules' from the 'code rules'[4] he possesses in order to achieve communicative effectiveness founder on a logical impossibility; at the start the learner has not acquired any 'code rules' and so cannot simplify what he does not have. In the initial stages 'simplification' cannot be a 'process whereby the language user adjusts his language behaviour in the interests of communicative effectiveness' (Widdowson, 1975; p. 196) because he does not possess any knowledge to adjust. The learner does not begin by acquiring rules of 'usage' which are then converted into rules of 'use'; rather he begins by constructing rules of 'use' from the start. The notion of 'simplification' cannot be applied to interlanguage in the same way as it has been used to describe registers such as motherese and teacher talk.

However, although it does not make sense to suggest that the L2 learner simplifies *grammatically* it is reasonable to argue that he simplifies *semantically*. He can do this by selecting which semantic role or roles from the elements present in a situational event to encode. Like the L1 learner, he knows how situational events are constructed and he knows that it is possible to communicate a proposition without encoding all the elements that constitute it. Simplification involves the reduction of linguistic information about a proposition according to the principle of informativeness and the availability of lexical resources, which together determine which semantic roles the learner encodes.

If this explanation is right—and more research is required to establish this, particularly with adult learners—the early stages of SLD, whether classroom or naturalistic, do not involve the acquisition of grammatical knowledge at all. Neither do they involve recourse to some 'basic language' as proposed by Corder (1981).[5] Rather they are dependent on the learner's knowledge of how to exploit the context of interaction and on his ability to memorise lexical items that are important for the meanings he wants to communicate.

From this it might be expected that the order of development of the different semantic roles is a reflection of the communicative value of each role in the typical settings in which the learner finds himself. This is what Brown and Greenfield and Smith have suggested for FLD. It also seems true in children's classroom SLD. The order of emergence and the frequency of use of the various semantic roles in the speech of the two Punjabi-speaking children seems to reflect the likely importance of each role for communication in a classroom. The Object role occurs early because the pupils have a constant need to obtain tools to perform pedagogic tasks. Likewise the Property of Object is encoded because it is often necessary to specify which of several objects is required. In contrast the Agent role is developed later because initially the children's messages are centred around their own activity so that the agency of events is a situational 'given'. Agents appear when the learner has sufficient vocabulary to encode events about other people. Datives are likely to occur before Agents because the roles of beneficiary or experiencer are particularly important in the classroom, at least from the pupil's point of view. Locatives are useful, but they are linguistically more complex as they require a Locative State (in the form of a proposition) and in many contexts can be easily substituted by a gesture. Not surprisingly, the first Locatives to appear are encoded using 'here'. State-Processes are typically represented by verbs such as 'have' and 'be', both of which convey little propositional information. Action-Processes, however, provide fuller information and are often the central element of a message; they are used in conjunction with the Object role most commonly, so it is to be expected that they develop later.

In conclusion, therefore, semantic simplification is motivated by the need to communicate when there are insufficient linguistic resources.

It both directs and is directed by the nature of communication. It also directs the course of early SLD itself. Its source is linguistic only in the sense that it relies on lexical knowledge (but not grammatical). Otherwise it resembles the same process in FLD by drawing on a conceptual base.

It would be wrong, however, to claim that FLD and SLD are entirely the same. There are a number of important differences. Ellis (1982a) proposes that early utterances in a L2 also demonstrate that the learner knows that language is syntactic and therefore seeks to use word order consistently. Thus all the semantically-reduced L2 utterances quoted in this chapter follow the 'universal' word order of subject + verb + object, whereas this is not the case in the L1 utterances (see pp. 48–49). A further difference between SLD and FLD lies in the fact L2 utterances, even in the early stages are characterised by a number of 'functors', although the learner may not use these in any consistently meaningful way. The L2 learner knows and understands such concepts as 'negativity', 'duration' and 'necessity' and he also knows that language is equipped to encode these meanings. The L1 learner almost certainly knows neither of these facts. The L2 learner can make limited use of this knowledge, however. He has limited production capacity and may only be able to encode functors such as prepositions or verb inflections at the cost of omitting a semantic role. Thus, for instance, if the learner is restricted in spontaneous communication to three-term utterances, he may have to choose between an utterance like:

The little boy

or one like:

Little boy cry.

Which one he chooses will be the product of his communicative intent, but on balance he is likely to find it more useful to encode propositional elements than modality elements. Although the L2 learner may have the *ability* to learn and produce grammatical features, he may find it more communicatively *useful* to stick to semantic roles in the majority of instances. For this reason, semantic simplification remains the dominant early process.[6]

Many teachers, however, may still be sceptical that *all* L2 learners resort to the kinds of propositionally-reduced utterances illustrated in the creative speech of the two Punjabi-speaking children. Surely, they might assert, *adult* learners are capable of producing utterances that are fully formed and grammatical from the start, providing they are given practice in automatising a number of basic grammatical features and patterns. This may prove correct—it is another matter for empirical research. But, if the argument presented in this chapter is on the right lines, it would seem likely that even adults will resort to semantic simplification to a substantial degree in their *creative speech*. When the learner is concerned with realising his 'meaning potential' rather than displaying his linguistic wares and when he is called on to do so spontaneously, the product will be speech that is propositionally reduced and relatively devoid of modality features. However, adult learners may possess a larger production capacity and so be able to give greater attention to encoding functors. Also adult learners will find it easier to 'engineer' utterances using alternative processes entirely to semantic simplification. Such utterances will probably be more grammatical. They are, however, the result of processes which have different conditions of application and which may not be available in spontaneous discourse.

There is an important outstanding question. How does semantic simplification help the learner to *acquire* knowledge of a L2 as opposed to using that knowledge that he already possesses? The answer to this lies in whether semantic simplification is to be seen as applicable to reception as well as production. Arguably, the learner is led to attend to the propositional elements rather than the modality elements of the input in the first place on the grounds that this is the best way to decode the meaning of utterances. He may also use his awareness of the constituents of situational events to predict which semantic roles in an utterance will be most informative within their own context. Semantic simplification, therefore, may direct acquisition by controlling the learner's intake.

Notes

1. According to Fillmore (1968) propositional meaning involves 'a tenseless set of relationships involving verbs and nouns'. Modal meanings are realised linguistically by functors such as determiners and verb inflections. Thus, for instance, the following two sentences have the same propositional meaning but different modality meanings:

    He hits the ball.
    He is hitting a ball.

    Later versions of 'Case grammar' made a number of changes which affected whether specific meanings were classified as 'propositional' or 'modality', but the basic distinction was adhered to.
2. The same utterance can have a different function depending on context and non-verbal behaviour. 'ball' said with a falling intonation while the child points at the object is an example of the 'indicative' function; 'ball' said to a higher pitch while the child is trying to reach it and hold it is an example of the 'volitional' function.
3. Pienemann's study, in fact, focuses on syntactic development. It is nevertheless relevant here because it throws light on semantic development in early L2 speech.
4. 'Code' rules are rules that characterise the learner's linguistic knowledge; 'context rules' are rules that characterise how the learner uses his linguistic knowledge to perform communicative actions. Therefore 'code rules' relate to 'usage' and 'context rules' to 'use'.
5. Corder proposes that the L2 learner may have recourse to the various stages of development through which he passes on acquiring his L1. The very earliest stages involve a 'basic' language which the learner reproduces in the L2.
6. Felix (1978) has pointed out another difference between early speech in FLD and naturalistic SLD. The L2 learners he investigated did not produce utterances that reflected a 'unique grammatical system'. Whereas L1 speech is marked by great structural diversity, L2 development is 'amazingly restricted'. These observations are also true for the kind of spontaneous speech produced by the two classroom learners referred to in this chapter.

Chapter 4
Special Constructions in the Classroom

NOT all the utterances that language learners produce are the result of using the 'creative' rule system. There are also utterances which seem to be produced as synthetic wholes and which have rather special properties. These utterances are often called 'formulas'.

Formulaic speech has often been observed in the speech of language learners but it is not restricted to them. It also occurs with native speakers. Formulaic speech consists of 'expressions which are learned as unanalysable wholes and employed on particular occasions by native speakers' (Lyons, 1968, p. 177). Examples given by Lyons are 'How do you do?' and proverbs such as 'Easy come easy go'. The all important characteristic of such utterances is that 'their internal structure, unlike that of genuine sentences, is not accounted for by means of rules which specify the permissible combinations of words' (Lyons, p. 177). In other words, formulas and grammatical sentences are alternative ways of expressing meaning. Steinberg (1982) captures this rather nicely by referring to these alternative means respectively as 'familiar sentences' and 'novel sentences'.

There has been a slowly growing interest in special constructions, fuelled by case studies of individual learners which show that formulas are very frequent in the early stages and also by neurolinguistic research which has tried to show that formulas are processed by the right hemisphere of the brain, in contrast to creative speech which is processed by the dominant left hemisphere.

This chapter will begin by discussing the problems of identifying formulaic speech. There will be a brief review of existing research into the use of formulas and a somewhat longer discussion of the role formulas play in the classroom. Some evidence will be provided to support Fillmore's (1976) claim that formulas evolve into creative rules. Finally the part that formulaic speech might play in classroom SLD will be considered.

Identifying formulas in learner speech

Most of the existing definitions of prefabricated patterns are functional in nature and/or refer to the method by which they have been internalised. Garvey (1977) for instance, gives this definition:

> Routines are predictable utterance sequences that serve a single or limited role, and are restricted to particular positions or specialised functions in respect to a conversation or interaction. A routine is highly conventionalised and is probably learned as a package. (p. 43)

It is clear that a full description formulaic speech needs to account for both functional uses and formal characteristics. However, despite the fact that formulaic utterances stand in close relationship to fairly ritualised social functions, there have been few attempts to classify them functionally. One such attempt is Yorio's (1980). He suggests the following classification of 'routine formulas':

(1) Situation formulas (i.e. those associated with a specific situation).
(2) Stylistic formulas (i.e. those associated with a particular style).
(3) Ceremonial formulas (i.e. those associated with ritualistic interactions).
(4) Gambits (i.e. those used to organise interactions and activities).
(5) Euphemisms

Most of the definitions focus on the formal characteristics. Huang and Hatch (1978) point to a number of criteria that could be used; formulas (or imitated sentences, as they call them) are fully formed, the learner displays no awareness of smaller units within the sentence and there is no recombination of words or morphemes into other sentences.

One of the principal problems in identifying formulas lies in the fact that they can be words, phrases or sentences and also they can be incorporated as constituent elements into the structure of rule-derived utterances. It was this that led Krashen and Scarcella (1978) to distinguish 'prefabricated routines' and 'prefabricated patterns'. The former refer to memorised whole utterances and the latter to partly memorised wholes and partly 'creative' utterances.

The notion of formulaic speech, however, need not be restricted to single utterances, as Garvey's definition above suggests. It can consist of learnt discourse stretches that are dependent for their existence on specific, easily identifiable contexts. One such example might be a greeting sequence. This particular interpretation of formulaic speech is closely related to the concept of 'script' in FLD research. Nelson and Gruendel (1979) suggest that children develop 'scripts' of regular conversational routines by forming a conceptual representation of a sequence of interactive events. These scripts are stored in long-term memory and activated in appropriate contexts. However, they claim that the child's script is general in structure rather than a detailed set of context-specific slot fillers. Their explanation of how scripts work indicates that they are to be conceived of formally as 'patterns' rather than 'routines'. This account of scripts closely mirrors the adult language learner's experience of trying to memorise whole conversational structures which correspond to their communicative needs and which they can easily 'lock' into.

Formulaic speech, then, can be described in terms of the communicative functions it serves. Formally, it is possible to distinguish 'routines', 'patterns' and 'scripts'. It should also be noted that formulaic language can occur in writing as well as speech. However, for the purposes of this chapter only speech will be considered.

Language learners' use of formulas

Referring to native speaker competence, Lyons (1968) considers formulaic speech relatively infrequent compared to 'the vast mass of more "normal" utterances'. The competence of native speakers, therefore can be represented as in Fig. 4. In contrast, L2 learners in the early stages of development know relatively few TL rules for either reception

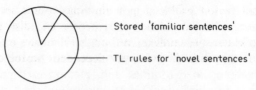

FIG. 4. Native speaker linguistic competence.

or production: Their linguistic competence therefore must be characterised by a much larger proportion of stored formulaic speech, as represented in Fig. 5. One way of characterising language development may be as the gradual replacement of a reliance on familiar sentences with an ability to understand and produce novel sentences.

The widespread use of formulas in early FLD has often been noted. Guillame (1927) in a discussion of one child's development of French observed utterances that were 'direct reproductions of ready-made sentences which cannot possibly be personal combinations of truly independent words' (pp. 137–8). Similar observations have been made by Leopold (1949) and Brown (1973). Brown notes that 'idiosyncratic and inflexible terms' become 'lodged' in the speech of children when they are perceptually salient and highly frequent (pp. 179–80).

Dulay, Burt and Krashen (1982) review much of the SLD research literature dealing with formulas. Formulaic speech figures prominently in the early acquisition of English by young children in informal environments (Fillmore, 1976; Hakuta, 1974; Huang and Hatch, 1978; Wagner-Gough, 1975) and also by adults (Hanania and Gradman, 1977). All these studies look at naturalistic SLD. Krashen and Scarcella (1978) claim that it is more likely that formulas will be widespread in learning contexts characterised by communicative pressure, i.e. when the learner is not allowed to develop naturally by means

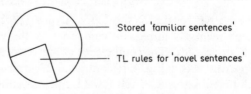

FIG. 5. Early L2 speaker linguistic competence.

of the 'silent period'. They suggest that classrooms are examples of such contexts. There have, however, been no studies of the use of formulas in classroom contexts, although Fillmore's study looked at learners who may have been heavily dependent on the classroom for input.

Formulas in classroom SLD

The communicative speech produced by the three classroom learners (see Ellis, 1982b) mentioned in previous chapters was examined for evidence of formulas. Only the first few months were considered, as after that time 'creative' utterances were likely to be more frequent and it would be difficult to distinguish familiar and novel sentences. Table 5

TABLE 5

Formulas Observed in the Speech of Three Classroom Learners (children)

Type of formula	Examples
(1) Situation formulas	Finished (spoken after completing a task) Very good (self-congratulating in a game or classroom task) What's the time? (spoken as breaktime was approaching)
(2) Stylistic formulas	Can I have rubber/colour etc, please? (Requesting goods from teacher or other pupil)
(3) Ceremonial formulas	How are you? (greeting) Good morning (greeting) Excuse me miss (attracting teacher's attention) Oh my God (exclamation)
(4) Gambits	This one or this one? (identifying nature of classroom task) What's this? (identifying object) I don't know? (referring to either lack of knowledge or inability to respond) That's all right. (confirming course of action)
(5) Euphemisms	Ø

gives sample formulas belonging to the various functional types identified by Yorio (see p. 66). This analysis gives some indication of the functional utility of formulaic speech in the classroom where the target language is both the medium and the goal of instruction. It is apparent that the early stages of classroom SLD are marked by frequent use of a small number of formulas which are important to the children as a means of meeting their basic communicative needs in the classroom when they have little 'creative' competence. Most of the formulas listed in Table 5 occurred in all three children's speech. There was also a high level of agreement in the order in which the different formulas appeared. The ritualistic formulas (i.e. 'Good morning' and 'Thank you'), 'finish' and 'I don't know' tended to occur before 'This one', 'Can I have _____ please?' and 'What's this?'. These formulas were used frequently, but their range was quite limited. Table 5 contains examples of both 'routines' and 'patterns'. An example of each will be discussed in some detail in order to show the uses to which formulaic speech was put and to shed some light on how they were acquired.

(1) *'Can I have _____ please?'*

This is an example of a pattern. 'Can' first appeared in this formula. It was also unique in a number of other ways; it manifested subject–verb inversion at a time when no other utterance did; it made use of the first person pronoun only and also the only verb was 'have'. The only open slot was that of the noun object, which typically referred to some common classroom tool (i.e. colour, pencil, pen, book, brush, ruler, paper, scissors).

'Can I have _____ please?' was used to request goods but it was not the only means of performing this function. Other simpler devices based on semantic simplification were used:

e.g. Colours, sir.
Give pencil.

There is some evidence to suggest that 'Can I have _____ please?' was a marked form, used when the pupil wished to be polite or to display 'good' English. One teacher made a deliberate effort to teach it by correcting the pupils whenever they used an imperative form.

It is interesting to note that the almost identical form required to request permission (e.g. Can I play noughts?) did not occur in the data for the Portuguese boy until much later and in the data for the two Punjabi-speaking children not at all during their first year. This suggests that the formula was not so much a *form* for the children as a device for performing a specific language *function*.

(2) '*I don't know*'

This is an example of a routine. The formula was very common in the speech of the two Punjabi-speaking children but less so in the Portuguese boy's. This may be because the latter's creative competence progressed at a much faster rate. It was explicitly taught to *R* and *T*'s class; when the teacher observed the pupils using 'no' to respond to a question they could not answer he instructed them to use 'I don't know' instead. This formula was particularly evident in situations where the teacher was questioning an individual pupil. A failure by the pupil to respond is conspicuous and conversationally unacceptable; 'I don't know' served to fill a turn and to take the pressure off the learner.

In many cases the children's use of 'I don't know' was ambiguous. It could be used to indicate that the learner had failed to understand the teacher's question or that despite understanding he could not answer because of linguistic insufficiency. Its main function seems to be to take up a discourse slot when the learner feels obliged to take his turn but cannot contribute to the propositional development of the conversation.

For all three children 'don't' was used monomorphemically and only occurred in this formula to begin with.

In the early stages the two Punjabi-speaking children's speech was predominantly composed of single words, routines and patterns. There was also evidence of the use of 'scripts'. *R* sought to escape the communicative pressure imposed by the classroom tasks set him by switching to those 'scripts' which he felt competent to realise linguistically. One such script, a colour identification routine, is illustrated below:[1]

T: I want you to tell me what you
   can see in the picture or what's
   wrong with the picture. Look at
   that.

R: a /poik/ (= bike)

T: A cycle, yes. But what's wrong?

R: /ret/ (= red)

T: It's red, yes. What's wrong with it?

R: Black

T: Black. Good.

In this example the teacher's conceptualisation of the task and the script the pupil uses do not match. The result is what Keenan and Schieffelin (1977) call 'discontinuous discourse'. But it is interesting to note that ultimately it is the teacher who adapts to the pupil's script rather than vice-versa.

Later development in the form of formulas

It has been suggested in both FLD and SLD research that formulas serve as the basis for 'creative' speech as the learner comes to realise that the formulas he first understood and used as unanalysed wholes consist of discrete constituents that can be combined with other constituents in a variety of rule-bound ways. Clark (1974) reports on the FLD of one child. She observes a number of 'routine unproductive sentences' (p. 4) that seemed to exist alongside a few productive rules. The former seem to be the result of a copying strategy and were rapidly used in the construction of more complex utterances. She gives several examples, including the following where the italics identify the embedded sentence structure:

I want *you get a biscuit for me.*
I don't know *where's Emma gone.*
I want *I eat apple.*

Clark points out that only well-practised sequences can be interrupted or added to in this way; new, unfamiliar ones have to be practised as integral sequences before they can be interrupted. Thus Clark considers that the child's speech becomes creative predominantly through gradual analysis of the internal structure of sequences which start out as patterns.

A very similar position is taken by Fillmore (1976, 1979). Fillmore documents a large number of formulas—a much wider range than that identified in the speech of the three classroom children described in the previous section—and suggests that over time they are submitted to an analytical process that releases constituent elements for use in other slots than those they occupied initially. She suggests that this analysis can occur in two ways; by the learner noticing variation in the formulaic structure according to the situation and also by the learner noticing similarities in parts of different formulas. It is this process that accounts for why later utterances seem less well-formed than the earlier ones. As constituent elements become freed the learners' utterances become rule-based, although not necessarily in terms of target language rules.

It is obviously important to establish to what extent formulas are converted into rules through a process of juxtaposition or embedding, as described by Clark and Fillmore. Is there any evidence of this in the use of formulas produced in the classroom? To this end the 'I don't know' formula will be considered developmentally.

In tracing the developmental route of 'I don't know' in the speech of the three classroom learners it is necessary to consider when 'don't' is first used in similar but different expressions, when an alternative subject to 'I' first occurs, when 'know' is released for use without 'don't' and when additional constituents occur. Table 6 below gives the first instance and the week of its occurrence in the children's speech of each of these developments.

When 'dont' first appears in structures other than 'I don't want' its use is still very restricted. There is no immediate release followed by productive use with a range of different verbs. It is, in fact, quite likely that many of the new forms (e.g. 'I don't understand' and 'I don't like . .') are also formulas and that only when the learners are able to perceive the syntactic similarity between the two routines will

TABLE 6
The Development of the Formula 'I don't know' in the Speech of Three Classroom Learners.

Developmental feature	Portuguese speaker	R	T
'don't' used in similar but different expressions	I don't understand. (14)	I don't like holiday. (22)	I don't like this book. (26)
Alternative subject to 'I'	You don't know where it is. (21)	ø	ø
'know' used without 'don't'	I know this (18)	I know 'five'. (26)	I know this one. (28)
Additional constituent	I don't know that big one. (18)	I don't know this one. (24)	I don't know this. (18)

completely productive use result. The data, which cover the first year the learners spent in the classroom, suggest that this point is not reached by any of the children.

Only the Portuguese boy develops the ability to replace 'I' with an alternative pronoun. This is perhaps a reflection of his more rapid overall development. His speech also manifests each developmental feature at an earlier date.

All three children used 'don't' with other verbs before releasing 'know' for independent use. In fact 'I don't know' precedes the structurally simpler 'I know' by as much as six months. This is surely a reflection of the comparative importance of the communicative uses of the two structures; in the classroom, at least, children prize the ability to express ignorance over the ability to express knowledge! It is all part of a defensive strategy for warding off the teacher's questions.

The most interesting of the developmental features is the use of additional constituents with 'I don't know' i.e. when the routine becomes a pattern. The data show a remarkable similarity with those provided by Clark. Here are some examples taken from the speech of the three children with the juxtaposed structure again italicised:

(1) *That one* I don't know. (Portuguese boy—week 21)
(2) You don't know *where it is*. (Portuguese boy—week 25)
(3) I don't know *how to play*. (Portuguese boy—week 27)
(4) I don't know *what is squirrel*. (R—week 24)
(5) I don't know *what's this*. (R—week 26)
(6) I don't know *'holiday' spelling*. (T—week 22)
(7) I don't know *what's this*. (T—week 25)
(8) I don't know *making*. (T—week 30)

These reveal at least two different strategies. One involves combining two routines into a single utterance. Definite examples of this strategy are (1), (5) and (7) and also the examples given in Table 6. (6) is also probably the result of this combination strategy as 'noun + item to be spelt' served as a common device for requesting assistance with written work. (2) and (3) may also represent the conjunction of two routines, although 'where it is' and 'how to play' could also be rule-derived constituents. (4) and (8), however, reflect a totally different strategy. In both cases the learner has incorporated a constituent from the teacher's previous utterance, attaching it as a single unanalysed unit to his/her existing routine. This is another example of what Scollon (1976) has called 'vertical structures' (see Chapter 1).

Although considerable development in the three children's use of 'I don't know' has taken place it is not clear how much of the grammatical information contained in the formula has been 'un-packaged' and made available for productive use. As the above discussion indicates, much of the apparent development can be explained either in terms of additional routines or by the conversion of routines to patterns. If such an analysis is correct, little real 'analysis' has taken place. The contribution that formulas make to SLD is discussed in the following section.

The role of formulas in classroom SLD

Any discussion of the role of formulaic speech in SLD must consider both its contribution to learner *performance* and its contribution to the *acquisition* of the 'creative' rule system. It is important to realise that these are separate issues. Thus it is possible to conclude that formulaic speech contributes positively to the learner's productive capacity but plays no part in the development of the rule system. On the basis of this separation it is possible to formulate a strong position regarding the contribution of formulaic speech (i.e. it aids *both* performance and acquisition) and a weak position (i.e. it aids *only* performance). Even if the weak position is adopted, however, a convincing case can be made out for allocating formulaic speech a more important role in SLD than is traditionally the case.

There is general acceptance that L2 performance is aided and enhanced by formulaic speech. Krashen (1982b) argues that it serves, like the use of the mother tongue, as a means of 'out-performing competence'. For Krashen the 'ability to perform' and 'competence' appear to be distinct, the latter relating solely to knowledge of the creative rule system. Krashen acknowledges, however, that L2 users need to communicate beyond the means provided by their competence and thus accepts that formulaic speech has a role, albeit a limited one, to play. It can improve overall performance both by compensating for deficiencies in knowledge of the TL rule system (Krashen's basic point) and also by helping to solve production difficulties. If Bialystok's (1982) position is to be accepted TL knowledge needs to be characterised not only in terms of *quantity* but also *quality*.[2] One aspect of the latter dimension is the degree of automaticity. Thus the user's TL knowledge (and presumably the native speaker's also) of a given rule can be more or less automatic and thus more or less available in contexts such as free conversation that call for instant processing ability. A reasonable hypothesis is that utterances produced with reference to the underlying rule system take longer to process than when they are produced as wholes. Thus formulaic speech is useful to the language performer because it relieves the burden placed on his processing mechanisms. This point is nicely put by Steinberg (1982):

> The fact that speakers are able to produce and understand sentences at the fantastic rate that they do could never be explained if we suppose that every sentence had to be constructed through application of all related rules. (p. 123)

Thus 'familiar phrases and sentences' facilitate processing by making available direct meaning-bound associations.

Steinberg's comments refer to native speaker performance. The need for processing relief in L2 speaker performance is that much greater. Thus the extent to which TL formulaic speech is used is a function of three factors:

(1) the user's need to 'outperform competence';
(2) the degree of automaticity of acquired TL rules; and
(3) the degree of pressure placed on his processing mechanisms by the type of discourse he is engaging in (i.e. the more unplanned the discourse type, the greater the need for access to ready-made utterances).

The extent to which formulaic speech is important to classroom learners is likely to be a reflection of the kind of linguistic environment the classroom constitutes. If there is little room for authentic communication, where the learner has to make do with whatever resources he possesses, there will be little need to 'outperform competence' and so formulas will not be learnt. This is likely to be the case in classrooms, where the teacher controls the language the learners are to produce and where the target language is not the medium of instruction. In contrast in classrooms where there is plentiful opportunity for authentic communication and in particular where the target language is the means of organising classroom behaviour, there will be communicative pressure and a consequent need for formulas in the early stages. This was the kind of classroom the three learners discussed in the previous sections participated in. The small range of formulas they acquired were a great help to them in coping with the regular demands of certain classroom situations. Without these formulas their communicative proficiency in the early stages would have been seriously impaired.

There is no unanimity regarding the nature and the extent of the contribution made by formulaic speech to the acquisition of the TL rule system. Two basic positions are possible. The first states that formulaic speech and rule-created speech are unrelated. The following might be considered evidence for this position:

(1) In the initial stages of language development (FLD or SLD) formulaic speech is by definition unrelated to rule-created speech i.e. routines or patterns contain structural elements which are *not* evident in propositional speech.

(2) There is neurolinguistic evidence (i.e. from cases of left hemispherectomy) of patients who lose the ability to speak but are nevertheless still able to produce automatic speech consisting of stereotyped expressions. This evidence is reviewed by Krashen and Scarcella (1978). Seliger (1982) in a review of research literature dealing with the role of the right hemisphere in SLD also suggests that there is a neurolinguistic basis for separating the kind of holistic processing required for learning formulas from the serial processing required for the acquisition and use of creative rules.

(3) The fact that adult native speakers continue to make extensive use of formulaic utterances and scripts indicates that these may be protected from analysis throughout the period of language acquisition. Thus a common utterance such as 'What's this?' could potentially be derivable from two sources; from the store of formulaic utterances available immediately to the speaker or from the store of rules internalised by the learner's 'language acquisition device'. Which source is used may simply reflect the amount of processing time available in different situations.

The alternative position is represented in Fig. 6. This represents the gradual analysis of formulaic utterances into their component parts, which helps to augment the learner's creative rule system. This occurs when the learner notices that the form of a formulaic utterance varies according to the situation or when he recognises similarities between the part of different formulas. This proposal effectively confers the analytical skills of the linguist on the language learner, that is he comes to understand the internal structure of utterances by realising that elements can be substituted, added, deleted or re-arranged. One of the Punjabi-speaking children, *R*, appeared to engage subconsciously in just such procedures in a form of 'semantic play' (Butzkamm, 1980).

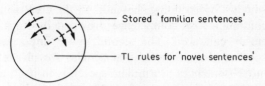

Fig. 6. The contribution of formulaic speech to the learner's creative rule system.

The utterances[3] he produced suggest that learners do indeed manipulate a 'whole' and through this discover its parts:

Book in the bin. (=basic utterance)
You book in the bin.
My book in the bin.
You in the bin.
No writing in the bin.
You bin .... in the bin, all right?
You writing in the bin.

Neurolinguistic evidence could also be cited to support the position represented in Fig. 6. Genesee (1982) reviews neurolinguistic research into the effects of stage of development on right hemisphere processing. If, as has been claimed the right hemisphere is responsible for processing the use of formulas and if, as has also been claimed, formulas are more prevalent in early SLD, it should follow that right hemisphere processing should occur to a greater extent in the non-proficient stages. However, this hypothesis receives little support from the available research. Also, as the neurolinguistic research tirelessly reiterates, the ability of the brain to interact across cortical areas ensures that there is no function that is entirely localised.

At the present moment, therefore, it is not possible to decide in favour of one or the other of these two positions. Neither is it easy to see how this issue can be resolved. On balance the longitudinal case-study evidence appears to favour the second position, although it does not answer the line of argument presented in (3) above. Two further points are worth making. The first is that there is general agreement that 'routines' do evolve into 'patterns' (i.e. notwithstanding whether by so doing they add to the creative rule system). Thus the communicative competence provided by formulaic speech is considerably enhanced. The second, more important point, is that, irrespective of whether 'familiar sentences' evolve into rules for performing 'novel sentences', formulaic speech is in itself an important aspect of communicative competence. The weak position alone warrants paying close attention to the place of formulaic speech in an instructional programme.

Finally, a few comments on whether formulaic speech can be actively taught to the L2 learner are in order. This is an interesting variant of the 'can-syntax-be-taught?' question, which is the subject of Chapter 6. Krashen (1982b), in a discussion of 'conversational competence' argues that although 'a small sub-set' of formulas can be taught, the total set of devices required is too complex to be 'learned' and can only be acquired' (p. 79). However, the evidence of the three classroom learners presented in this chapter suggests that at least some of the formulas they mastered were the result of successful teaching. Below is an extract from a lesson in which the first recorded instances of 'I don't know' by the two Punjabi-speaking children occurred. It was followed almost immediately by fairly regular use, possibly as a result of the teaching that took place.

T: Now, what's that? (Teacher points at a picture of a tree.)

T: No sir.

T: Do you know? Do you know? What's this?

T: No.
R: No.

T: No. Say, 'I don't know'.

R. I don't know.

T: Do you know? Do you know?

T: No.

T: I don't know.

T: I don't know.

T: Do you know?

R: I don't know.

The learners may respond to this direct teaching because it provides them with the linguistic means of expressing a function that pupils find communicatively important in the classroom i.e. admitting ignorance. This rather anecdotal evidence of the success of teaching one formula must be considered in the light of evident and repeated failure to teach the same learners various syntactical rules (e.g. plurals; WH interrogatives). It may be possible to memorise useful formulas in much the same way as any other useful information.

In conclusion, then, it can be said that formulas are important for SLD. They help to reduce the learner's processing difficulties in the performance of communicative functions that are important to the learner. They may also aid the development of the creative rule system, although this is less certain. They may be 'teachable' when creative rules are not.

Notes:

1. The teacher and pupil were together looking at a What's Wrong Card. This depicted a picture of a bicycle without any pedals. The conversation took place in the third week of *R*'s stay at the Language Unit.
2. Bialystok's point is that the learner's linguistic competence has a quantitative aspect (i.e. how many rules the learner knows) and a qualitative aspect (i.e. how well the learner knows the rules.) With regard to the latter Bialystok suggests that L2 knowledge can be more or less automatic and more or less analytic (i.e. the learner has varying degrees of consciousness of the knowledge he possesses). Bialystok's framework is taken up later in Chapter 6.
3. These utterances were produced in conversation with another pupil, a Vietnamese boy. It was evident that the two boys enjoyed playing with language and using it to tease each other.

Chapter 5

Types of Classroom Interaction and their Role in Classroom Second Language Development

So far classroom SLD has been explored in terms of the learner's linguistic output. The specific question addressed was whether the kind of language-learner language produced by classroom learners was the same as that produced by naturalistic learners. Chapters 2, 3 and 4 have shown that the output of classroom learners can be very similar to that of naturalistic learners. Both types of learners appear to process grammatical data in similar ways and even where differences are apparent these may only be temporary. Also both types of learners employ 'semantic simplification' and formulas in the early stages, in order to overcome the linguistic problems of communicating with very limited resources. These characteristics are evident in 'communicative' speech, which is predominant in naturalistic SLD but which can be found in varying degrees in different types of classrooms. However, 'modelled' speech, which is common in many classrooms, appears to involve different processing mechanisms which are not related to those responsible for 'communicative' speech.

The purpose of this chapter is to examine the role played by the input in classroom SLD. More specifically it is to consider in what ways different types of classroom interaction involving the teacher and the pupils contribute to SLD. The chapter will begin with a review of literature dealing with the relationship between input/interaction and naturalistic language development—both FLD and SLD. It will then report on studies of input/interaction and classroom SLD. Following this, a framework will be proposed for analysing the different kinds of interaction in a language classroom. Each type of interaction will be illustrated and its potential for facilitating SLD be discussed. Finally, a number of aspects of interaction that seem to be important for SLD will be described.

The role of interaction in naturalistic language development

Chomsky (1965) argued that the input served merely as a trigger to operate the 'language acquisition device'. Furthermore, he argued that the input was degenerate and could not, therefore, explain how the child came to acquire linguistic competence. However, in the seventies this view of language development was challenged. First it was shown that the speech addressed to children was in fact extremely well-formed. Secondly, studies were conducted to show that certain features of this speech helped FLD. More recently, it has also been hypothesised that input is important in naturalistic SLD and that the route that learners follow when acquiring grammatical competence grows out of the interactions they take part in.

Interaction and FLD

Brown (1968) had this to say about the way a child acquires a knowledge of language:

> It may be as difficult to derive a grammar from unconnected sentences as it would be to derive the invariance of quantity and number from the simple look of liquids in containers and objects in space. The changes produced by pouring back and forth, by gathering together and spreading apart are the data that most strongly suggest the conservation of number and quantity. (p. 287)

Brown is suggesting that the child's grammatical competence grows out of conversational interactions with his caretakers. It is precisely this issue which the Bristol Language Development Study[1] has set out to investigate. Wells *et al.* (1979) pinpoint three related aspects of this study:

(1) What are the main characteristics of caretaker–child interaction?
(2) What aspects of the child's linguistic development does inter-action influence?
(3) In what ways does caretaker–child interaction influence FLD?

Each of these is considered separately below.

(1) *The characteristics of caretaker–child interaction*

There is now a wealth of literature describing the linguistic and communicative features of 'motherese'. Motherese is characterised by a lower mean length of utterance than in adult–adult speech, by various kinds of syntactic simplification (e.g. a high frequency of simple, one clause utterances), by modifications in the pronunciation of certain sounds, voice pitch and intonation, by a high frequency of certain language functions such as instructions, by frequent use of topic incorporation devices such as repetitions and expansions and also by various topic constraints such as the 'here-and-now' principle.

However, caretaker–child interaction cannot adequately be ac-counted for in terms of properties of just the adult's language. It needs to be seen as a process involving the joint contributions of child and adult. One of the main contributions of the Bristol Language Devel-opment Study has been to recast the study of motherese in a more interactive framework using an adaptation of Halliday's (1980) model of discourse. This has led to the identification of strategies used by both participants for building a shared field of attention through language and for sustaining discourse (see Wells *et al.*, 1979).

An important question regarding the contribution of the caretaker is whether her speech is 'finely tuned'. Krashen (1981b) argues that it is only 'roughly tuned' (i.e. the caretaker does not adjust her speech to suit the precise stage of the child's development but makes only approximate adjustments). There is some evidence for this. Newport *et al.* (1977) found that with the exception of the mothers' yes/no questions and deixis there were few significant relationships between the mothers' speech and the child's linguistic knowledge. They concluded that fine tuning is not a requirement for universal aspects of language although it may aid some language-specific items. Other studies (e.g. Furrow *et al.*, 1979) have found evidence of fine-tuning on a wide range of measures. But to talk about fine or rough tuning in this way is unsatisfactory because it conceives of tuning in terms of input rather than interaction. A far more subtle and complex relationship between caretaker speech and child speech is involved. Wells and Robinson (1982) emphasise that the density of adjusted features varies from utterance to utterance as a result of interactional decisions:

> Finely tuned adult speech does not consist of utterances which are uniformly simple in form and semantically redundant. Rather it is influenced by the particular purpose of the interaction and the context of activity in which it occurs and is characterised by a dynamic utterance-by-utterance adjustment to the communicative demands of the conversation, as these are assessed on the basis of the continuous feedback that the adult receives in the form of the child's behaviour, both verbal and non-verbal (p. 19)

If the caretaker's speech is facilitative it is so, not because it is finely or roughly tuned, but because it helps the child to express his meanings just when he needs it.

(2) *Aspects of FLD influenced by caretaker–child interaction*

Two mutually compatible hypotheses have been put forward. The first is that universal characteristics of caretaker–child interaction determine the *order* of the child's linguistic development. The second is that differences in the *rate* of FLD are the result of differences in specific characteristics of caretaker–child interaction. At the moment, however, there is insufficient evidence to consider the first hypothesis. The following discussion will be limited to the second.

The available research suggests that it is the interactional rather than the formal adjustments of caretaker language that help to accelerate development. Fast learners receive substantially more directives (Ellis and Wells, 1980) and polar questions that serve to sustain and extend the child's involvement in conversations (Wells *et al.*, forthcoming). Therefore, when the adult acts as the initiator of interaction she can best do so in a directing mode but when the child initiates discourse the adult can facilitate development by acknowledging, clarifying and confirming through polar questions. Another feature of caretaker–child interaction associated with rapid development is talk about topics related to contiguous objects and ongoing activity in which both participants are engaged. Only as the child increases his mastery of the language system does the range of topics expand to cover past and future events and displaced activity. It is predominantly discourse features which are related to fast development.

Wells and Montgomery (1981) suggest that it is when the caretaker adopts a *supportive* style that development accelerates. In this style the child is allowed to initiate conversations and the adult helps to maintain a unitary topic and purpose through the use of continuing moves that acknowledge and request further information. It contrasts with a *tutorial* style where the child is the respondent and the mother controls the discourse through the use of closed questions and evaluations of the child's contributions.

(3) *Explaining how interaction aids FLD*

Wells (1981) provides the following account of how the child utilises the interactive context to obtain information about the linguistic code:

> ... the general principle involved seems to be one of constructing a linguistic representation on the basis of the speech signal that he hears, and comparing that with the conceptual representation of the situation to which he believes the spoken message applies, using any available cues to help him along with the task. (p. 109)

Listening and being able to relate one sensory modality (the aural) to another (the visual) is of central importance, therefore. The child may not always successfully discriminate the signal or he may fail to effect the modality matching. As a result the discourse may become disorderly or epistemological concerns for truth, accuracy and relevance be ignored. It is because of this that the child needs an accommodating partner who is prepared to make meaningful whatever contributions he is capable of. The task of modality-matching which is of central importance in all types of language development, is made easier by the interactional routines in which mother and child participate in both pre-linguistic and linguistic exchanges. As Ferrier (1978) explains:

> The small baby finds himself with monotonous regularity in routine interactional contexts in which his mother produces a fairly limited and predictable set of utterances. (p. 302)

It is the regularity and invariance of the caretaker's utterances together with the fact that they are tied to objects and activity of shared attention that enables the child to relate what he can see to what he can hear. This allows him access to both the phonological representations he requires and also to how objects and actions are coded in language.

Krashen (1981b) places great store by listening in the early stages. He emphasises that SLD is the result of comprehension not of production. Wells, however, considers speaking also very important in FLD. He points out that there is no guarantee that the modality matching process described above will always result in linguistic knowledge that matches the adult's. Ferrier notes that 'errors' of interpretation often occur when the child either overextends the reference of a given item or underextends it by linking it to the specific action through which it was originally learnt. It is by using his linguistic resources in production that the child is able to clarify both the semantic and grammatical systems of language. To this end it is important that he can get into conversation and play his part in sustaining it. There are a variety of devices for achieving this; one way is to chain a series of topically-related exchanges and another is by combining the responding move in one exchange with the initiating move in the next (see Wells *et al.*, 1979). The child is motivated to become a communicator. He develops discourse skills for achieving this, but in the process he obtains feedback on how meaningful his efforts are and subsconsciously adjusts his linguistic representations to match those of the adult.

Assuming for the moment that SLD takes place in much the same way as FLD, the question can be asked, how does a study of caretaker–child interaction help to understand classroom SLD? Krashen (1981b) draws attention to three points that he considers important about caretaker speech; it is roughly tuned and so casts a wide 'net' to ensure that 'i + 1' is available, it is designed to ensure communication and not to provide teaching and it follows the 'here-and-now' principle. This, however, constitutes a limited, static and therefore inaccurate view of the role of caretaker speech. From an interactional perspective which takes into account discourse features as well as syntactical features, caretaker speech, at least in some adults, seems very well adjusted to the child's needs. There is evidence that even some syntactic features are closely related to the child's linguistic development. Rather than emphasising the *input* provided by care-takers, Wells focuses on the need for reciprocity of *interaction*, which ensures that potentially facilitative features such as directives and polar questions used to maintain intersubjectivity are made available. This is the basis for the modality matching that must occur in all types of language development and for which both listening and speaking are necessary. Classroom SLD may be successful, therefore, not when the teacher provides an input with x features but when reciprocal inter-action occurs.

Interaction and SLD

Investigations of the relationship between interaction and SLD have tended to follow in the footsteps of FLD research. Not surprisingly, therefore, the same kinds of questions have been considered, although the bulk of the empirical research has focused on the nature of the adaptations made by native-speakers when talking with L2 learners and the other issues—the aspects of SLD affected by these adaptations and the explanations of these effects—have been largely a matter of speculation. The literature can be summarised under the same three headings used in the discussion of interaction and FLD.

(1) *The characteristics of native-speaker–learner interaction*

Native-speaker speech adjustments are often referred to as 'foreigner talk' (Ferguson, 1971). Like motherese, foreigner talk involves a range of input modifications. It is characterised by an exaggerated enunciation, greater overall loudness, the use of full forms rather than contractions, parataxis in preference to hypotaxis, reduction of inflections and absence of function words and also a special lexicon (see Ferguson and Debose, 1977). Discourse characteristics include a high proportion of topic-incorporation devices such as expansions repetitions, clarifications and paraphrases and some topic simplification (Long, 1981a).

Foreigner talk is not a discrete register. Like motherese it is continuum of adjustments.[2] At one end of this continuum there are both extensive formal and discourse modifications, while at the other end the speech may be entirely grammatical and contain only discourse adjustments. Which type of foreigner talk is used depends on a number of factors such as the status relationships between the conversational participants (Arthur *et al.*, 1980) and the age of the L2 learners (see Scarcella and Higa, 1981).

It is not only the native-speaker, however, who adapts his speech. The learner also uses various strategies to maximise his potential for communicating in the L2 when he has limited resources. These strategies are referred to as communication strategies (Varadi, 1973). These are not easy to identify or to define, but two criteria are commonly applied. The first is that the strategies are *consciously* employed or, at least, that they are *potentially conscious* (Faerch and Kaspar, 1980). The second criterion is that the strategies are *problem oriented*. That is, they are employed by the learner because he lacks the linguistic resources to express his intended meaning, or, as Corder (1978) puts it, when there is a lack of balance between means and ends.

Various typologies of communicative strategies have been produced (e.g. Corder, 1978; Faerch and Kaspar, 1980; Tarone *et al.*, 1976, Varadi, 1973). Most of these typologies make a distinction between *reduction* strategies, where the learner reduces either or both of the formal and functional properties of the intended message, and *achievement* strategies, where the learner develops an alternative plan for accomplishing his original goal. Examples of the former include topic-switching and message-abandonment. Examples of the latter include word-coinage, circumlocation and mime. Achievement strategies appear to have a similar function to foreigner talk, that is to facilitate communication when the learner's linguistic competence is limited.

Foreigner talk and the learner's communicative strategies are, in fact, two sides of the same coin. When there is a communicative problem the solution is not sought separately by the native-speaker modifying the formal and discourse characteristics of his speech or by the learner resorting to communicative strategies. It is sought jointly by the native-speaker and learner working together to establish and maintain a mutually acceptable topic. What is important, therefore, is the 'negotiation of an agreement on meaning' (Tarone, 1981). In order to study this negotiation it is necessary to look at the joint contributions of native-speaker and learner by considering the discourse that they construct. In other words, it is through discourse analysis that the characteristics of native-speaker–learner interaction can best be established.

Hatch (1978b, 1978c) discusses the different types of discourse found in conversations involving both child and adult L2 learners. Where children are concerned conversations typically commence with attempts by the learner to 'open the channel' by calling for the adult's attention. The adult responds by identifying the object that has attracted the child's attention and the child then repeats the name of the object. The sequence may end there and a similar 'nominating' sequence be embarked on. Alternatively, the conversation might move into the development stage, stimulated by the adult demanding some comment on the nominated topic by the child. This may result in an attempt at elaboration by the child. Further developments can occur if the adult calls for further comments or requests clarification. These child–adult conversations follow the 'here-and-now' principle. In contrast conversations involving adult learners are more likely to be rooted in displaced activity. As a result the learner has difficulty in identifying the topic and often resorts to requests for clarification (e.g. 'huh'?) or to echoing part of the native speaker's question in order to establish the field of reference. Repair strategies are also common in the native-speaker's speech. These involve moving the topic to the beginning or end of the sentence where it is more salient, simplifying lexis, adding gestures or even translating or switching to foreigner talk. The native-speaker also tries to help out by modelling what he thinks the learner wants to say.

The account of native-speaker–learner conversations, which Hatch provides (see also Scarcella and Higa, 1981), reinforces the point which Wells and Robinson (1982) made about motherese. Adjustments are the result of utterance-by-utterance attempts of both the native-speaker and the learner to achieve intersubjectivity.

(2) *Aspects of SLD influenced by native-speaker–learner interaction*

As in the case of FLD, it can be hypothesised that native-speaker–learner interactions can influence the *route* or the *rate* of SLD or both.

A strong case for the effect of interaction on the route of SLD has been made by Hatch and her fellow researchers. Hatch *et al.* (1979) make three claims. First they argue that the frequency of specific syntactic forms in the speech directed at the learner influences the language forms he produces. Both the forms and their frequency can be accounted for by the basic rules of conversation (i.e. as described in the previous section). Secondly, they argue that conversations provide the learner with large units which are incorporated into sentence structure. The learner builds utterances as 'vertical' structures (see Chapter 1, p. 14). Thirdly, they argue that conversations with different interlocutors (children *vs* adults) provide the learner with a variety of input which is of benefit to language development in different ways.

It is with regard to the third point, however, that a logical difficulty arises. If the route of development is determined by the types of interaction in which the learner participates and if these types are substantially different depending on whether the native-speaker and the learner are children or adults, why is it that both children and adults appear to follow the same 'natural' order of development? It is clear that the discourse which child learners and adult learners take part in is very different. Therefore, the frequency of the syntactic forms in the input is likely to vary. The developmental route, however, is the same. This suggests that input frequency may not be the most important determinant of the route of SLD.

It seems more likely that interaction plays a more important role in the rate of SLD. Interactional modifications, whether in the form of foreigner talk or communicative strategies, are motivated by the need to stay on topic. Where they are successful the learner will obtain both more input and input which he can understand. It would seem highly likely that this will facilitate rapid development, in much the same way as it appears to do so in FLD. It must be emphasised however, that this has yet to be clearly demonstrated by empirical research. The study of interaction has focused almost entirely on describing the different kinds of adaptations that take place and, unlike FLD research, has not investigated the relationship between different kinds of interaction and rate of SLD. One highly suggestive study, however, is Scarcella and Higa's (1981). They compared a number of interactional features in conversations involving children and adolescents. They found that the child learners received the simpler input, but that the adolescents engaged in more negotiation of meaning. They hypothesised that as adolescents have been shown to be the more rapid learners (Snow and Hoefnagel-Höhle, 1978), interaction may facilitate rate of SLD, but that it is negotiation that results in a more optimal input than simplification. This supports Long's (1981) claim that it is the discourse modifications rather than the formal adjustments in foreigner talk that aid development.

(3) *Explaining how interaction aids SLD*

If interaction determines the route of SLD, as Hatch suggests, then it does so by constraining the forms to which the learner is exposed and by providing the learner with ready-made chunks of language which he can incorporate into his utterances. Hatch argues that the learner is concerned to communicate and it is by learning to do this that he systematically acquires the grammar of the L2. As Hatch (1978b) puts it:

One learns how to do conversations, one learns how to interact verbally, and out of this interaction syntactic structures are developed. (p. 404)

This is perhaps the strongest claim that can be made for interaction. It is a claim that emphasises the role of the linguistic environment, as shaped jointly by learner and native-speaker, and plays down the role of internal processing factors.

A somewhat weaker position is that advanced by Krashen (1981b, 1982). Krashen argues that it is important that the learner obtains input that is roughly suited to the level of development he has reached. When this happens the learner's internal processing mechanisms can operate efficiently. In other words, development will take place providing the learner obtains 'comprehensible input' as this will ensure that the input is at the right syntactic level. As long as the learner is able to understand what is said to him he will be exposed to 'i + 1' (i.e. input consisting of the grammatical feature that is next in line according to the 'natural order' of acquisition). According to this position, therefore, it is the internal processing factors that are responsible for SLD, but the process of development can be facilitated or retarded according to how regularly the input is comprehensible. Input controls the *rate* of development.

Krashen emphasises the importance of listening over production. He suggests that production ability emerges from attending to input and is not a factor in SLD. This seems wrong on two counts. First, the learner's own contribution to a conversation provides the native-speaker with information about how effectively he is making himself understood. The native-speaker needs feedback on how successful his speech adaptations have been. Secondly, the learner's output also serves as input to his language processing mechanisms. This may be a particularly valuable type of input if it enables the learner to work on it in some way by attending to the kind of response it elicits from the native-speaker. As was argued for FLD, it is not *input* in itself that is important but *interaction* and ideally this involves the learner contributing actively to the interaction. It may be, however, that comprehension is most important right at the beginning of acquisition as a way of developing some minimal competence that can then be used in two-way interaction.

In conclusion, this review of the role of interaction in naturalistic language development suggests the following:

(1) When learners are addressed by fully competent speakers of a language, the latter adjust both the formal and discourse levels of the language they use. Learners also employ certain strategies to enable communication to take place.

(2) There is insufficient evidence to decide whether these interactional modifications are responsible for the *route* learners follow in FLD or SLD, although it would seem unlikely that they are the major determining factor. There is evidence to suggest that the types of interactions learners participate in facilitate development by influencing the *rate* of progress.

(3) Interaction contributes to development because it is the means by which the learner is able to crack the code. This takes place when the learner can infer what is said even though the message contains linguistic items that are not yet part of his competence and when the learner can use the discourse to help him modify or supplement the linguistic knowledge he has already used in production.

When a learner is interacting naturally with a fully competent speaker (or even another learner) he is trying to use language to accomplish actions. Linguistic knowledge, therefore, is a by-product of communicative competence.

The role of interaction is classroom SLD

The traditional view of classroom SLD is that it is different from naturalistic SLD. The difference which is envisaged is that between a 'free' learner who uses language to convey messages and a 'captive' learner who approaches language as if it is a formal puzzle (Corder, 1976). This view of classroom SLD can also be found in the research publications emanating from CRAPEL, University of Nancy. Gremmo, Holec and Riley (1978), for instance, state:

> .... when we analyse classroom discourse it becomes clear that the very presence and participation of the teacher distorts the interaction to such an extent that it no longer provides even the basic raw materials from which a learner can construct his competence. (p. 63)

Implicit in the position these authors take up is the belief that learners need the opportunity to participate in the same kinds of interactions as naturalistic learners in order to develop the capacity for what has earlier been called 'communicative' speech.

A starting point, then, is to ask to what extent the classroom does constitute a different linguistic environment. Once again this question can be tackled by examining the nature of the *input* provided by the teacher and the kinds of *interaction* which are typically found in the classroom.

Teacher-talk

'Teacher-talk' is the special language the teacher uses when addressing L2 learners in the classroom. It shares a number of common characteristics with foreigner-talk. There is systematic simplification of the formal properties of the teacher's language. Gaies (1977, 1979) found that teachers' utterances were simpler on a range of measures of syntactic complexity when they addressed pupils than when they were talking amongst themselves in a seminar. Henzl (1979) notes lexical, phonological and grammatical modifications in a teacher's language depending on the level of the learners he was teaching. For example, the teacher avoided lexical items with narrow semantic fields (e.g. 'young gal') in preference for general words (e.g. 'woman'). There is, however, one difference between the formal adjustments in teacher-talk and foreigner-talk. Whereas the latter permits deviations from the adult native-speaker's grammar, the latter usually does not.

Teacher-talk is also characterised by functional adjustments. Gaies (1977) found evidence in his teachers' speech of the same 'training strategies' characteristic of adult input to children. He gives examples of repetition, prompting and prodding, modelling and expansions. Wesche and Ready (1983) found that both an English-speaking professor and a French-speaking professor used significantly more self-repetitions when addressing L2 students in university psychology classes than when teaching the same content to L1 students. This finding is similar to that reported for foreigner talk by Long (1983).

It is clear that teacher-talk involves many of the same adjustments found in foreigner-talk. It might be hypothesised, then, that these adjustments facilitate SLD in the classroom in much the same way as foreigner-talk adjustments are hypothesised to facilitate SLD in naturalistic settings. From the point of view of teacher-talk, therefore, the linguistic environment provided by the classroom is not so different from that found outside. In Krashen's terms there is likely to be plenty of 'comprehensible input', even in the language classroom where the focus of the teaching is on form.[3]

Classroom discourse

It is when interaction is seen as discourse rather than input that the differences between classroom and naturalistic settings becomes apparent. In classrooms the predominant type of discourse is three phase—a teacher initiation, a pupil response, teacher feedback. The prevalence of IRF in classrooms has been well-documented by Barnes (1976) and Sinclair and Coulthard (1975). In the language classroom the IRF framework is also common, although a number of differences from content classrooms have been noted (see McTear, 1975). The important point, however, is that the basic pattern of classroom discourse differs considerably from the discourse patterns found in normal conversations outside the classroom. For example, Long and Sato (1983) found that ESL classrooms were characterised by more 'display' questions (i.e. questions which require the learner to demonstrate his knowledge of something) than naturalistic native-speaker discourse. Sinclair and Brazil (1982) observe that there are also differences in the discourse contributions from the pupils:

> The pupils have a very restricted range of verbal functions to perform. They rarely initiate, and never follow-up. Most of their verbal activity is response, and normally confined strictly to the terms of the initiation. (p. 58)

The question that follows is whether these differences in discourse are important where SLD is concerned. There are grounds for thinking that they are. Wells (1981) has argued that where FLD is concerned:

> The sort of interaction that will be beneficial for his (i.e. the child's) development . . . is that which gives due weight to the contribution of *both* parties, and emphasises mutuality and reciprocity in the meanings that are constructed and negotiated through talk. (p. 115)

If this is also true for SLD—and this would seem likely—then the IRF type of interaction of the classroom may deprive the learner of just those facilitative features which both FLD and SLD researchers have claimed are important. For example, Long and Sato (1983) argue that display questions do not invite the learner to respond at length or to initiate new topics. They are not likely to lead to sustained discourse.

However, as will be shown later, not all classroom discourse involves IRF exchanges and display questions. Many other types of discourse are possible. The main aim of this chapter is to explore these different types and to suggest in what way they might facilitate SLD in the light of what is known about the relationship between interaction and language development in general. Beforehand however, it is important to clarify what 'facilitate' means where classroom SLD is concerned.

Aspects of classroom SLD influenced by interaction

As with FLD and naturalistic SLD the question of the role of interaction can be explored with regard to both the route and the rate of classroom SLD.

In the previous three chapters it has been suggested that with a few minor exceptions the route of SLD manifest in learners communicative speech is the same as that observed in naturalistic SLD. There are two possible explanations for this. One is that interaction is not an important determinant of the order of development. It is the internal processing mechanisms which determine the acquisitional route. Another possibility is that, despite the differences between typical classroom and naturalistic interaction there are common characteristics and these determine in what order grammatical knowledge is internalised. It could be that the speech modifications which are found in both foreigner talk and teacher talk determine the developmental route. At the moment, however, it is not possible to decide between these two explanations. The focus of this chapter, therefore, will be on how different types of classroom interaction facilitate the *rate* of development.

Fillmore (1982) is one of the few researchers to have investigated how classroom interaction affects the rate of SLD. Fillmore carried out a longitudinal study of 60 children learning English in four different classrooms. She found that neither the difference in classroom composition (i.e. whether the classrooms were mixed English-speaking and non-English-speaking children or whether they contained mainly non-English-speaking children) nor the difference in the type of teaching offered (i.e. whether the teaching was 'open' or teacher-directed) influenced the success of language learning when considered separately. However, when considered together, it was apparent that these two factors interacted to influence language learning. Fillmore observed that successful language learning occurred in two different kinds of situation:

(1) In classes that were mainly teacher-directed and that had high proportions of non-English-speaking children.
(2) In classes that were taught through an 'open' organisation and that had mixed English-speaking and non-English-speaking children.

Conversely, Fillmore observed that language learning failed to take place in two other types of situation:

(3) In classes that had an 'open' organisation and that had high proportions of non-English-speaking children.
(4) In classes that were teacher-directed and that had mixed English-speaking and non-English-speaking children.

Fillmore outlines a number of reasons for her findings. She suggests that in the case of (3), where the type of teaching places great emphasis on one-to-one interaction, there was insufficient contact with English in a class of 30 pupils. Only those pupils who interacted frequently with the teacher progressed. With regard to (4) the main difficulty is that because the language proficiency of the class is mixed the teacher finds it difficult to tailor her instructional language to provide a suitable input for the L2 learners. In (1) the teacher serves as the main source of input and the pupils are prevented from practising imperfectly learned forms. The English the pupils learned, however, resembles teacher-talk rather than natural children's language. (2) appears to foster language development because the teacher grouped the pupils by language but taught each group in both languages. The teacher made special efforts to assure that the children understood the content. Also because the class was mixed there were opportunities for the non-English-speaking children to interact with the English-speaking children.

Fillmore's study is insightful because it shows both what factors influence SLD in a classroom and, most importantly, how these factors interact. However, Fillmore does not offer any illustrative evidence of the kinds of interaction she considers facilitative, so it is not possible to decide precisely *how* the kinds of discourse typically found in each of the four situations she investigated influence development. Earlier it was suggested that in FLD *formal* adjustments parents make in the speech they address to their children have no effect on the rate of development, whereas *interactional* adjustments involving pragmatic and topic-incorporation features do. Some evidence was also given for the importance of interactional variables in SLD. In order to examine the relationship between the *process* of classroom SLD and classroom discourse it is necessary to consider the various opportunities for interacting in the L2 that are available.

This discussion of the relationship between interaction and classroom SLD has raised a number of issues. In order to investigate these, a number of different types of classroom discourse will be identified to show how these might hinder or foster successful SLD.

Investigating types of classroom interaction: a framework

The approach that will be adopted for investigating the different types of interaction found in language classrooms is an exploratory one. No attempt will be made to quantify measures of language development and interactive opportunities in order to 'do something correlational'. Instead, a number of discourse samples involving different kinds of learner will be inspected in order to suggest in what way their communicative efforts might contribute to development. The chosen means for analysing the different interactions is discourse analysis. However, no attempt will be made to follow any particular theory of discourse or to utilise any specific descriptive framework. Politzer (1980) has argued that for pedagogical purposes discourse analysis needs to be 'motivational' rather than 'structural' and that this requires a higher level of speculation than most discourse analysts encompass. In line with this view, the descriptions offered are eclectic, drawing on techniques from different approaches according to whatever seems best suited to throw light on the developmental process itself.

A framework was required in order to sample different kinds of interactions. This was created by juxtaposing two aspects of face-to-face conversation:

(1) *The interactive goal*

It is possible to distinguish three major goals that motivate interaction in the language classroom. The first two derive from a distinction made by Black and Butzkamm (1978):

> Normally, in the foreign language classroom, organisation of classroom activity is used as a *framework* to achieve performance by the pupils in formal language exercises. The exercises are considered the *core* of the language teaching. (p. 271; italics added)

In the language classroom where the TL also serves as the medium of everyday communication, a third type of goal can be identified associated with the *social* needs of the interactants. The three goals are therefore: core goals, framework goals and social goals.

(2) *Address*

The term 'address' is used to refer to the interactive roles that are adopted in the classroom. Following Phillips (1972) the interacting participants can have one of four identities: teacher (T), pupil (P), class (C) i.e. when all the pupils are addressed as a single entity, and group (G), i.e. when any number of pupils less than the whole class is addressed.

Interacting participants can adopt different interactive roles. Gremmo, Holec and Riley (1977) give three such roles: speaker, addressee (i.e. the person to whom the message is addressed) and hearer (i.e. a person other than the addressee who hears the message).

Permuting the interactive identities and the roles listed above gives a number of 'address' types. Not all the possible combinations will be examined, however. Only the most frequently occurring will be illustrated.

This framework is designed to provide a basis for discussion, not to code the interactions that can occur in a language classroom. It must be emphasised that the distinctions that have been made do not constitute discrete categories as many of the interactions will be multi-purposive. Stubbs (1976) has shown that the way in which the teacher organises activities relating to 'core' goals provides a 'framework' in which communication (and hence learning) can take place. 'Core' and 'framework' goals tend to blend into one another.

Interactions involving 'core' goals

Three types of 'core' goals can be distinguished:

(1) Goals where the teacher's primary target is the teaching of the TL. Butzkamm and Dodson (1980) describe these as 'medium-oriented'.
(2) Goals where the teacher's primary target is the teaching of some subject content that is part of the school curriculum. Butzkamm and Dodson refer to these as 'message-oriented' goals.
(3) Goals where the teacher's primary target is to achieve specific pupil behaviours that result in some non-verbal product. These can be called 'activity-oriented' goals.

As the language learning opportunities afforded by these three types of 'core' goals are rather different, each will be considered separately.

'Medium-oriented' goals

The types of address typically associated with classroom interactions where the 'core' goals are medium-oriented are T-C, T-P(C) (i.e. teacher addresses an individual pupil with the rest of the class as hearers) and to a lesser extent T-P (e.g. when the teacher moves around the class helping individual pupils) and T-G. It is the teacher who generally operates as Speaker and the pupil who operates as either Addressee or Hearer. It is likely that the vast bulk of interactions involving language teachers around the world will have medium-oriented goals.

The kind of interaction that results from medium-oriented goals and teacher-centred patterns of address is very familiar. Below is an episode[4] taken from a lesson where the goal was the use of plural and singular forms. It was taught to the two Punjabi-speaking children referred to in earlier chapters approximately one month after they had started learning English at the Language Unit. The class has already been engaged in drilling activities for several minutes.

```
 1  T. Now T.....
 2      What is this? (The teacher holds up a pen.)
 3                              T. This is a pen.
 4  T. What are these? (The teacher holds up two pens.)
 5                              T. This are a pen.
 6  T. These are _____?
 7                              T. Are pens.
 8  T. What is this? (The teacher holds up a ruler.)
 9                              T. This is a ruler.
10  T. What are these? (The teacher holds up two rulers.)
11                              T. This is a (.) are (.)
12                              This are a rulers.
13  T. These are rulers.
14      What are these?
15                              T. This are a rulers.
16  T. Not 'a'.
17      These are _____?
18                              T. Rulers.
19  T. Rulers.
20                              T. Rulers.
```

The exchange structure of this episode is IRF until the final exchange. It is in this way that the teacher seeks to control and guide '*T*'s responses which are evaluated on entirely formal criteria. The task of processing plural sentences is however, beyond '*T*' at this stage of her development. In order to produce the required sentence (i.e. 'These are pens/rulers') '*T*' needs to encode a number of plurality markers:

(1) the plural demonstrative article ('these');
(2) the plural form of the copula ('are');
(3) the zero article;
(4) the plural form of the noun ('rulers', 'pencils', etc.).

However, as at this stage '*T*'s early communicative speech is characterised by the reduction of both grammatical and propositional elements (see Chapter 3), the requirements (1) to (4) above are clearly contrary to her chosen processing strategies. The most likely response she would give to the question 'What are these?' should it occur in a context calling for 'use' rather than 'usage' would be 'Pencil' or 'Ruler'. As it is '*T*' fails to produce one or more of the plurality markers in each of her utterances, as shown in Table 7. The teacher uses a number of discourse devices to help '*T*' in her task. She frames the sentences that are required, (6) and (17), she models the correct answer, (13), and she corrects, (16). Despite these efforts, '*T*' never succeeds in producing a fully correct sentence. The episode ends with '*T*' offering only a single word response, (18), which the teacher appears to accept by her imitation, (19). *T*'s final repetition breaks the IRF mould. It is common in medium-oriented interactions involving L2 learners (Ellis, 1980; McTear, 1975) and may reflect a strategy for acquiring or consolidating vocabulary. It constitutes *T*'s only 'optional' utterance in the entire episode.

TABLE 7
Production of Plurality Markers by T in One Episode

Utterance	Missing plurality marker
5	(1), (3), (4)
11	(1), (2), (3)
12	(1), (3)
15	(1), (2), (3)

It would be unwise to claim that no SLD occurs in '*T*' as a result of participating in this and similar episodes, but from what has been shown about the nature of her development of English in the early stages, it is evident that there is a mismatch between the teacher's goals and the learner's subconscious developmental strategies. '*T*' tended to tire very rapidly of this kind of interaction and only attended to what was being said when the teacher put a question directly to her. As a result little of the total 'input' provided by these interactions was converted into 'intake'.

In medium-centred lessons considerable time can be taken up in establishing the specific goal. This is apparent in the episode below. Here adult EFL students in a private language school in London are being taught a lesson on noun clauses with the past tense. The teacher began by telling them what she had dreamt about.

1	*T*. What did I dream?	
2	*T*. Can you remember?	
3		*P*1. You turned into a toothbrush.
4	*T*. Can I have a full sentence, Hugo?	
5		*P*1. That you turned into a toothbrush.
6	*T*. OK	
7	You ____?	
8		*P*2. You turned into a toothbrush.
9	*T*. You ____?	
10		*P*2. You turned into a toothbrush.
11		*P*3. You dreamed.
12	*T*. You dreamt.	
13		*P*3. You dreamt.
14	*T*. Everyone.	
15		*Chorus*. Dreamt.
16	*T*. OK	
17	I dreamt that I turned into a toothbrush.	

For the learners interactions such as these constitute a puzzle—not a linguistic one, as most of the students had no difficulty in producing correct exemplars of noun clauses later in the lesson, but a cognitive one. They need to discover what the target structure of the day is. The teacher adopts an inductive approach by trying to elicit this structure without actually letting on what it is (i.e. utterances (1), (7), (9)) but her cues are misleading (i.e. 'You _____' does not unambiguously cue 'You said that . . . .') and her correction in (4) is unhelpful, as student 1 did in fact produce a full sentence in (3). Ultimately it is the teacher who models the required sentence, (17). In addition to this 'primary' goal of the episode there is a 'secondary' goal which arises when student 3 uses the wrong past tense form of 'dream'. It is interesting to speculate, that if anything is learnt from this episode, it is from the 'secondary' rather than the 'primary' goal.

It may be that in medium-centred interactions the most valuable input is not that provided by the 'primary' goal but that which occurs in 'side-sequences', when the teacher deviates from the main goal to deal with some issue that has cropped up. This is evident in the 'I don't know' episode quoted on p. 80. Here the main goal was labelling objects in pictures, but the teacher took the opportunity that arose to teach a useful formula. One reason why learning may result from 'side-sequences' is that the teacher's input occurs as a *response* to something the pupils have said rather than as a pre-planned teacher-initiated exchange. By following the communicative direction taken by the pupils, the teacher has in some small way conferred 'rights' on the pupils. In general, however, medium-centred interactions require the teacher to lead and the pupils to follow.

The main problem with medium-centred interactions is that there is little room for any genuine 'teacher-talk' or negotiation of meaning. The structure of the discourse is rigid in the three-phase mould, offering little opportunity to the pupil to exercise his own communication strategies. As Riley (1977) puts it:

> By evaluating, suggesting, correcting, commenting, criticising, managing—that is by 'teaching'—the teacher falsifies or distorts the discourse . . . (p. 12)

Although it would be premature to state that SLD cannot take place from such discourse, what is known about the role of interaction in FLD and naturalistic SLD suggests that SLD is not likely to be facilitated.

Message-oriented goals

Widdowson (1978) has argued that one of the most effective ways of teaching a second language is through teaching the content of ordinary subject lessons. In such cases the interactions will be characterised by message-oriented goals. However, such teaching can only be effective for language learning purposes if the teacher adapts his speech to ensure that meaningful exchanges take place. This is much easier to achieve with intermediate and advanced students than with elementary students. The three beginners in the Language Unit all took part in lessons where the goal involved content to be transmitted to the pupils. The interactive pattern of these lessons tended to be characterised by teacher domination through the use of 'closed' questions. Often there was insufficient adjustment on the part of the teacher to ensure understanding. As a result little was probably learned.

As an example of a message-oriented episode involving a beginner consider the sample below. This occurred about $2\frac{1}{2}$ months after the Portuguese speaking boy's arrival at the Language Unit. The teacher's goal is to familiarise the pupils with the Green Cross Code. She begins by explaining the basic regulations and, then, after some fairly unsuccessful questioning, invites one pupil to mime how to cross the road.

1   *T*. Anan, you start over there.
2   And walk along pretending
        you're crossing the road.
                (Anan begins to mime crossing the road.)
3   That's it.
4   Now, are you going to stop there?
5   Now look down and see why you
        shouldn't stop there.
6   Why shouldn't you stop there?
7   *P*. Looking.

8 *T.* Pardon?
9   *P.* Looking.
10 *T.* Pardon?
11   *P.* Looking.
12 *T.* Yes, but why can't you see?
                        (*The Portuguese boy is expected to*
                        imagine chairs representing cars.)
13   *P.* Two cars.
14 *T.* There's two cars.
15   Right.
16   So what do you do?
17   What do you do?
18   *P.* Walk.
19 *T.* Walk, yes.
20   Further on.

The general impression created by this episode is of a teaching goal
that is beyond the linguistic abilities of the pupils. There are two
reasons for this. The first is that there is nothing in the immediate
context to help the pupils decode the teacher's meanings. The second
is that the teacher's language is very ambitious for pupils at this stage
of development. The episode quoted above is one of the very few in
the whole lesson where any pupil ventures a response. The teacher has
a clear content that she wishes to communicate but the dominating,
interrogating style she chooses appears inadequate for her purpose.

It is instructive to consider how the teacher deals with the pupil's
responses: (7), (9) and (11). The boy seems to be answering some other
question than that actually asked by the teacher in (6). This is not
surprising. 'Why' questions are developed relatively late by both L1
and L2 learners and (6) is particularly difficult as it requires an
understanding of the modality encoded by 'should'. He appears to be
answering a 'What' question and in order to do so may be operating
a strategy of retrieving items from the previous discourse (MacLure
and French, 1980)—in this case, 'look'. The teacher cannot make any
sense of his response at first, but even when she is sure of what he said,
she does not accept it. Instead she repeats her 'Why' question, (12).
This time the boy answers it, after a fashion, perhaps because he has

been clued to attend to the furniture symbolising the two cars (i.e. 13). This utterance is the longest produced by any pupil in the whole lesson.

Not all language lessons are medium-centred. Language teachers often make use of a subject content (e.g. in comprehension lessons) and at times this is not only a means of conveying samples of the TL but takes over as focus of attention. Below is an episode taken from Allwright (1977) in which the 'message' appears to replace the focus on 'medium'.

1 *T*. ... You say he he did, he killed that man.
2   OK.
3   You claim that, but you, if you can't prove it, it's only a claim.
4   Yeah?
5   *P*. He claims ....
6 *T*. Yeah.
7   *P*. I think they'd better produce electric machine for car to use.
8 *T*. For, for to to end the pollution problem?
9   *P*. Yeah.
10   Yeah.
11 *T*. Yeah.
12   OK.
13   What does this mean—'get to'?
14   Uh.
15   *P*. X X
16 *T*. OK.
      It says the group has been trying
      to get the government, to help uhm
      draw special lanes, lanes like this (*Teacher draws on board*)
      on the street.
17   OK.
18   These are for cars.
19   These are for bikes. (*Pointing to board.*)

20	*P.* You know, in Moscow they reproduce all all cab.
21 Uhm?	
22	*P.* They reproduced all cabs X X
23 *T.* They produce?	
24	*P.* Reproduce.
25 *T.* D'you mean uh they they use old cabs, old taxis?	
26	*P.* No, no, no.
27	The reproduced ALL cabs.
28 *T.* All the cabs?	
29	*P.* Yeah.
30	All the cabs for electric (electric you know) electric points.
31 *T.* Cab.	
32 Oh you mean they made the cabs in down in downtown areas uh uh use uh electric motors?	
33	*P.* Yeah.
34	No downtown.
35	All cabs in Mos<u>c</u>ow.
36 *T.* Where?	
37	*P.* In Moscow.
38 *T.* Oh, and it's successful?	
39	*P.* Yeah.
40 *T.* OK.	
41 Uhm, just a second Igor.	
42 Let's see what does this mean?	
43 If you get someone to do something.	
44 Uhm.	

This episode is taken from a lesson taught to a low-level ESL class in the University of California, Los Angeles. The lesson begins as a medium-centred interaction with the teacher trying to explain the meaning of 'claim', but the pupil shifts the focus on to content, (7). The teacher accepts the shift, (8), but the pupil does not pursue the topic, so he returns to a medium-goal, (13). Later, (20), the pupil reintroduces the previous subject and this leads to an extensive series of exchanges in which the teacher requests clarification, (21), (28), offers a correction, (23), requests further information, (25) and attempts to paraphrase what the pupil intended to say, (32). The need to repair the discourse after the potential breakdown caused by (20), leads to a pattern of interaction not so dissimilar from that occurring between adults in naturalistic acquisition (Hatch, 1978a; see p. 91). It is noticeable that in terms of quantity of speech there is far greater equality between teacher and pupil when the focus is on the 'message' than when it is on the 'medium' (compare the teacher's utterances in his first turn, (1) to (4), fifth turn, (16) to (19) and final turn, (41) to (44) with his utterances in the rest of his turns).

Allwright discusses this episode at length but of particular interest here are his comments on the contribution such an interaction might make to language learning. Allwright points out that the pupil has in fact 'disrupted' the lesson by causing the switch from 'medium' to 'message'. This can only be considered detrimental to language learning if 'medium-oriented' goals are more facilitative than 'message-oriented' goals. Allwright in fact suggests that 'real attempts at communication' may be more useful for language learners. He also suggests that the benefit is not only reaped by the participating pupil but also by the 'hearers'. Allwright is reluctant to affirm that the pupil's 'extra participation' is a 'good thing' but it is clear that he feels more is to be learnt from constructing meaningful 'messages' than practising or talking about the 'medium' (see also Allwright, 1979).

What can be said in conclusion about the value of 'message-oriented' interactions for classroom SLD? Clearly, it is not just a matter of the type of goal but also of the accompanying patterns of address. Where the teacher occupies the role of Initiator and the pupils the role of Responder there may be relatively few opportunities for the learners to 'test' the limits of their productive competence. Also, where the teacher is not especially good at 'teacher-talk' and has a tendency to refer to displaced activity rather than the here-and-now of the classroom itself, the pupils may not achieve any 'intake' that they can use to extend their receptive competence. This may prove to be the case with beginners who are children. However, when the focus on content offers the learners the chance to negotiate meaning they are interested in on a basis of equality, real opportunities for extending receptive and productive competence can arise. This may be more likely to occur when the pupils are post-beginners and adults.

Activity-oriented goals

Medium and message-oriented interactions are normally associated with T-C address and so are likely to be teacher-dominated. Activity-oriented interactions result in a greater variety of address-types and offer the pupil the opportunity to act as the Initiator to a much greater extent. Lessons where such interactions occur are PE, handicraft, cookery, woodwork etc. Activity-oriented goals can also be introduced into language lessons through the use of various communicative games (e.g. Byrne and Rixon, 1979) and even through language games such as word bingo or hangman. Another approach is to introduce problem-solving activities involving skills such as map-making (Prabhu, 1980). Activity-oriented interactions are perhaps more typical of the primary than the secondary school or adult education, but they are becoming more common in the latter, as a result of the growing recognition that fluency in the use of a L2 requires opportunities for speaking and listening in communicative situations. The main feature of such interactions is that the focus is on the completion of specific activities rather than on the display of knowledge, linguistic or otherwise. Language becomes a means to an end not an end in itself; communication becomes part of the learning process.

As an example of the kind of discourse that can result from activity-oriented goals consider the following sample taken from Ellis (1981a). It is part of a lesson involving a group of 8-year-old Asian children and a native-speaking teacher. The lesson began with a story-telling session but in the episode below the teacher is negotiating the changeover to a meal activity by organising the laying of the table.

1	*P.* Can we do cookin?
2	*P.* Can we do cookin?
3 *T.* Oh, we're going to do some eating.	
4	*P.* I can do.

5 *T*. All right.

6   *P*. X X X

7   *P*. I only had one go.

8 *T*. Oh, you're moaning.

9   Your turn.

10   Belinda, put the bowls on the table.

                                           (*Teacher offers pupil the bowls.*)

11   *P*. Can I?

12   *P*. Can I?

13 *T*. Careful! (*Teacher hands over the bowls.*)

14   *P*. Can I?

15 *T*. Arkesh, put the milk on the table.

                                        (*Teacher gives pupil the bowl of milk*)

16   *P*. Can I?

17   *P*. Can I?

18 *T*. Sha, put the sugar on the table.

                                        (*Teacher gives pupil the sugar bowl.*)

19   *P*. Can I?

20   *P*. Can I?

21 *T*. Nina, put the spoons on the table.

                                        (*Teacher gives pupil the spoons.*)

22   *P*. (*Noise*)

23 *T*. Now shh!

24   Let's go and sit down. (*Teacher starts to get up.*)

This interaction is different from the kinds discussed previously in a number of ways. First, it is initiated by a pupil rather than by the teacher. This is quite common in activity-oriented interactions. Second, it involves a speech act of a very different kind—there are no examples of giving information, only of requesting permission. Third, the pupils' utterances are volunteered rather than elicited. The teacher functions more like a mother than a teacher, seeing her task principally as an organisational one. Her first act is to establish the intended activity, (3), which she does by drawing attention to the key item 'eating' by contrastive stress. Later she embarks on a series of instructions, (10), (15), (18) and (21). Each utterance has the same syntactical pattern with a different nominal. Each utterance is also related to objects that are visible to the children. Ellis compares this episode to that between a mother and a child, noting that although the interaction is not as rich because of the classroom limitations, it contains many of the same interactional features that have been shown to facilitate FLD. Although the repetition of the formal pattern in the teacher's directives is reminiscent of a language drill, the focus in this episode is on what language does rather than what it is.

In order to make comparisons of the effects of different address-types in activity-oriented interactions, a number of samples based on the symbol-drawing activities[5] in the Concept Seven Nine Communication Pack (Wight, Norris and Worsley, 1972) will be discussed. The main purpose of communication games such as symbol-drawing is, as Dickson (1982) puts it, 'to elicit from children (or adults) higher frequencies of various speech acts serving specific communicative functions than would occur naturally in other classroom settings' (p. 145). However, as will become apparent from the samples discussed below it is not the games themselves but the types of address involved in playing them that dictates the richness of the interactions.

The first sample involves the Portuguese boy approximately one month after he joined the Language Unit. He is communicating with a Vietnamese girl who is giving him instructions about a drawing she can see but the boy cannot.

1	*P*1. Draw big red circle.
2	*P*2. Big red circle.
	(*He draws the circle as instructed.*)
3	*P*1. And a small blue circle.
4	*P*2. In here?
	(*He indicates the circle he has already drawn.*)
5	*P*1. I don't know.
6	*P*2. A big?
7	*P*1. I don't know.
8	A square in circle.
9	*P*2. Big or small?
10	*P*1. Small.
11	And in the square draw a big circle.

The task is not easy for the two pupils. Not only do they require linguistic means to encode their instructions with precision but also to maintain the discourse when a communication breakdown occurs. The discourse that results is far removed from the three-phase pattern illustrated in T-C interactions with medium and message-oriented goals. The pupils have to shoulder the burden of both initiating and sustaining the discourse and this requires the performance of a variety of speech acts. Thus, the boy (i.e. Pupil 2) works to keep the communication channel open in (2), to clarify communicative uncertainty in (4) and (8) and to solve a communicative impasse in (6). The successful outcome is the result of negotiation made by the participants working together. This requires that they remain flexible in their use of address (e.g. the boy acts chiefly as the Responder but in (6) takes on more of an Initiating role) and also that they jointly establish *what* constitutes a relevant propositional content and *how* this is to be communicated through speech acts.

Gumperz and Herasimchuk (1972) make an interesting comparison of the interactive styles occurring in P-P and T-P interaction. They suggest that whereas the former is 'co-operative' and characterised by 'syncopation', equal contributions and swift and direct exchanges, the latter is 'hierarchical', involving monotony and teacher-dominated exchanges in which the teacher tries to guide the pupil through a series of pre-determined, pseudo-logical steps. The 'co-operative' style of P-P interactions may be better suited to SLD than the 'hierarchical' style of teacher-dominated interactions in so far as it gives the learners the opportunity to perform different interactive roles and a range of speech acts. In general, however, Krashen (1981b) excepted, teachers and researchers do not consider 'interlanguage-talk' a suitable model for classroom SLD.[6] Also, it should be pointed out that whereas interactions elicited by a communication game played by L1 speakers tend to reflect both an 'analytic mode' and a 'metaphoric mode'[7] (Dickson, 1982) a similar richness is not so apparent in interactions between L2 learners, who rely instead, as illustrated in the above sample, on only the 'analytic' mode. To benefit to the maximum from P-P exchanges, the L2 learner needs to communicate with someone who has sufficient proficiency in the TL to ensure an input that is pitched not just at the learner's level but, at times, slightly beyond it.

T-P interactions offer the pupil the chance to communicate with a linguistically mature partner and they need not be as monotonous as those described by Gumperz and Herasimchuk if the teacher abandons the role of the 'knower'. Below is another episode involving symbol-drawing, this time between the Portuguese boy and a teacher about 12 weeks after the boy arrived at the Language Unit.

1 T. Right, J....
2   Tell me the first picture.
3   P. Pick /∂/ up a crayon.
4   A green crayon.
5   And draw (.) draw a dog.
6   No very big.
7 T. A dog.
8   Not very big.
9   Okay.
10   P. Number one, that's all right.
11   Um, draw a black dog.
12   A small dog.
13 T. Smaller than the green one?
14   P. No.
15   Black.
16 T. A black dog.
17   Smaller than the green one or
        bigger?
18   P. Small.
19 T. Small.
20   P. Not very very very small.
21 T. Very very small?
22   P. Not very ....
23 T. Not too small.
24   Okay. (*Pupil looks to see what he has drawn.*)
25   P. No.
26   Beside.
27 T. Beside.
28   Ah, beside.
29   P. This one go this way.

30 *T.* Which one?
31   This one is going this way? (*Pupil starts to show him.*)
32   Don't show me.
33   *P.* No.
34   This one is all right.
35   This one face here. (*He gestures*
                                     where.)
36 *T.* Oh, the face should be here.
                              P. Yeah.

Although in this episode the teacher still insists on some of the conversational rights that are canonically his (e.g. the right to announce when the interaction will commence, (1), and the right to insist that the 'rules' are followed, (32)) he has forfeited a number of other rights. Thus the teacher does not initiate all the exchanges, does not control the length of the exchanges and does not invariably close them. There is in this episode the same quality of negotiation that was apparent in the previous P-P episode. The pupil performs a wide range of speech acts (directives, corrections, evaluations, confirmations and descriptions) in his role of discourse Initiator, and, although the teacher uses a number of interrogatives ((13), (17), (21), (30), (31)) these function as requests for clarification rather than for information and occur in response to something that the pupil has said. By relinquishing his traditional rights, the teacher creates 'space' into which the pupil is able to move. As a result the pupil's share of the discourse is both quantitatively different (he produces a total of 12 structured utterances, the same number as the teacher) and qualitatively different both with regard to formal and functional aspects from his share in the *T-C* interactions discussed earlier.

It is not possible to demonstrate how this pupil's interlanguage system changed as a result of participating in this interaction, but an inspection of the language he used suggests a number of hypotheses that he might have been able to test out. In (6), for instance, he produces a negative utterance in accordance with an early interlanguage rule (see Chapter 2). The teacher corrects this by way of confirming he has understood the pupil's instruction. Subsequent negative utterances, (20) and (22), are produced in accordance with a later interlanguage rule; they conform to the adult native speaker's form, which is again modelled by the teacher in (23). In this sequence of utterances, therefore, the learner may have received data that will help him in the process of replacing an early with a late rule. This occurs in a context of communication that seeks to resolve a semantic challenge and not a formal one.

This episode also illustrates a particularly productive learner strategy. In (3) the pupil produces a directive and then in (4) expands one of its constituents. (5) is likewise expanded by (6) and (12) builds on (11). In each pair of utterances an initial constituent is developed by means of an expansion strategy. This may be one of the principal ways in which a learner extends the generative power of his interlanguage rules. It is perhaps significant that this strategy only occurs when the pupil initiates. The freedom this gives him to encode his own meanings from his own resources may be crucially important for expanding and automatising the interlanguage system.

When the address pattern in an activity-based interaction is *P-P* (*T*) (i.e. the teacher is listening in while two pupils interact), the freedom apparent in the other interactions discussed above disappears.

1 *T*. See if you can tell him to draw that.
                                     (*The teacher gives Pupil 2 the card.*)
2   *P*1. No pencil.
3 *T*. Here's a pencil.
4   *P*2. P . . . , draw a big square.
5   *P*1. XXX
6 *T*. Listen.
7   *P*2. P . . . , draw a big square.
8   *P*1. Red square?
                                           (*He looks at the teacher.*)
9   *P*2. P . . . , draw a big square.
10 *T*. Draw a big square.
11   *P*1. Big square.
12   Four square?
13 *T*. Four squares, *J* . . .?
14   *P*2. One
15 *T*. One.

16   *P*2. Finished?
17   *P*1. Yes.
18 *T*. No, he hasn't.
19   *P*2. Not finished.
20 *T*. No.
21   A big square

Although *P*1 is supposed to be addressing *P*2, he is for the most part addressing the teacher. The teacher acts as a kind of master of ceremonies, claiming the right to monitor the pupils' meanings and behaviours. As a result he deprives them of the opportunity to negotiate their own way through the task. Thus, it is the teacher who establishes which directives are to count (i.e. (10)), who authorises the pupils to seek clarification (i.e. (13)), to keep open or terminate each activity sequence (i.e. (18)). Not surprisingly there are no obvious interlanguage hypotheses that the pupils could be testing out in this episode.

This discussion of activity-oriented interactions has attempted to show that when certain conditions are met regarding the sharing of discourse rights, it is more likely that language will be experienced as communication similar to that found outside the classroom. It has been suggested that this may help the learner to reconstruct and expand his interlanguage system. Bernstein (1981), writing about early mother–child conversations, has this to say:

> ... a critical developmental function of dialogue is to provide the child with opportunities to participate in creating linguistic relationships of which she/he would be incapable alone. (p. 117)

This may be more likely when the focus of communication is activity in which the participants are mutually engaged and when the learner has control over both what he says and how he says it. *P-P* and perhaps even more so *T-P* discourse in the classroom allows for a negotiation of meaning and consequently linguistic experimentation. It would seem likely that SLD will be facilitated when the learner has the opportunity to perform a variety of speech acts.

Interaction involving framework goals

An efficient teacher is normally thought of as one who can get the pupils to respond instantly (and probably silently) to the organisational requirements of the lesson. Organisational language is only a 'framework' for achieving the pedagogic goals.

In the language classroom where the TL serves as the medium of communication, organisational language can be considered 'natural'. As such it contrasts with the 'artificial' language that is imported into the classroom as or along with the pedagogic goals. The classroom provides its own rationale for communicating about the materials and tools required to carry out an activity, for conducting routine classroom business such as getting out and putting books away or discovering who is absent, for organising outings, for getting on and staying on task and for ensuring that law and order is maintained. It is partly for these purposes that the asymmetrical social structure of the classroom, so often commented on in the literature (e.g. Edwards and Furlong, 1978; Stubbs, 1976) arises. Only by establishing a 'framework' can the tasks that constitute the 'core' goals be undertaken. It is not surprising, then, that classrooms contain an amazing amount of negotiation on the materials needed for a task and that children in particular spend a lot of time getting what is needed. The need to establish an adequate framework has implications for the kinds of talk that take place, both with regard to the interactional roles adopted by the participants and also the speech acts they perform. Accounts of classroom interaction that only consider language relating to 'core' goals (such as those provided by CRAPEL researchers) are incomplete. SLD, particularly in the early stages, may owe much to the discourse that derives from 'framework' goals, where these are negotiated in the TL.[8]

One set of 'framework' goals are the teacher's 'systems-management mechanisms' (Stubbs, 1976). A large proportion of the teacher's total communicative efforts can be taken up with 'coaxing along the communicative process itself' (p. 162), especially when the learners are relative beginners. The teacher has to get the pupils' attention, monitor their understanding by constant checking, clarify, explain, define and when appropriate summarise.

Below are a series of short episodes taken from a lesson involving the Portuguese boy about two weeks after he arrived at the Language Unit. The teacher is trying to get him started on a textbook exercise and then to monitor his progress.

1 *T.* Where have you got up to?
2   Where did you finish?
3   Have you done this? (*The teacher points at an exercise in the*
                              textbook. The pupil shakes his head.)
4   You haven't?
5   Good.

6 *T. J . . .*, no paper for you.
7   Do it in your book.

8 *T.* Have you finished this? (*The pupil nods*)
9   Have you started this? (*The pupil shakes his head.*)
10   You haven't?
11   Good.

12 *T.* I want you to write 'Is this a bus?'
13   And you draw a picture and write 'Yes, it is'.

14 *T. J . . .*, have you finished? (*The pupil looks up. The teacher waits.*
                                      The pupil shakes his head.)

15 *T. J . . .*, have you finished? (*The teacher stoops to the pupil's level*
                                      and looks him firmly in the eye until
                                      the boy shakes his head.)

16 *T. J . . .*, have you nearly finished? (*The pupil shakes his head.*)
17   Where are you up to?
18   Have you finished this?
19   Finished this? (*The teacher points at the exercise.*)

Two points can be made about these samples. The first is the repetitive nature of certain kinds of teacher requests. For example requests relating to finishing an activity occur in (2), (8), (14), (15), (16), (18) and (19). Such requests are related to specific contexts that are the classroom equivalent of the 'routine interactional contexts' that Ferrier (1978) identified as important in FLD (see p. 88). The second point is the context-dependency of the teacher's utterances. Rarely is any reference made to non-contiguous objects or events in 'framework' language. This is reflected in the frequent use of 'this' (often accompanied by a non-verbal identification of the referent) in the episodes quoted above. It is not surprising that two of the earliest forms to appear in the Portuguese boy's (and also the two Punjabi-speaking children's) language were routines with 'finish' and 'this'. The repetitiveness and the obvious communicative utility of these forms clearly contribute to their development.

Repetitiveness and context-dependency are features of almost all types of organisational language in the classroom. Another regular feature is the use of various kinds of directives. Ellis (1980) gives examples of the two most common types; need statements (e.g. 'I want you to finish this exercise for homework'.) and imperatives (e.g. 'Finish this exercise for homework'). Below are two interactions (one involving the Portuguese boy and the other the Punjabi-speaking girl) that illustrate the pervasiveness of directives in classroom interaction.

1 T. J . . . , could you collect the scissors
       for me?   (*Pupil picks up his own scissors only. The teacher goes to his table.*)
2 T. In the box.
3   Go round and collect the scissors
       in the box.   (*The teacher points at the box. Pupil picks up his scissors and puts them in.*)
4 T. All right.
5   Put the scissors in the box.   (*Pupil starts to go round and collect the scissors.*)

---

6 T. T . . . , can you collect the
       scissors for me?   (*Pupil does not move.*)

7 *T. T...*, collect the scissors
for me.   (*The teacher points at the
                                 scissors. Pupil does not move.*)
8 *T. T...*, collect the scissors
for me.   (*Pupil begins to collect the
                                 scissors.*)

In both episodes the teacher's directive is not immediately successful
but by dint of repetition or paraphrase and with the help of contextual
clues he is able to make the children understand. There are a number
of reasons why such interactions might aid SLD. First, they occur in
standard action-frames, i.e. familiar and frequently-occurring contexts.
Second, they refer to the 'here-and-now', which keeps the decoding
task simple. Third, like the L1 learner, the L2 learner may be equipped
with an 'action-strategy'. (Schatz, 1978) which makes him particularly
responsive to directives. Fourth, directives in the imperative form are
morphosyntactically simple and so may be ideally suited to the
learner's limited processing capacity in the early stages of SLD. Fifth,
directives require a non-verbal response and so are more likely to result
in 'successful' communication than requests for information, which
require the learner to draw upon his productive competence. Although
it is not clear what aspects of development directives foster it can be
speculated that they facilitate development of the propositional component of the learner's grammar (see p. 47) by giving salience to how
the TL encodes events that are already cognitively available to the
learner through visual perception. As discussed earlier there is now
considerable evidence available (Ellis and Wells, 1980; Wells *et al.*, in
press) that directives, at the very least, facilitate the *rate* of FLD.
Politzer (1980) and Politzer *et al.* (1981) have also found the frequency
of direct imperatives is related to the success of medium-centred goals
in the classroom.

If the predominant speech act in the teacher's organisational language is the directive, the speech act that has the greatest frequency
in the children's contributions is the procedural interrogative. This
occurs when the purpose is to clarify or confirm something that the
teacher (and sometimes another pupil) has said. Procedural interrogatives constitute the vast majority of interrogatives produced in

learners' 'communicative' speech in the classroom. Here are some examples, taken from the speech of the Portuguese and Punjabi-speaking children:

> This one or this one?
> Writing?
> Put name sir?
> Miss, this one draw?
> Number one?
> Sir, this one cutting?

They often occur in a stream. They are realised by means of 'intonation questions' (i.e. declarative statements spoken with a rising intonation) which constitute the first developmental types of interrogatives to appear in SLD (see p. 33). Three points are important. The first is that they occur because of a strong communicative need (the pupils just have to find out how to get on task). The second is that they often occur as pupil initiations in the middle of an activity. The third is that, like other types of 'framework' language, they have an immediate locus of reference.

A rather different kind of pupil-talk related to 'framework' goals is what Atkins (1978) calls 'task-talking'. This involves verbal commentaries that learners use to help shape the activities in which they participate. They are far more common with young children than with adolescents or adults, but even the latter use them on occasions. 'Task-talking' is a form of self-initiated practice; it is learner-autonomous and repetitive in nature. It may be an important means of automatising partially developed interlanguage rules. Here is an example of the kind of language that can occur; it was produced by the Punjabi-speaking boy about 6 months after he came to the Language Unit.

1	*P.* This one no colour.
2	This one colour.
3	Not red colour.
4	Oh no good!

5	Oh yes, no colour.
6	Here's no colour.
7	No here colour.
8	Yes colour here.

So far classroom 'framework' language has been illustrated separately from the teacher's and the pupil's perspective. It would be wrong, however, to suggest that there is no *negotiation* involved. The interaction below shows how the teacher and the pupil sometimes need to co-operate in decision making. The pupil (the Portuguese boy) has gone to the front of the classroom to get a new piece of paper because he has made a mess of his first piece.

1 *T. J*..., try and rub it out.

2   *P.* No very good.
                                           (*Pupil waves his paper in the air.*)

3 *T.* Try and rub it out. (*Teacher mimes the action of rubbing out.*)
                                           (*Pupil goes to get a rubber and starts to rub it out. Then he abandons the attempt and goes to get another piece of paper.*)

4 *T. J*..., did you try rubbing it out first?

5   *P.* No very good.

6 *T.* It wasn't very good?

7   All right.   (*Pupil gets a new piece of paper.*)

Conversations such as these, simple as they are, are far removed from the IRF pattern of interaction observed in interactions with 'core' goals. They demonstrate that 'everyday talk' such as that experienced by the child at home in FLD can and does occur in the classroom, although not in the same quantity. Both the amount and the quality of the discourse that occurs in 'framework' interactions may be important for SLD and may help to explain why the classroom SLD of the Portuguese speaking and two Punjabi-speaking children is so similar to naturalistic SLD.

Interactions involving social goals

Classrooms are places where people socialise as well as learn. In classrooms where all the learners share their mother tongue or a lingua franca, socialising is unlikely to take place in the TL. But in classrooms where there is no common language in which all the pupils are fluent, the TL may be used for purely social matters.

In many classrooms, however, social exchanges are not encouraged; they take place in time that is 'borrowed' from the pursuance of pedagogic goals. Pupils form an expectancy that the kind of discourse they will engage in in classrooms will be 'pedagogic' rather than 'natural' and, as a result, may be reluctant to make use of social opportunities for talk. This was so in the case of the Portuguese boy in his first weeks at the Language Unit. He was the only Portuguese speaker in the class and so had to use English whenever he needed to interact with the other pupils. But he initially showed little inclination to take part in pupil–pupil informal talk. English was treated as a 'transactional' language. Most of the social utterances addressed to his fellow pupils were directives borrowed from classroom routines:

1   *P.* Dinner time you out. (*To a pupil who wanted to stay in the classroom.*)

2   *P.* Be quiet please. (*Other pupils were interfering during a game of word bingo.*)

Later on, however, he used English extensively to communicate with other pupils and also with his teachers about purely social matters.

In many language classrooms there is no need to use the TL for social purposes. This was the case for the two Punjabi-speaking children, who were taught in classrooms containing other Punjabi-speaking children. What social English they used was addressed to the teacher in most instances, although there were interactions with other pupils involving complaints and the protection of property and rights, as in the sample below where the boy is arguing with another pupil who has taken all the coloured pencils:

1   *P.* Not this colour!

2   Give me colour one.

3   Not this one colour.
4   You four colour.
5   Give me colour one.

This was said at great speed and with great determination. The sequence of utterances constituted the lengthiest this learner had produced in the first three months. However in classroom SLD there is often little opportunity for this kind of spontaneous child–child conversation, although in an adult class where the learners have mixed mother tongues, social talk may be more common.

Conclusions

Successful SLD can take place in a classroom, i.e. learners can develop the knowledge and skills required for spontaneous communication in the TL. The extent to which this occurs depends on various psycho-sociological factors that influence the learner's attitudes and motivation towards learning the TL. However, even where these factors are favourable, successful development will only take place if the learner is afforded the interactional opportunities to modify and extend his interlanguage system by 'pouring back and forth', 'spreading apart' and 'gathering together'.

The purpose of this chapter has been to examine some of the discourse processes involving teacher and pupils which *might* contribute to the route and rate of SLD. The discussion has been explanatory and speculative but strong theoretical grounds and some illustrative evidence have been advanced to suggest that the classroom does afford, in some types of discourse, very similar kinds of 'input' to that occurring in naturalistic FLD and SLD. The similarity can be graphically represented as shown in Fig. 7. The shaded area shows the extent of the similarity. The reason why classroom SLD appears to follow a similar path to that in naturalistic SLD may be because in both types there are the same, facilitative types of interaction; the reason why classroom SLD so often does not seem to lead to an ability to communicate spontaneously in the TL may be because often the environmental conditions of the classroom are not those that foster the development of 'communicative' speech. What, then, are the

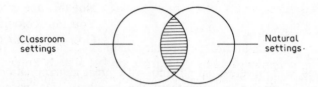

FIG. 7. The relationship between classroom discourse and that occurring in natural settings.

environmental conditions that encourage SLD and how are these made available to the learner? An examination of the literature in both FLD and SLD research together with the analysis of classroom interactions provided in this chapter suggests the following aspects of discourse may be important:

(1) *Quantity of 'intake'*

Wells (1979) found that the amount of adult speech addressed to the L1 learner helped rapid learning. This would also seem likely for SLD. One effect of social and psychological distance (Schumann, 1978) is to reduce the amount of speech that the learner comes into contact with. It is, however, not merely a question of the amount of speech made available to the learner but of the amount that is converted into 'intake'. In the classroom a lot of the language addressed to the class may not be 'comprehensible' and/or may not be attended to. Wells' research has also shown that quantity of speech itself is not sufficient for rapid development; qualitative aspects are also important.

(2) *A need to communicate*

The L1 learner needs to communicate in order to understand his environment, but this is not so with the L2 learner. In naturalistic SLD the learner is likely to need to interact socially, but in classroom SLD this need is greatly reduced. A third kind of need, however, can exist very strongly in the classroom when the TL serves as the medium as well as the target of instruction; the need to communicate for transactional purposes.

(3) *Independent control of the propositional content*

Unless the learner is free to express his own meanings, there can be no need to communicate. A corollary of this requirement is that the meanings communicated by the learner are not already known by the other interlocutors. If the learner is merely asked to supply responses to fit the teacher's pre-determined template of the communicative task, there will not be the opportunity for him to use his resources in a flexible manner. This flexibility may be crucial for shaping the interlanguage system.

(4) *Adherence to the 'here-and-now' principle*

In the early stages of both FLD and SLD the locus of reference for communicative events should ideally consist of contiguous elements in the interactive context. Blank *et al.* (1978) have shown how the 'perceptual-language distance' controls both the cognitive and linguistic complexity of the task. The greater the distance between what can be immediately perceived and what is being talked about, the more difficult it becomes to encode and decode propositional meaning.

(5) *The performance of a range of speech acts*

This is related to (2). When there are different communicative needs a wide range of speech acts will have to be performed. Only if the learner has the chance to initiate as well as to respond in communicative exchanges, will he be able to perform a full range of illocutionary meanings. In the home contexts of FLD it is the child who initiates most conversations (Woll, Ferrier and Wells, 1975), and when the child is not allowed to initiate discourse, communication often breaks down. In the classroom the learner is often cast in the role of responder with a corresponding restriction in the range of speech acts he is able to perform (Ellis, 1980; Gremmo, Holec and Riley, 1977).

(6) *An input rich in directives*

Various reasons for the facilitative effects of directives have already been given (see p. 123).

(7) *An input rich in 'extending' utterances*

'Extending' utterances are defined by Wells *et al.* (in press) as those utterances that 'pick up and elaborate, or add to the meaning that the child has just contributed'. They consist of various topic-incorporation devices such as expansions, extensions, imitations and paraphrases. These often have the form of polar interrogatives. One of their main functions is the maintenance of intersubjectivity. As such they differ from the 'Feedback' move in IRF exchanges, which is typically used in the classroom to keep the teacher's meanings 'in play' rather than to develop those of the pupil.

(8) *Uninhibited 'practice'*

'Practice' refers to the autonomous right to use language without communicative intent and also to the opportunity to repeat utterances that are meaningful to the learner. It corresponds to the egocentric talk that many children engage in in FLD. In this sense, therefore, there is no connection with the kind of 'practice' provided by audio-lingual teaching methods.

There are other factors that could have been mentioned. One is the importance of two levels of 'input', one pitched at the learner's current level and the other in advance (see Cross, 1977), although this can be taken as implied by the eight factors listed. One factor that has been deliberately excluded is 'an input rich in requests for information'. Wells *et al* (in press) and Ellis and Wells (1980) could find no facilitative effect for the frequency of this kind of question in FLD. 'Teacher-talk' contains high frequencies of such questions. Long (1981b), in an analysis of foreigner-talk discourse suggests that questions are favoured by the native speaker because they signal to the non-native speaker that a speaking turn is approaching, they require an answer and they lighten the conversational burden for the addressee. There is, however, no evidence that questions aid SLD; Long, in fact, reports a very low correlation coefficient between frequency orders in the input and the L2 users' accuracy orders. Questions tend to be frequent when a large proportion of the topic-initiating moves is taken up by the native speaker, and, as has been argued in (5), this is not conducive to rapid language development.

Fillmore's (1982) study discussed earlier showed that the availability of facilitative discourse types is not entirely dependent on the type of classroom organisation adopted by the teacher. Pupils will learn most successfully when they are given ample opportunities to interact in conversations characterised by the eight conditions described above. But *how* these opportunities are provided will depend on various other factors such as the stage of SLD the pupils are at (i.e. whether they are beginners or more advanced) and the composition of the class (i.e. whether the class is mixed or composed mainly of L2 learners and whether or not they have access to a common language other than the TL). Thus the type of classroom organisation that is most facilitative in one situation may not be so successful in another. Table 8 is an

TABLE 8

The Facilitative Characteristics of Different Types of Classroom Interaction Involving Three Learners in a Language Unit

Types of classroom interaction	Aspects of discourse							
	(1)	(2)	(3)	(4)	(5)	(6)	(7)	(8)
1. 'Core' goals								
(a) Medium-oriented								
(i) grammar (T-C)				+				
(ii) formulae (T-C)		+		+				
(b) Message-oriented (T-C)								
(c) Activity-oriented								
(i) P-P	+	+	+	+	+	+		
(ii) P-T	+	+	+	+	+	+	+	
(iii) P-P(T)				+				
2. 'Framework' goals								
(a) Teacher language (T-P)	+	+		+		+	+	
(b) Pupil language (P-T)	+	+	+	+	+			+
3. 'Social' goals		+	+	+	+	+		+

+ Potentially facilitative.

attempt to suggest how different types of classroom interaction were successful in providing an input that met the eight conditions described above for the three children at the Language Unit, whose conversations have been used extensively to illustrate the role that verbal interaction can play in classroom SLD. In the case of this particular learning situation the types considered to be most facilitative have activity-oriented, framework and social goals, although social interactions do not meet criterion (1) (i.e. quantity). The types that are shown to be least facilitative have medium-centred and message-centred goals. It must be emphasised that the profile provided by Table 8 is specific to the three children. It would seem likely that when the learners are adults or when the class is mixed the profile will be different. The extent to which this proves to be the case is a matter for further research.

Notes

1. The Bristol Language Development Study was part of a larger project called 'Language at Home and at School'. This was directed by Gordon Wells and was SSRC funded. It involved the longitudinal study of 128 children from a wide range of homes and was concerned with describing their development of language and conversation.
2. There are differences between foreigner talk and motherese. Freed (1980) identified differences in the frequency of a number of language functions. Motherese contained higher frequencies of questions and instructions, whereas foreigner talk contained higher proportions of statements. Freed suggests that whereas the main purpose of motherese is to direct the child's behaviour, in foreigner talk the main purpose is to exchange information.
3. There is a general assumption that the adjustments which take place in teacher-talk facilitate communication. However, this need not always be the case. Chaudron (1983) illustrates how lexical and grammatical simplification and the teacher's use of specific discourse strategies may sometimes lead to ambiguity and over-elaboration which actually hinder understanding by L2 learners.
4. Appendix A lists the conventions used in transcribing the conversations quoted in this chapter.
5. Symbol drawing activities involve pupils communicating in pairs about a diagram or picture. In each pair only one of the pupils can see the diagram; the other pupil has to draw it. When he has done so he shows it to his partner so they can check how successful their communication has been.
6. Fillmore (1982), for instance, argues that pupils need exposure to the standard speech of the teacher and that interlanguage-talk can lead to a pidgin-like competence. However, because interlanguage-talk is likely to involve equality of roles it affords opportunities for language use not typically available in T-P talk.

7. Utterances that describe the physical features of a diagram are in the 'analytic mode':

   e.g. It goes out but then it sort of curves a little bit.

   Utterances that involve a comparison between some feature of the diagram and some other object are in the 'metaphorical mode':

   e.g. This one sort of looks like two fingers coming up.

8. I believe there are strong arguments for ensuring that classroom management and organisation are conducted in the L2 rather than the learners' L1. In the ESL classroom, which the interactional extracts chosen for this chapter principally illustrate, the L2 was inevitably used for these functions. In the EFL classroom, however, teachers sometimes prefer to use the pupils' L1 to explain and organise a task and to manage behaviour in the belief that this will facilitate the medium-centred goals of the lesson. In so doing, however, they deprive the learners of valuable input in the L2.

Chapter 6

Teaching Grammar and Classroom Second Language Development

So far, the focus has been the classroom language learner. However, as traditionally it is the teacher who determines both the content and the nature of the interactions, it is also necessary to take a look at classroom language development from his point of view. In general the teacher is likely to conceive of his task as one of teaching and practising grammatical items in order to help the learner internalise the generative rule system in the shortest possible time. From the teacher's point of view, therefore, the central question is: What is the relationship between formal instruction and SLD? Can syntax be taught?

These questions have already been partially considered in Chapter 5, where it was suggested that teacher-dominated interaction that results from 'medium-centred' goals may restrict some learners' ability to construct and amend hypotheses about the L2. It was also pointed out, however, that learning can take place when 'secondary' goals arise as a response to something that the learner has said. An example was the 'I don't know' formula which was explicitly taught in this way to the two Punjabi-speaking children. In general, though, medium-centred interactions do not allow the kind of negotiation which appears to foster language development. The role of teaching was also considered in Chapter 2. It was reported that the order of development of a number of grammatical structures did not appear to be substantially influenced by formal instruction in the case of 10+-year-old children in both a 'pure' and an 'impure' classroom environment. The drift of the previous chapters has been that accurate and automatic performance of 'modelled' speech, which is the target of formal grammar teaching, is not related to the spontaneous 'communicative' speech which develops as a result of discourse processes required for the negotiation of meaning.

There are still a number of important issues relevant to the role played by grammar teaching that are outstanding. The purpose of this chapter is to consider directly if and how classroom SLD can be influenced by formal instruction. To this end it will be necessary to examine exactly what is meant by 'formal instruction', what the learner variables are that may determine the extent and the nature of its effects and what these effects are. Finally, this chapter will discuss the validity of the non-interface hypothesis which Krashen (1981b) has advanced to account for the relationship between the kind of learning which results from formal instruction and that which derives from participating in spontaneous 'communicative' speech.

Instructional variables

A conventional grammar lesson has a 'structure of the day'. This is presented either inductively or deductively by the teacher and then practised to help the pupils automatise its use. During the practice stage the teacher is likely to try to reinforce well-formed utterances and to correct deviant utterances. Further instruction on a remedial basis may well be offered at a later date. The essence of grammar teaching is 'consciousness-raising' and practice.

'Consciousness-raising' is a term used by Sharwood-Smith (1981), who argues that allowances must be made for degrees of explicitness and of elaboration in grammar teaching. Explicitness refers to the extent to which the teacher makes use of the metalanguage of formal grammars (e.g. the teacher can hint with the help of examples or he can state a formal rule). Elaboration refers to the amount of space and time taken up by the presentation of the rule. Using these two dimensions, which Sharwood-Smith represents as continua, he distinguishes four basic types of 'consciousness-raising' as shown in Fig. 8. Sharwood-Smith points out that before it is possible to decide that grammar-teaching does not contribute to SLD it is necessary to consider the different types of consciousness-raising. 'Formal instruction', then, needs to be differentiated at the level of presentation.

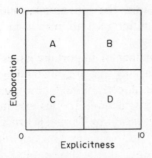

Fig. 8. Consciousness-raising in language learning (Sharwood-Smith, 1981, p. 161).

It also needs to be differentiated at the level of practice. There is a battery of techniques, mechanical and contextual, that are available to the language teacher for practising a grammatical rule. There are also a number of different strategies for correcting pupils' responses (see Allwright, 1975; Long, 1977). Although the evidence of the comparative method studies suggests that there is little to choose between the effectiveness of one set of techniques and another (see Krashen, 1982, chapter 5) the possibility that the manner in which formal instruction is handled is an important variable influencing the success of SLD cannot be overlooked. The difficulty of testing the comparative effectiveness of different methods in the classroom has long been recognised.

The effectiveness of formal instruction may also be dependent on the nature of the grammatical rule that is being taught. Krashen (1982) suggests that the learnability of rules is probably a product of their formal and functional simplicity. Thus the 3rd person singular of the present tense is formally and functionally simple, the definite and indefinite articles formally simple but functionally difficult and WH interrogatives formally difficult. Krashen suggests that even the best pupils can only 'learn' a small subset of those taught, which in turn is only a small subset of the applied linguist's knowledge. There are cognitive limitations on the extent to which pupils can consciously attend to formal language rules. If the teacher tries to exceed these limits successful SLD is not likely.

The target of formal instruction need not be a 'rule'; it might be a 'formula'. Sharwood-Smith provides an interesting illustration of how explicit knowledge can be used to plan some aspects of L2 performance:

> ... a good oral example of this would be preparing a short question, a speech or telephone conversation where certain things can be predicted in advance. You know what you will have to say. You have attended an effective course of formal instruction giving you a range of procedures which allow you to put together utterances in a completely conscious manner. (p. 166)

Sharwood-Smith does not distinguish between consciousness-raising involving 'rules' and that involving 'formulas', but the example he gives suggests that what he has in mind is the kind of 'script' discussed in Chapter 4 (see p. 67). It is possible that formulaic speech may be more amenable to formal instruction than creative rules.

The formal linguistic environment that arises as a result of grammar teaching involves far more than consciousness-raising and formal language practice. As Bialystok (1981) puts it:

> ... a formal learning situation encompasses many more features than those which are explicitly designated as the goal of the lesson, such as extraneous conversation, the social context in which the lesson occurs, and so on .... (p. 65)

This was the assumption of the previous chapter, where the various kinds of contexts created by the classroom were examined. Thus lessons that have the learning of a particular grammatical rule as their goal will also involve interactions with 'framework' goals and perhaps also with 'social' goals. Furthermore even medium-centred goals will provide far more than knowledge of a rule. For example, a lesson on plurality markers might require pupils to produce sentences like:

These are pencils.

But even if the pupils are unable to internalise or use the plurality markers in this sentence, they may obtain useful information about some other feature of the sentence (e.g. the use of the copula in equational sentences). Although the pupils have had their consciousness raised with regard to the *target* structure, they will not have had it raised with regard to other features, which must inevitably co-occur in sentences devised to model the target structure. In this sense then the 'focus on form' is never absolute. Formal instruction, therefore, needs to be seen as a matrix in which various kinds of input are made available to the learner.

A corollary of the above argument is that it is perfectly possible to acquire knowledge of a grammatical rule in a classroom without consciousness-raising and formal practice. Rules can be 'picked up' in the classroom as in any other setting. Empirical evidence for this can be found in a study of 43 classroom learners of Spanish as a foreign language by Terrel *et al.* (1980). They investigated whether these learners successfully developed rules for interrogatives without having received any explicit teaching in them. They found that 82% of the questions they elicited from the higher grade pupils and 74% from the lower grade pupils were well-formed. They argued that, as the teaching methods the students had been exposed to involved extensive use of questioning by the teacher, the pupils had been provided with an input rich in interrogatives which had been sufficient for development to take place.

SLD research has not always recognised that language lessons centred on grammar teaching also provide incidental exposure to target language data. Felix (1981), in the study discussed in Chapter 2, makes no mention of classroom exposure as a potential source of input for SLD. Krashen *et al.* (1978) equate the number of years of formal study (which will involve both formal teaching and exposure) with formal instruction. They found that 116 ESL students' proficiency correlated more strongly with the number of years of formal English study than with the number of years they had spent in an English speaking environment. Their conclusion is hardly justified, however:

> . . . formal instruction is a more efficient way of learning English for adults than trying to learn it in the streets. (p. 260)

The difficulties of separating out the effects of instruction and of exposure that arises from the instruction may be insuperable. Certainly they cannot be resolved without paying careful attention to the process of interaction that occurs in the classroom.

Another important variable is the learner's perspective. What for the teacher may be an attempt to practise a rule may be something else entirely for the learner. Loveday (1982) has noted that the teacher's conscious insistence on norms has less to do with learning and speaking a language than with the kinds of operation activated by mathematical problems, memorisation and the methods of analysis used in natural science. From the pupil's point of view formal practice calls for what Felix (1977) has called 'reproductive competence'. Hosenfeld (1976; reported in McDonough, 1981) investigated the ways in which pupils set about performing language drills by asking them to instrospect and report on the strategies they used. She concluded that what was being practised were procedures for getting right answers rather than the grammatical items themselves. McDonough comments:

> ... from the pedagogical point of view we need to decide
> whether the problems given to the students encourage the
> development of language proficiency or merely make further
> problems of the same type easier to solve. (p. 25)

'Formal instruction' cannot be glossed simply as a 'focus on form'. The extent and nature of this focus is variable in terms of both 'elaboration' and 'explicitness'. Even greater variability exists in the techniques for practising and correcting, while the choice of rule is another factor that may influence the success of training. Also formal instruction will inevitably offer 'exposure' to L2 data which have not been designated targets for learning by the teacher. Finally, from the learner's perspective formal instruction may be treated as a cognitive puzzle calling for general problem-solving strategies rather than language learning. All these are necessary caveats when it comes to examining the effectiveness or otherwise of formal language training.

Learner variables

It is an everyday experience of language teachers that where teaching succeeds with one pupil, it fails with another. To talk monolithically of the success or failure of formal instruction is, therefore, very dangerous. What, then, are the learner variables that may affect the ability of the individual pupil to benefit from formal training?

The variable most frequently referred to in arguments refuting the ineffectiveness of formal instruction is the learner's stage of development. As James (1980) has suggested, grammar teaching needs to be timed to just precede or to co-occur with the emergence of a specific form in the learner's interlanguage, if it is to be successful. This is in line with Vygotsky's (1962) assertion that instruction must be related to the learner's 'zone of proximal development' (p. 103). It is the difficulty of ensuring this in classrooms that contain learners at different stages of development that led Krashen (1981b) to argue that 'rough tuning' derived from attempts to communicate meaningfully is the safest way of ensuring that 'i + 1' is covered.

The learner's stage of development may affect the success of formal instruction in another way. *Beginners* may benefit to a greater extent than intermediate or advanced pupils. This is the position adopted by many language teachers, including those who advocate a methodology that emphasises the natural, fluent use of the L2 (e.g. through communication games). Before the learner can begin to be communicative, it is argued, he needs to obtain at least some minimal competence in the L2 and this can be provided most effectively through the presentation and practice of formal language items. Later on, development can take place through the process of communicating itself. This is an important argument, and although it is challenged in Chapter 8, it highlights a potentially significant learner variable.

Another learner variable often invoked is age. Various reasons have been put forward for suggesting that adults and adolescents are more likely to benefit from formal instruction than children. Lenneberg (1967) proposed a neurolinguistic explanation. As a result of lateralisation, language learning functions become specialised in the left hemisphere (in most learners) which affects the operation of the

'Language Acquisition Device'. Thus after about the age of 12 the learner resorts to alternative strategies in language learning. This neurolinguistic explanation has been challenged on a number of grounds (see Genessee (1982) and Seliger (1982) for a review of the literature) and there is now general agreement that adults are neu-rolinguistically capable of learning a L2 in much the same way as children. It is also generally accepted, however, that adults are more amenable to formal study in language learning, perhaps as a result of Formal Operations (Krashen, 1981b; Rosansky, 1975). Rosansky argues that cognitive development leads to a progressive decentration and flexibility accompanied by a meta-awareness. Whereas the young child does not know he is learning a language, the adult and adolescent are always aware. It is this awareness that blocks natural language learning and encourages viewing the acquisition task as 'a problem to be solved using hypothetico-deductive logic' (p. 98). Rosansky suggests that the only route open to the adult is via instruction which treats the TL as a 'subject'. This explanation founders, however, on the growing evidence from empirical studies of adult SLD (e.g. Bailey *et al.*, 1974; Schumann, 1978; Shapira, 1978) that adult SLD follows the same route and uses the same processes as child SLD. It is possible that the phenotypical similarity of adult and child SLD masks different devel-opmental strategies, but the available evidence suggests otherwise. It would seem, therefore, that although adults have a capacity for formal study that is greater than that of children, they also continue to have access to the same informal learning processes as in child SLD. It must be admitted that adults are better equipped to benefit from formal instruction in a L2. The central question is whether knowledge they gain in this way is knowledge that can be used 'communicatively'.

A third variable is motivation. Despite the slipperiness of this concept, it is recognised that motivation, whether instrumental or integrative (Gardner and Lambert, 1972) or whether global, situational or task-oriented (Brown, 1981) or whether part of the act of commu-nication itself (MacNamara, 1973) is a determining factor in SLD. Sharwood-Smith (1981) suggests how motivation may be important where formal instruction is concerned. He argues that the explicit knowledge derived from consciousness-raising may not be automatised (and so available as implicit knowledge) unless the learner is disposed to spend the energy and extra time that is required to effect this transfer. 'Fossilisation' occurs when the learner is not so disposed. Thus the overall effectiveness of formal instruction may depend not only on the learner's preparedness to invest effort in consciousness-raising but also in his preparedness to practise until automaticity is achieved.

Personality may also influence the effectiveness of instruction. Learners who see mistakes as threats to their egos may be more inclined to treat the task of learning as a hypothetico-deductive task than to risk spontaneous communication. With regard to performance in a L2 Krashen (1978) has suggested that extroverted learners are likely to underuse the Monitor (i.e. the knowledge the learner uses to consciously edit his errors) and introverts to overuse it. In general, however, the relationship between personality and learning-styles is very speculative and it is not clear what type of personality will or will not benefit from formal instruction.

A final variable worth considering concerns the availability of different kinds of learning environment. Chapter 2 (p. 73) reviewed the literature dealing with the effects of classroom exposure on different kinds of learners. Krashen (1982) argues that the differences in the findings of a number of research projects can be explained in terms of the availability of opportunities for naturalistic exposure to the TL. Formal instruction has little effect if the learner has the chance to communicate in the L2 outside the classroom. This argument suggests that in the case of 'pure' classroom SLD formal instruction may be more effective than in 'impure' classroom SLD. This view, however, is challenged by Long (1983a)—see also the next section.

This review of potential learner variables that may influence the success of formal instruction is not complete (see Altman, 1980 for a comprehensive list). It has been suggested, however, that variables which may be particularly important are the learner's stage of development, his age, motivation and personality and the availability of opportunities for naturalistic SLD. Table 9 speculates on the kind of learner who is the most and the least likely to benefit from formal instruction.

The effects of instruction

There have been a number of studies of the effects of instruction on SLD. It is useful to divide these into three groups; (1) those that

TABLE 9.

Characteristics of L2 Learners Likely to Benefit the Most and the Least from Formal Instruction

Characteristics of learner more likely to benefit from formal instruction	Characteristics of learner less likely to benefit from formal instruction
1. The learner is in the early stages of SLD.	1. The learner is in later stages of SLD.
2. The learner is an adult or adolescent.	2. The learner is a child (i.e. below 12 years old).
3. The learner is prepared to invest energy in automatising explicit knowledge.	3. The learner is not prepared to spend time automatising explicit knowledge.
4. The learner is introverted and does not like taking risks.	4. The learner is extroverted and is prepared to take risks.
5. The learner is totally reliant on the classroom environment for input.	5. The learner is exposed to the TL outside the classroom.

investigate the effects on the *route* of development, (2) those that examine the effects on the level of proficiency achieved (i.e. the *success*) and (3) those that consider the effects on the *rate* of development. As has been constantly pointed out in the previous chapters it is possible that teaching influences both the route and the rate (which is the view taken by the language teaching profession) or that it does not influence the route but does speed up the process. In the case of the latter possibility it is also likely that instruction will contribute to the overall level of proficiency achieved by different learners.

Effects on the route of SLD

Lightbown's research shows that instruction may influence the order in which classroom learners acquire grammatical competence. Lightbown (1983) found that verb morphology (specifically -*ing*) was acquired in a different order than in naturalistic SLD and argued that this was because of 'overlearning' which resulted from both direct instruction and classroom exposure. The effects, however, were short-lived as the 'natural' order appeared to eventually reassert itself (see Chapter 2). Lightbown *et al.* (1980) investigated the effects of classroom teaching on 175 French-speaking students' use of a number of formal features of English grammar. They found that the direct teaching of {s}, the copula in equational clauses and locative prepositions of motion influenced performance. Scores on a grammatical judgement test improved on average 11% in comparison with a 3% improvement in a control group. However, once again the effects were short-lived. The overall scores fell back to an intermediate level in a third administration of the test six months later. It might also be noted that a grammatical judgement test is likely to test the ability to produce 'modelled' rather than 'communicative' language. Lightbown's studies are among the few that find some positive effect of instruction on the route of SLD. The effects reported do not seem long-lasting.

There are several studies that show that formal instruction failed to alter the order of grammatical development in SLD. Schumann (1978) found that his subject, Alberto, was unable to benefit from formal instruction in the use of English negatives, or at least, that his 'communicative' speech was not affected. He concluded that this was because Alberto had 'fossilised', but an equally tenable conclusion would be that instruction did not help. Turner (1978) investigated three ESL learners and found that the order of instruction of a set of grammatical morphemes did not correlate very highly with their order of acquisition. The subjects acquired a number of syntactic patterns in a different order from the teaching order. Further evidence of the failure of formal instruction to influence the order of SLD comes from the longitudinal research projects of Ellis (1982b) and Felix (1981), which were considered in detail in Chapter 2. Whereas these research findings do not provide conclusive evidence for rejecting Bailey et al.'s (1974) assertion that 'years of experience in language learning and teaching show instruction is directly related to English language proficiency in adults' they do suggest that this direct relationship is not the result of attempts to manipulate the developmental route.

None of the studies reported above took pains to ensure that the rules that were being taught were within the learners' 'zones of proximal development'. In an attempt to control for this important variable, Ellis (1984) used his longitudinal study of the two Punjabi-speaking children to decide when to investigate the effects of formal instruction in WH interrogatives. He chose a point when WH questions had begun to appear on a regular basis in the speech of the two children (and others in the same class who were estimated to be at the same or a more advanced stage of development). Inversion in WH questions, therefore, was within the pupils' 'zones of proximal development'. The 13 pupils in the class were given three hours teaching aimed at ensuring a clear understanding of the meaning of 'what', 'who', 'where' and 'when' and the use of subject–verb inversion with all four pronouns. For the class as a whole no significant development in the ability to produce inverted WH questions in an elicitation game designed to obtain samples of 'communicative' speech was observed. When the amount of formal instruction directed at each individual pupil was measured (in terms of teacher-nominated exchanges involving each pupil in the practice stage of one of the lessons), it was found that this was significantly *inversely* related to development of 'when' questions, the last of the four interrogatives to appear in the longitudinal study. In other words those children who developed the most were the ones who were given the least opportunity to practise in formal exchanges.[1] Ellis suggested that individual pupils who did appear to develop their knowledge of WH interrogatives did so not because of the formal instruction that was provided but because they took the opportunity to participate in interactions involving negotiated communication in both the elicitation sessions and also in the classroom. Ellis also noted that the order of development of the four interrogatives observed in this study was the same as that occurring in naturalistic SLD, i.e. the instruction did not effect the route.

Although the difficulty of controlling all the independent variables precludes any firm conclusions regarding the inability of formal instruction to influence what order classroom learners learn the grammar of a L2, the available research suggests that the route, at least where 'communicative' speech is concerned, cannot be altered except temporarily.

Effects on proficiency levels achieved

Long (1983) reviews a number of studies that investigate the effects of instruction on ultimate attainment, as measured using a variety of tests. The results of this review are summarised in Table 10. It should

TABLE 10.

Relationships between Instruction (I), Exposure (E) and Second Language Acquisition (see Long, 1983, p. 375)

Study	SLA Type	Subjects	Proficiency (B, I or A)	Acquisition Environment	Test Type (DP or I)	Instruction helps?	Exposure helps?	I > E or E > I?
Studies showing that instruction helps								
1. Carroll (1967)	FLL in USA & SLA abroad	adults	B I A	mixed	I	yes	yes	E > I
2. Chihara and Oller (1978)	EFL (Japan)	adults	B I A	poor	DP I	yes	no	I > E
3. Brière (1978)	SpSL (Mexico)	children	B	mixed	DP I	yes	yes	I > E
4. Krashen, Seliger, and Hartnett (1974)	ESL in USA	adults	B I A	rich	DP I	yes	no	I > E
5. Krashen and Seliger (1976)	ESL in USA	adults	I A	rich	I	yes	no	I > E
6. Krashen, Jones, Zelinski, and Usprich (1978)	ESL in USA	adults	B I A	rich	DP I	yes	yes	I > E
Ambiguous cases								
7. Hale and Budar (1970)	ESL in USA	adolescents	B I A	rich	DP I	?	yes	E > I?
8. Fathman (1976)	ESL in USA	children	B I A	rich	I	?	yes	E > I?
Studies showing that instruction does not help								
9. Upshur (1968; Experiment 1)	ESL in USA	adults	I A	rich	DP	no	—	—
10. Mason (1971)	ESL in USA	adults	I A	rich	DP I	no	—	—
11. Fathman (1975)	ESL in USA	children	B I A	rich	I	no	—	—
Additional study showing that exposure helps								
12. Martin (1980)	ELS in USA	adults	I A	mixed	DP I	—	yes	—

Note: B = beginning   DP = discrete point
       I = intermediate   I = integrative
       A = advanced

be pointed out that Long's own interpretation of some of the studies differs from that of the original researchers. For instance, Hale and Budar (1970) and Fathman (1976) both concluded that instruction did not influence ultimate attainment. Long reworks their data to show that they support the opposite conclusion.

Long's review indicates that on the whole learners achieve higher proficiency if they have received some instruction. Long notes that this holds (1) for children as well as adults, (2) for intermediate and advanced learners, not just beginners, (3) on integrative as well as discrete-point tests[2] and (4) in acquisition-rich environments (i.e. in settings where learners receive substantial exposure to communicative language use) as well as acquisition-poor environments. Long also points out that instruction has a stronger effect than exposure in five of the studies which examined both.

The evidence that Long compiles is impressive. However, there are a number of problems with this kind of evidence. The first problem has to do with the tests of proficiency that were used in the various studies. Long is careful to note that the effects of instruction are seen on integrative as well as discrete point tests. It is not certain, however, to what extent the integrative tests reflect the kind of performance found in 'communicative' speech. It is possible that the tests tap 'modelled' data, in which case a positive effect for instruction is to be expected. The second problem has to do with the possibility that in some of the studies (e.g. Krashen et al., 1978) instruction was confounded with other related factors, which interact to jointly determine SLD proficiency. For instance, adult students who are highly motivated can be expected to seek out instruction, while those that are not will content themselves with natural exposure. The crucial factor, therefore may be the level of motivation.[3] A third problem is perhaps the most serious. The studies Long examines do not discuss precisely what took place in the name of 'instruction'. In fact 'instruction' appears to be equated with the amount of time spent in a classroom. However, as has already been argued 'instruction' involves both 'exposure' and consciousness raising/practice. Because the classroom is treated as a 'black box', it is not possible to determine what took place in the 'instruction' provided. It is conceivable that it was classroom exposure rather than consciousness raising/practice that facilitated SLD.

Classroom learners in general do better than street learners. But the available quantitative research does not enable us to explain why this is so. Instruction (i.e. inductive/deductive teaching of language rules) may be the reason, but so too may be motivation or classroom exposure or a combination of all three factors.

Effects on the rate of SLD

If instruction can be seen to have an effect on the level of proficiency ultimately attained by learners, it would follow that instruction in some way helps to speed up SLD. One reason why this is the case is that instruction serves to draw the learner's attention to the features of the language which need to be developed. As Sharwood-Smith (1981) puts it:

> It may be 'naturalistic' to learn languages in a purely intuitive manner, but how long will it take to amass a sufficient amount of implicit knowledge and the appropriate skills for using it? .... The short-cut, a ready-made *a priori* explanation (partial or otherwise), is attractive; at the very least it provides an insight into the task and means of labelling and specifying the problem. (p. 160)

What is the evidence to support such claims?

Perkins and Larsen-Freeman (1975) calculated accuracy orders for five morphemes produced by 12 adult Venezuelan students who had recently arrived in the USA, both before and after two months of classroom instruction. They found very little difference in the rank orders of the morphemes on the two occasions, suggesting that the instruction the students had undergone had had little effect on the route. They did observe a gradual improvement in performance in an elicitation task, which may have been due to instruction. They concluded that whereas instruction does not influence the route of SLD it may influence the rate. However, as they did not examine the nature of the interactions that took place in the name of 'instruction', it is once again not possible to tell whether consciousness-raising and practice or 'exposure' facilitated development. Ellis (1984), in the study referred to above, argues that for the 13 children he investigated it was the quality of certain kinds of interaction rather than the focus on form that contributed to the development of 'when' interrogatives in those children who showed some improvement.

There is insufficient evidence to decide whether SLD can or cannot be accelerated by instruction. Surprisingly, although there have been several studies which have examined the comparative effectiveness of different methods to promote learning, there have been few which have investigated whether the presence or absence of instruction in whatever form affects the rate of development of specific L2 forms. Ideally what is required is a controlled study involving matched learners, one group of whom receives instruction in a set of rules (and/or formulas) while the other does not. The time taken for each group to acquire the rules/formulas could then be compared.

To summarise, instruction does not appear to influence the order of development. No matter what order grammatical structures are presented and practised in the classroom, learners will follow their own 'built-in syllabus' (Corder, 1967) as far as 'communicative' language performance is concerned. There is, however, considerable evidence to suggest that classroom learners achieve higher levels of proficiency than naturalistic learners, although precisely why this is so is not clear. It is also likely that instruction makes SLD quicker, but few studies have investigated rate of development. In general the available evidence is not conclusive and so it is not surprising that there is disagreement between those who argue in favour of consciousness-raising (e.g. Sharwood-Smith, 1981) and those who argue that successful SLD only needs exposure that provides 'comprehensible input' (e.g. Krashen, 1982). It is to the theoretical debate that the next section turns.

The non-interface hypothesis

Krashen (1981b) distinguishes 'acquired' and 'learnt' knowledge. 'Acquired' knowledge arises when the learner takes part in natural communication which provides him with 'comprehensible input'. 'Learnt' knowledge derives from conscious study of the formal characteristics of the language. When the learner performs in a L2 he initiates utterances by means of 'acquired' knowledge.[4] 'Learnt' knowledge can only be used to Monitor the output from 'acquired' knowledge and only providing the learner is focused on form, knows the rule and has sufficient time. In normal communication—whether speech or writing—the learner relies on 'acquired' knowledge. Krashen argues that 'acquired' knowledge and 'learnt' knowledge are distinct and unrelated sources so that there is no transfer of knowledge from one to the other. Krashen (1981c) refers to this as the *non-interface hypothesis*.

The alternative position might be called the interface hypothesis. This acknowledges a differentiation of types of knowledge as in the 'acquired/learnt' dichotomy but argues that the sources of knowledge are related. That is, it posits that knowledge can be transferred from one source to the other. This position is represented in the model of SLD proposed by Bialystok and Fröhlich (1977) and is strongly argued by Sharwood-Smith (1981).

Both the non-interface and the interface hypotheses are based on a dual competence model of SLD. In such a model the variability of the learner's performance commented on in Chapter 1 (see p. 3) is accounted for in terms of two separate competencies, one of which is responsible for what has been called 'communicative' language use and the other 'modelled' language use. There are other models of SLD, however, which do not rest on a simple dichotomy of types of knowledge but seek to explain variability in terms of a stylistic continuum which reflects the use of different strategies drawing on a single knowledge store. Such a model is proposed in Chapter 7. For the time being, however, the discussion will be limited to the 'interface' controversy.

Krashen (1981c) reviews the arguments in favour of the non-interface hypothesis. He argues that learners such as 'P' who are intelligent, hard-working and highly-motivated, nevertheless are still unable to utilise 'learnt' knowledge in spontaneous communication. Even where the learner is strongly motivated to automatise 'learnt' knowledge, this knowledge remains unavailable in normal conversations. Support for the inability of learners to utilise 'learnt' knowledge in face-to-face interaction also comes from Seliger (1979), who showed that there was no relationship between his subjects' ability to use 'a' and 'an' before a noun and their ability to state the rule involved. The separateness and primacy of 'acquired' knowledge is also, according to Krashen, apparent in learners who have access to rules that they have never been consciously 'learnt'. Krashen also claims that learners who 'learn' rules before they 'acquire' them do not avoid having to 'acquire' them at a later date. Another argument advanced in favour of the non-interface hypothesis is the invariant order of development. It has been argued that learners follow a fixed route in SLD, which cannot be substantially altered by instruction. Because 'learnt' knowledge cannot be converted into 'acquired' knowledge, consciousness-raising and formal practice have only a minor role to play in SLD:

> The use of the conscious grammar is limited. Not everyone Monitors. Those who do only Monitor some of the time and use the Monitor for only a sub-part of the grammar ... the effect of self-correction on accuracy is modest. Second language performers can typically self-correct only a small percentage of their errors, even when deliberately focused on form ... and even when we only consider the easiest aspects of grammar. (Krashen, 1982, p. 112)

The non-interface hypothesis runs counter to the traditional assumption of language teaching and also to the intuitions of countless language teachers. Teachers distinguish 'skill-getting' and 'skill-using' (Rivers and Temperley, 1978, p. 4) on the grounds that the pupil needs to discover what the TL consists of (in terms of perceiving, internalising and practising rules) before he can go on to use the TL in real communication. 'Skill-getting' should come before 'skill-using', particularly with adults. Teachers accept, however, that there are many students who study a L2 for many years but who are unable to participate in even simple spontaneous communication when called upon to do so. These students do not need to start the process of development from scratch but only to activate that knowledge that was developed in the classroom by 'skill-getting' activities. This process of activating existing knowledge can occur quite quickly. Thus, even if the classroom fails to develop 'skill-using', the instruction is not wasted provided the student has the opportunity later on to participate in authentic communication. Teachers are strongly committed to an interface position.

The main theoretical argument in favour of the interface position is that the 'acquisition/learning' distinction is a reflection of whether L2 knowledge is automatised. James (1980) for instance argues that 'rule formation' must be distinguished from 'rule automatisation' and that incorrect usage may occur after a rule has been assimilated because automatisation lags behind. Sharwood-Smith (1981) makes a similar point and offers a model of SLD that allows for an interface between 'explicit' and 'implicit' knowledge (see Fig. 9). In this model internalisation is explained as the result of attending to 'input' which is seen to consist of both the language user's own 'output' and other speakers' utterances. Storage is represented in terms of 'implicit' and 'explicit' knowledge sources and performance can occur by calling on each knowledge source separately or together. Thus, implicit knowledge converts into explicit knowledge via 'input' and vice-versa. This model is very similar to that proposed by Stevick (1980), who also seeks to explain how 'seepage' from the 'learnt' to the 'acquired' knowledge store takes place.

An alternative to conceptualising the interface as 'seepage' is to view the role of 'learnt' knowledge as sensitising the learner to rules which can then be more easily 'acquired'. By providing instruction involving consciousness-raising and practice the learner has his attention directed to specific linguistic phenomena in his environment and is therefore less likely to ignore them. This argument suggests that although formal instruction may not be responsible for the immediate assimilation of new rules, it can facilitate the process indirectly. In

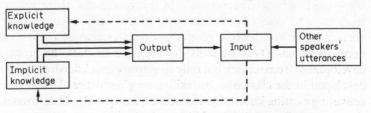

FIG. 9. Sharwood-Smith's model of linguistic input and output.

Seliger's (1979) terms the role of pedagogical rules in SLD is as 'acquisition facilitators'. The effects of formal instruction from this point of view are not immediate, but delayed. It is difficult to see how such a view can be empirically investigated, particularly if no limits are placed on the 'delay' in effect that can occur (but see note 5). It is, however, a commonly held view among teachers.

The statements of the interface position so far considered have all been based on the *a priori* acceptance of a *single* dichotomy of knowledge. Bialystok (1982) offers a more complex picture involving two separate continua. She suggests that there is an 'analysed factor' which concerns the degree to which the learner is able to form a 'propositional mental representation' of TL knowledge and an 'automatic factor' which concerns the relative ease of access the learner has to TL knowledge irrespective of the degree of analysis. Figure 10 illustrates how these two factors can realise four basic types of L2 knowledge.

The advantage of this model is that it avoids conflating the notion of automaticity with that of explicitness. One of the assumptions of single-factor models such as Sharwood-Smith's is that as 'explicit' knowledge becomes automatised so it transforms into 'implicit' (= 'acquired') knowledge. But it is perfectly possible to talk about 'explicit' knowledge that has been automatised to a greater or lesser degree i.e. the learner remains conscious of what rule he is using but is able to process it rapidly without undue effort. This would constitute Type B knowledge in Figure 10, and might arise as the result of

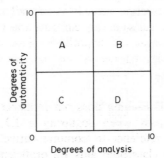

FIG. 10. Types of L2 knowledge (based on Bialystok, 1982).

'overlearning' rules that have been formally presented and practised. Type D knowledge occurs after initial consciousness-raising and limited practice. In contrast Types A and C, which involve little or no rule-awareness, might occur through participating in meaningful communication. They are distinguished in terms of the ease and immediacy with which the rules can be recalled and processed This elaborated view of the nature of L2 knowledge suggests that formal instruction may mainly succeed in making available to the learner knowledge that is analysed (i.e. B and D). The internalisation of unanalysed knowledge (i.e. A and C) may call for a different kind of linguistic environment, one that emphasises the opportunity to negotiate meaning.

This discussion of the interface hypothesis has highlighted the generally speculative nature of the various positions. It is difficult to see how the hypothesis can be reliably investigated, mainly because of the problems in devising a testing or elicitation instrument that can accurately tap the different kinds of knowledge posited. It is likely, therefore, that the discussion will continue to be speculative. Of the positions discussed Bialystok's is the most promising because it avoids the simplification inherent in single-factor models.

Conclusions

It is difficult to reach any firm conclusions regarding the role of grammar teaching in SLD at the moment. The available empirical evidence must be treated circumspectively because of the difficulty of controlling potentially important instructional and learner variables. In general, the issue has been tackled theoretically in terms of what has become known as the interface controversy. It is more appropriate, therefore, to speak of hypotheses than conclusions. The following constitute 'best guesses' about the role of instruction in SLD.

(1) Formal grammar teaching does not influence the route along which learners pass when acquiring a L2 if this route is determined with reference to 'communicative' speech.
(2) Time spent in a classroom aids L2 proficiency and probably facilitates rapid learning.

A dual-competence model of SLD struggles to accommodate both these hypotheses. (1) suggests that the kind of knowledge developed by formal grammar teaching is not available for use in 'communicative' speech. (2) suggests that what happens in a classroom does facilitate learning. Protagonists of a non-interface position argue that this is because of the exposure to 'comprehensible input' provided by the classroom. Protagonists of the interface position argue that formal grammar teaching makes new knowledge available to the learner which eventually can be used in 'communicative' speech.[5] At the moment it is not possible to decide between these arguments. However, irrespective of whether formal instruction has a direct effect or an indirect effect (i.e. in terms of the 'exposure' which it constitutes) it is clear both from what is known about naturalistic SLD (and FLD) and from studies of the effects of time spent in a classroom that SLD can be enhanced by the opportunity to take part in interactions in the L2. The answers to many of the issues raised in this chapter are to be found by inspecting the kinds of interactions which take place in classrooms including those that involve pedagogic grammar rules (i.e. as in Chapter 5).

It may be better, however, to model SLD in terms of a variable competence rather than as a dual competence. In this case performance will be explained with reference to a single knowledge store which is drawn on differently according to the type of language use involved. Formal grammar teaching can then be linked to the development of particular kinds of language processes which differ from those found in ordinary communication. Such a model—available in part in Bialystok's dual dichotomy—is advanced in the next chapter.

Notes

1. Ellis's finding is the opposite of that reported by Seliger (1977). Seliger found that the amount of interaction engaged in by individual adult intermediate ESL students in the classroom correlated significantly with scores on achievement tests administered at the end of the course. However, Seliger's study does *not* show that classroom interaction changed the order of development (nor was it intended to). Also, as Seliger points out, his 'high input generators' were likely to seek out input outside the classroom. Seliger's study, therefore cannot be used to show that formal instruction affected either the order of development or increased accuracy in the use of specific language forms.

2. Discrete point tests test whether specific items of knowledge (e.g. the 3rd person singular) have been learnt. An example is multiple choice questions. Integrative tests test global language proficiency. Examples are cloze passages and free composition.
3. The predictive value of motivation is well attested. For example, Gardner (1980) finds motivation accounts for 14% of the variance in the proficiency of English-speaking students of French as a L2 in Canadian high schools. He claims this is a substantial figure.
4. Krashen also suggests that utterances can be initiated using patterns borrowed from the learner's L1 and through the use of formulas.
5. The argument here is that instruction has a *delayed* effect. There is some evidence to support this. Lightbown (1983) found that the effects of 'overlearning' of the progressive -ing form in Grade 5 were evident in Grade 6 and that the effects of higher frequencies of uninflected verb forms in the input in Grade 6 were not seen until Grade 7. Seliger (1977) found that the amount of interaction his students engaged in did not correlate significantly with test scores at the beginning of the study but did with those at the end. Seliger's (1979) argument that pedagogical rules function as 'acquisition facilitators' is also an argument for the delayed effect of instruction (see p. 154).

Chapter 7

A Variable Competence Model of Second Language Development

SLD research has not been short of theorising. It has been argued, in fact, that researchers have been over-ready to propose models of SLD. Schouten (1979) for instance suggests that 'in second language learning too many models have been built and taken for granted too soon, and this has stifled relevant research' (p. 4). He argues that there is a need to make 'axioms' (= 'untestable statements') and 'assumptions' (= 'untested but testable statements') as modest as possible. However, it could also be argued that SLD research has suffered from the lack of a sound theoretical base, with researchers often happy to investigate researchable but unrewarding hypotheses. Ideally, of course, careful empirical investigation needs to go hand in hand with theorising so that the model of SLD that is proposed both informs and is informed by research.

What aspects of SLD need to be accounted for in a theory? Schumann (1976) identifies three sets of factors which require consideration. The first set consists of 'initiating factors'. These help to answer the question 'why', e.g. why does SLD take place? and why does it stop short of native-like competence? The second set involves 'cognitive processes'. These are the internal learner mechanisms that are responsible for the internalisation of data from the input and also for the use of internalised rules in actual performance. The cognitive processes can only be inferred from an examination of the third set of factors—the 'linguistic product', the actual utterances the learner produces. The function of a theory of SLD, then, involves the description and explanation of SLD in terms of these three sets of factors. It can be likened to a theory of how a washing machine works. Just as a theory powerful enough to account for the operations of a washing machine must be able to describe the various programmes performed by the washing machine (i.e. the output), how the internal parts operate (i.e. the cognitive processes) and what causes the parts to run (i.e. the initiating factors), so too a theory of SLD must be able to describe the utterances the learner produces at different stages of development, how these are processed and what fuels the entire process.

Existing theories vary in the extent to which they deal adequately with each of Schumann's sets of factors. For example, the *acculturation theory* (Brown, 1980) which attempts to explain SLD as part of the process of becoming adapted to a new culture, is an attempt to account for the role played by initiating factors. It does not, however, examine the internal processing mechanisms. In contrast, early *interlanguage theory* (e.g. Corder, 1967; Selinker, 1972) was primarily concerned with how the learner's internal processing mechanisms led to particular types of output. Perhaps the most comprehensive theories to date are those proposed by Dulay and Burt (1978) and Krashen (1981b). Both the *creative construction theory* and the *Monitor Model* represent attempts to account for all three sets of factors. They offer explanations of the relationship between input and internal processing and also between internal processing and output. It is for this reason that they have had such a strong impact on SLD research. Any alternative model must be just as comprehensive and must avoid the problems which arise from these models (see below).

There is no theory of classroom SLD. Theorising about how SLD takes place in a classroom has either derived from general learning theory (e.g. the contrastive analysis hypothesis was rooted in behaviourist learning theory) or from theories of naturalistic SLD such as the creative construction theory. A separate theory for classroom SLD, however, will only be required if the process of language learning can be shown to be different in the classroom than in a natural setting. The previous chapters have argued that this need not be the case. Both naturalistic and classroom learners use the same internal processes. However, classroom learners also afford evidence of processes which are different from those normally found in natural settings. The position that has been adopted is that where 'communicative' language use is concerned the process of development is the same in both settings, but that where 'modelled' language use is involved classroom development differs from that usual in natural settings. However, this difference is not absolute; just as 'communicative' language use can and does occur in classrooms, so 'modelled' language use can occur in natural settings (for example when adults study formal language rules in their own time).[1] A theory of SLD needs to explain both 'communicative' and 'modelled' language use. In so doing it will be applicable to both naturalistic and classroom SLD.

This chapter will commence by looking at a number of criticisms of Krashen's Monitor Model in order to show that a dual-competence model of SLD is not entirely satisfactory. A variable-competence model of SLD will then be proposed. This will be shown to account for the variable nature of the linguistic output, including that reflected in the 'communicative/modelled' distinction, the cognitive processes responsible for this output and the initiating factors which influence the rate of development and the overall levels of proficiency achieved.

The Monitor Model: a critique

Krashen's Monitor Model is a dual-competence model of SLD. That is, it seeks to explain, the L2 learner's variable performance in terms of two separate systems of knowledge, which the learner draws on depending on various conditions of use. These separate systems are referred to as 'acquisition' and 'learning' (see p. 150). Krashen argues that the manner in which these two knowledge systems are internalised, stored and used in the production and reception of utterances is different. Table 11 summarises the principal differences in internalisation, storage and performance, as discussed by Krashen (1981, 1982).

Krashen gives as evidence for a dual-competence model the results of the morpheme-studies. In a series of studies of the development of grammatical morphemes such as the plural {s}, articles, regular and irregular past tense, 3rd person singular, Dulay and Burt (1973; 1974), Bailey *et al.* (1974) and Larsen-Freeman (1976) among others discovered that the accuracy of use of these morphemes was invariable

TABLE 11.

Internalisation, Storage and Performance according to Krashen's Monitor Model

	Acquisition	Learning
1. Internalisation	This occurs through subconsciously attending to comprehensible input in spontaneous communication.	This occurs as a result of conscious study of the formal properties of language. A prerequisite is that the learner has reached the stage of Formal Operations.
2. Storage	'Acquired' knowledge is stored in the left hemisphere (in most users) in 'language areas' (see Krashen, 1981a, Chap. 6). It is available for automatic processing.	'Learnt' knowledge is also stored in the left hemisphere (in most users) but not necessarily in the language areas. It is only available in controlled processing.
3. Performance	'Acquired' knowledge serves as the major source of knowledge for initiating the encoding and decoding processes. The reported invariant order of learning is the result of using 'acquired' knowledge in production.	'Learnt' knowledge is only available for monitoring output derived from 'acquired' knowledge or from the mother tongue. There are three conditions concerning its availability: (1) sufficient time (2) focus on form (3) knowledge of the rule.

irrespective of the age or the L1s of the learners. If this accuracy order is equated with order of acquisition (as Dulay and Burt claim it can be), then a strong case can be made out for arguing that there is a 'natural' order in which grammatical functors are developed. However, some studies found that when data were collected using discrete-item language tests a different accuracy order emerged. Krashen (1977) sought to explain the alternative orders in terms of whether the learner made use of 'learnt' metalinguistic knowledge of grammatical rules. In other words, if the learner relied on L2 knowledge that was subconscious (i.e. 'acquired' knowledge) the 'natural' order would be observed, but if he made use of his Monitor (i.e. the device learners use to edit their utterances using 'learnt' knowledge) a different order would appear.

Variability in language-learner language, then, is the result of whether the learner is Monitoring or is not Monitoring. Krashen conceives of two types of learner behaviour:

(1) Spontaneous or 'normal' language behaviour
     This occurs when the learner is focused on meaning rather than form and is the result of 'acquired' knowledge
(2) Monitored behaviour
     This occurs when the learner is focused on form and is the result of the learner using his metalinguistic knowledge of L2 rules.

Which type of language behaviour occurs is the result of whether the learner has time to search through his repertoire of metalinguistic rules to edit 'normal' language behaviour and also of the extent to which he is oriented to accuracy or fluency, which may be a product of his personality (see Krashen, 1977). The Monitor functions as an on–off mechanism; the learner is either Monitoring or is not Monitoring.

Krashen does allow for a number of other mechanisms which are likely to lead to further performance types. He suggests that learners who possess little 'acquired' knowledge can substitute for this by (1) using 'formulas' (2) generating utterances in the L1 and slotting in L2 vocabulary. He also suggests that learners can pay attention to language form without using metalinguistic knowledge and this can lead to editing by 'feel'. In such cases the learner will not be able to state the rule he has used, but will be vaguely conscious that the initially-formulated utterance does not sound right. Potentially, therefore, the Monitor Model allows for different types of variability in language-learner language over and above that explained by the 'acquisition/learning' dichotomy, but it is clear from Krashen's publications that these other types are only peripheral. The notion of monitoring by feel, in particular, although potentially an important factor, is not developed to any extent. In general, Krashen views the learners' intuitive knowledge of the L2 system as a homogeneous competence.

There are two major problems with the Monitor Model. The first is that even when the learner is focused on meaning (i.e. is drawing on 'acquired' knowledge) his performance is clearly not homogeneous. The second is that the Monitor Model does not allow for any 'seepage' from one knowledge system to the other.[2] Each of these criticisms will be considered in turn.

The non-Monitored performance of learners is variable. Learners frequently produce utterances which are formally different even when it is evident that they are focused on meaning. Consider these two utterances produced by the Portuguese-speaking learner referred to in Chapters 2–6. They occurred within seconds of each other when he was clearly using language for behavioural purposes:

No look my card.   (*instruction to another pupil in a game of word*
Don't look my card. *bingo*)

Data such as these require an explanatory apparatus which acknowledges that even in 'communicative' language use alternative L2 rules exist. They cannot be explained by claiming that one utterance is derived from an 'acquired' rule (e.g. negative utterances are formed using 'no + verb') and the other utterance represents the application of a 'learnt' rule (e.g. negative imperatives are formed using 'Don't + verb'). They can only be explained by positing the existence of two separate rules within the learner's store of intuitive knowledge, both vying with each other for use in production at this stage of the learner's development. In other words, such data constitute counter evidence of a homogeneous rule system. Nor is such evidence an isolated example. Cancino *et al.* (1978) found similar variation in their subjects' negative utterances. They wrote:

> Our attempts to write rules for the negative proved fruitless. The constant development and concomitant variation in our subjects' speech at any one point made the task impossible. (p. 209)

In fact the case studies of naturalistic SLD are full of examples of the inherent variability of the learner's language.[3] Language-learner language reflects variable and not categorical rules even in performance where the learner is focused on meaning.

It would be possible to immunise the Monitor Model against the evidence of learner variability by developing a fuller theoretical account of editing by 'feel'. For example, the conditions under which implicit use of a new 'acquired' rule to modify an utterance containing an older 'acquired' rule occurs could be examined. This is in fact what McLaughlin (1978) does when he suggests that the learner's knowledge needs to be viewed in the light of the distinction between 'controlled' and 'automatic' processing. 'Controlled processing' requires some degree of active attention. It occurs because the user lacks the ability to attend to every single aspect of performance at the same time. 'Automatic processing' does not require active control. It occurs because the learner has access to knowledge that is thoroughly automatised through use. When a new L2 rule first enters the learner's competence it is only available for use through 'controlled processing'. As it is practised it becomes more automatic and so is available for use through 'automatic processing'. However, if the Monitor Model is immunised in this way it will be necessary to abandon the view of 'acquired' knowledge as homogeneous. It must instead be seen as variable, depending on the degree of automatisation of individual rules that make up the system. But once the claims of homogeneity are abandoned, it makes little sense to maintain a dual-competence explanation. The kind of performance that results from the use of metalinguistic knowledge (i.e. 'learnt' L2 rules) is best seen, not as a separate system, but merely as one aspect of a single but variable competence which contains rules that are more or less automatic and, also, as Bialystok (1982, see p. 154) has suggested, more or less analytic. By abandoning the claims about the separateness of 'acquisition/learning', it is no longer necessary to distinguish editing by 'feel' (= small-'m' monitoring) and editing by using explicit knowledge (= big-'M' Monitoring). Monitoring becomes the process by which the learner adjusts his performance by resorting to 'controlled processing' using rules which vary in their level of automaticity and analycity.

A dual competence model such as the Monitor Model rejects the possibility of 'learnt' knowledge turning into 'acquired' knowledge and vice-versa. Krashen is adamant on this point. Krashen (1982) writes:

> A very important point that also needs to be stated is that learning does not 'turn into' acquisition. The idea that we first learn a new rule, and eventually, through practice, acquire it, is widespread and may seem to some people to be intuitively obvious . . . . Language acquisition happens in one way, when the acquirer understands input containing a structure that the acquirer is 'due' to acquire . . .' (pp. 83–84)

This is a view which is rejected even by those who accept a dual competence model of SLD (e.g. Sharwood-Smith, 1981, see p. 153; Stevick, 1980). They argue that explicit knowledge can become implicit over time providing it is sufficiently practised. However, it is hard to see how these alternative positions can be reliably investigated, particularly as Krashen argues that when a rule which has been originally 'learnt' occurs in spontaneous 'communicative' language use it is because it has been newly 'acquired'. It is claims such as this that have led to criticisms that the 'acquisition/learning' distinction is 'theological' (James, 1980), that is has been formulated in order to confirm a specific goal, namely that successful SLD is the result of 'acquisition' only.

A variable competence model, such as that based on the distinction between 'controlled' and 'automatic processing', posits that L2 knowledge can exist in various forms, spanning a continuum from totally explicit to totally implicit knowledge. It is not necessary to show how one type of knowledge turns into the other but only to show that different L2 rules are related to different contexts of use in much the same way as the native-speaker's use of L1 rules varies stylistically according to social conditions (Labov, 1970). SLD is accounted for by demonstrating that structures which are initially stylistically restricted to formal contexts of use are gradually available for use in more informal contexts. Thus the psycholinguistic distinction between 'controlled' and 'automatic processing' is explained within a sociolinguistic framework which distinguishes styles of language use on a formal–informal continuum (see Tarone, 1982, 1983).

A variable competence model of SLD

This section will develop a model of SLD which views language use/and language development as two sides of the same coin. It will propose that the learner's competence is a variable one and that this can best be understood by hypothesising a single knowledge store which is drawn on differently by the learner depending on the type of language use he is participating in. The learner employs different strategies according to the type of discourse he is helping to construct. Thus the variability of language-learner language is to be explained in terms of different strategies which are related to different types of language knowledge. The learner's L2 competence consists of (1) his knowledge of L2 rules and (2) his ability to use this knowledge in different ways by means of various strategies. The so-called 'natural' order of development is a reflection of strategies of use associated with a particular kind of discourse. The rate at which the learner progresses along this natural route are the product of various affective factors and also the opportunity afforded the learner to participate in relevant discourse.

The model of SLD proposed will consist of (1) an account of the variable nature of language-learner language (2) an explanation of this variability in terms of discourse processes and (3) an explanation of variation in the rate of development in terms of individual learner differences and opportunity for the negotiation of meaning in discourse. The frame of reference will be the classroom, but the theory is also applicable to naturalistic SLD.

Describing the learner's output

Any description of the learner's output must account for both *vertical* and *horizontal* variability. Vertical variability refers to the use of alternative L2 rules at any single point in the learner's development. It is synchronic variability. Horizontal variability refers to the changing pattern of the learner's interlanguage system over time. It is diachronic variability. Later it will be argued that vertical and horizontal variability are inter-related, but first it is necessary to describe the two types.

Vertical variability

Vertical variability is a characteristic of language use in general. It is not peculiar to the output of language learners. The study of language-learner variability, in fact, owes much to Labov (1970). Labov argued that all speakers possess several 'styles' which they use in order to adapt to the social context. These styles can be ranged along a single dimension according to the amount of attention the learner pays to the language he is using. The degree of monitoring that is possible varies according to the context of situation. It is least in the 'vernacular' style, which is the style associated with informal, everyday speech. Labov argues that the vernacular style provides 'the most systematic data' for linguistic study. It is heaviest in contexts that call for careful, formal language use. The data associated with such contexts are not so systematic as they depend on which features of an utterance the learner has chosen to monitor. Labov shows that there are a number of 'speech markers' which vary according to the degree of attention the learner pays to his speech.

Vertical variability in general language use is a function of the level of formality. Informal use is associated with low levels of attention to language form and formal use with high levels. Another way of capturing this variability, then, is in terms of the distinction between *unplanned* and *planned* discourse (Ochs, 1979). Unplanned discourse is discourse that lacks forethought and preparation. Planned discourse is discourse that has been thought out and organised prior to expression. These are not alternatives but poles on a continuum. The kind of discourse encountered in everyday communication falls near the unplanned end of the continuum. The kind of discourse involved in giving a lecture falls near the planned end of the continuum. However, as Ochs points out, discourse differs not only in the degree to which it is planned but also in the extent to which it is plannable. Conversation constitutes relatively unplanned discourse because it is not usually plannable. Ritualised events lead to planned discourse because they are by definition plannable. Ochs also points out that there are constraints on the user's ability to plan discourse. Situational demands may require constant attention, so that the user is unable to attend to the form of communication. Also the conceptual demands of a proposition may interfere with planning.

Just as the vernacular style was considered by Labov to be basic, so unplanned discourse can also be thought of as primary. It is so both from a chronological point of view—the ability to participate in unplanned discourse is what children acquire first—and also from a functional perspective—the ability to take part in unplanned discourse is for most people more important than the ability to construct planned discourse.[4]

Ochs describes four features of unplanned discourse:

(1) Speakers rely on the immediate context rather than on syntax to express propositions. As she puts it, 'context is an alternative to syntax'. (p. 62)
(2) Speakers rely on morphosyntactic structures that were developed in the early stages of FLD.
(3) Speakers repeat and replace lexical items when expressing a new proposition.
(4) The form and content of sequentially-arranged speech tends to be similar.

The distinctions between formal/informal and planned/unplanned apply to language-learner language just as much as they do to native-speaker performance. They are echoed in the distinction between modelled/communicative data, which was described in Chapter 1. The modelled data so common in classroom SLD are characterised by attention to form and occur in carefully-planned discourse. In contrast, communicative data are restricted to the real-life exchanges associated in particular with social and framework goals (see Chapter 5). In order, therefore, to account for the patterns of variable language use in the classroom it is only necessary to posit a continuum between entirely communicative and entirely modelled speech. As Figure 11 indicates, this continuum can be divided into three broad bands: (1) communicative language use involving informal exchanges in un-planned discourse, (2) a mixture of communicative and modelled language use, involving attention to selected features of the language system in partly planned discourse, (3) modelled language use in-volving careful monitoring of speech in order to satisfy the formal norms of correctness established by the teacher in planned discourse (e.g. drills). The classroom is characterised by a constant shifting from discourse where the focus is entirely on meaning and which, as a result, is spontaneous and informal to discourse which is mechanical and where meaning is not involved at all. There are also mid-way types (e.g. where language use is contextualised but no real information conveyed or where genuine information is conveyed but in a way that would be unlikely to occur outside the classroom). As McTear (1975) observes problems of communication can arise when the pupils are oriented towards one type of discourse and the teacher to another.

At any single stage of his development, therefore, the learner has access to a series of alternative rules. Which rule he uses in any given context will be the result of the type of discourse he is being asked to take part in. Some rules will only be available in modelled speech, when he has the opportunity to focus on form and to plan utterances before they are uttered. Other rules will be characteristic of communicative speech, when he is focused on meaning and is required to plan and produce utterances more or less concurrently. Many actual instances of language use, however, will reflect both sets of rules in varying proportions depending on which features of an utterance he is attempting to monitor.

Unplanned informal	+ communicative − modelled	+ communicative + modelled	− communicative + modelled	Planned formal

FIG. 11. Types of language use in L2 speech.

In conclusion, vertical variability is an inevitable consequence of language use and will be observed in both classroom settings, where it is almost institutionalised, and in natural settings. Vertical variability constitutes a continuum of language use, which in language-learner language is manifest in fluctuating linguistic output depending on whether the learner is engaged in unplanned or planned discourse.

Horizontal variability

The learner's linguistic output changes over time. In order to describe these changes it will be necessary to consider both the learner's communicative speech and his modelled speech. That is, development can be expected to occur in both types of speech. However, given the primacy of communicative speech it is this which has received the greatest attention in SLD research, including that reported in Chapters 2–5 of this book.

As far as communicative speech is concerned classroom SLD follows the same route as naturalistic SLD (but see below). This route is characterised by five kinds of linguistic output:

(1) *Formulaic speech*

The occurrence of formulas in the speech of language learners is well-documented. They perform language functions that are frequent and communicatively important in the contexts the learner is required to interact in. They occur very early in the communicative speech of classroom learners and carry on without modification for some time. Eventually 'routines' develop into 'patterns', which may then be analysed out into the constituent parts. In this way formulas may contribute to the 'creative' rule system, although there is considerable disagreement whether this is in fact the case. There is general agreement, however, that formulas are an aid to performance in a L2 (see Chapter 4).

(2) *Propositionally-reduced speech*

The learner's first utterances that are both communicative and creative consist of strings of lexical items strung together without regard for word-order rules or for morphological requirements. These strings are likely to be propositionally reduced i.e. lexical items that would be observed in the equivalent adult native speaker utterance are omitted. It has been suggested in Chapter 3 that these strings correspond to the deep-structure generated by Fillmore's (1968) case grammar. To produce such strings the learner needs only a lexicon consisting initially of signifiers of objects and their attributes (i.e. arguments) and later of signifiers of action or state processes together with some lexicalised modality markers e.g. 'yesterday' (i.e. predicates). These utterances are, therefore, non-syntactic, they follow a 'universal' order which matches perception. They vary developmentally according to the degree and nature of propositional reduction. Initially, reduction is extensive as a result of the lack of lexical resources and the processing difficulties the learner experiences. Whenever possible the learner will choose to encode those cases which are maximally informative in terms of the context in which an utterance is produced. This may be why most early utterances do not contain an agent.

(3) *Syntactic utterances*

Utterances can be considered 'syntactic' when the learner is able to exploit the contrast between an 'unmarked' and a 'marked' word order. This distinction is evident in negative utterances where the initial 'unmarked' word order consists of external negation (i.e. the negative particle is attached to either the beginning or the end of an utterance) and the later 'marked' word order consists of internal negation (i.e. the negative particle is incorporated into the structure of the utterance). It is also evident in   interrogatives when the learner distinguishes intonation questions (= 'unmarked' word order) from questions with subject–verb inversion (= 'marked' word order). The learner cannot be said to have mastered word-order as a meaning carrying device until he has access to the contrastive use of both the 'unmarked' word order, consisting of Subject + Verb + Object, and 'marked' word order patterns.

(4) *Morphologically marked utterances*

Morphological development enables the learner to use bound

(e.g. *-ed*) and free (e.g. the definite and indefinite articles) grammatical functors. These are part of the component of grammar that Fillmore (1968) calls 'modality'. They encode a range of meanings that are often language-specific, for example past and future time, modal meanings such as intentionality and ability, number, gender and definiteness. Naturalistic SLD research has focused almost exclusively on morphological development, although there are some studies (e.g. Fillmore's, 1976) which have investigated early, non-morphological development. Early learner speech that is creative and communicative is not typically morphologically marked. Although a number of functors are developed early on, the different meanings they encode are not clearly distinguished until much later and many functors (e.g. those relating to tense) may not appear in some learners for over a year. Whereas all L2 learners will probably develop functional control over a number of functors, many will not master the entire range and some will develop only a small number. In this sense, therefore, morphological development can be considered the 'icing on the cake' (Leopold, 1954).

(5) *Complex utterances*

Complex utterances are utterances that express two or more propositions by means of various logical connectors, embeddings and clefting processes. Complete control over the full range of these devices may elude some native speakers. They contribute to what Slobin (1977) calls rhetorical expressiveness. They enable the learner to increase the number of devices he can use for information focus and thus are important for stylistically developed communication. The learner is now able to present information in a variety of ways in accordance with his assessment of what will achieve the greatest social and communicative effect.

It is suggested that where communicative speech is concerned, in both classroom and naturalistic SLD, these five kinds of linguistic product reflect a developmental progression, as represented in Fig. 12. Initially, the learner relies on non-syntactic and propositionally reduced utterances. During this stage he extends his lexicon, adding those items he needs to meet his basic communicative needs. As his vocabulary grows and as the effort of processing TL utterances

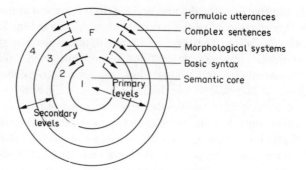

FIG. 12. Types of linguistic product in 'communicative' speech.

becomes less, he is able to fill out more of the case slots of each proposition and reduce his reliance on presupposition. The propositional expansion that takes place continues into the subsequent stage, when word order is used to distinguish one meaning from another. Likewise mastery of the various ordering devices of syntax continues into the third stage, when grammatical functors begin to be systematically and meaningfully used. This in turn overlaps with the fourth stage, when complex sentence patterns are mastered. Throughout all four stages the learner employs a number of formulaic utterances and may slowly separate out the grammatical elements that constitute them and so fuel the processes of morphosyntactic development. This is represented in Fig. 12 by the arrows emanating from the segment marked F.

These stages of development have been divided into 'primary' and 'secondary'. The 'primary' levels are reflected in speech which is pidginised. They are primary because they are chronologically first and because *all* learners complete the first two stages and at least enter the third. The 'secondary' levels arise in the natural process of development after the 'primary' levels and not all learners will reach this far. The third stage (i.e. the development of morphological systems) is shown as falling within both 'primary' and 'secondary' levels. This is because whereas some morphological features are easily acquired with minimal attention to the input (e.g. those that correlate with the learner's L1), others require considerable effort and perseverance to acquire because they are specific to the target language. Learners fossilise at different points within the third stage. One way of capturing the difference between the 'primary' and 'secondary' levels is to picture the learner using two resources to develop a knowledge of the L2; he can use his knowledge of language together with his general world knowledge (i.e. draw on 'internal input') or he can work on cracking the code by attending to the language addressed to him (i.e. draw on 'external input'). To begin with the learner faces inward and regresses to a set of primitive semantic categories, but as he becomes exposed to external input he extends his competence by incorporating language specific features of the target language.

This account is designed to provide a broad framework in which to interpret existing descriptions of the developmental route in SLD. For instance, the 'natural' order of acquisition, as reflected in the accuracy orders of the morpheme studies, can be understood as detailed account of stage (3).[5] The descriptions of the development of transitional structures such as negatives and interrogatives fits into stage (2). Little is yet known about stage (4) but research into relative clauses (Schumann, 1980) suggests that these also may be developmentally ordered.

Little is known about the developmental nature of modelled speech. It is unlikely that clear stages can be identified as for communicative speech. Which rules the learner learns how to process in modelled speech are likely to simply reflect the rules that are chosen for attention by the teacher. It is likely, however, that the mastery of each rule will involve (1) perception of the formal properties of the rule, (2) controlled processing of the rule and (3) more automatic processing of the rule. When (3) is reached—and this may require 'overlearning'—it is possible that the rule will begin to appear in communicative speech. But unless the rule is maintained at a high level of automaticity by constant practice, it is likely to disappear from communicative speech to be replaced by alternative rules that derive from natural discourse processes involved in the production of unplanned discourse.[6]

The relationship between modelled and communicative speech (i.e. vertical variability) and the developmental path which occurs in communicative speech (i.e. horizontal variability) is central to a variable competence model of SLD. It will involve:

(1) Identifying the strategies of language use that are involved in the production of unplanned and planned discourse;
(2) Identifying the types of knowledge which are typically processed by the strategies in (1).

The discourse processes involved in using L2 knowledge provide an explanation of *how* SLD takes place.

Explaining the learner's output

The output is the product of taking part in discourse. In order to explain the output it is necessary to examine how the learner takes part in discourse. In so doing it will be possible to explain how the learner acquires new rules, for these derive from the processes of interaction that are responsible for the construction of discourse. In this way an account of language use is at the same time an account of language development.

Widdowson (1979b) provides an elegant description of how 'rules' derive from 'procedures' for using existing knowledge:

> We draw upon our knowledge of rules to *make sense*. We do not simply measure discourse up against our knowledge of pre-existing rules, we create discourse and commonly bring new rules into existence by so doing. All competence is transitional in this sense. (p. 62)

In other words, the process of language development is the same as the process of language use. The learner develops procedures for using whatever knowledge he possesses to 'make sense'. In so doing he develops new rules to add to his existing knowledge.

The procedures—or processes, as I shall now call them—are social. They enable the learner to take part in verbal interaction. They will be called *discourse processes*. However, each process involves certain mental operations. Thus relating to the different discourse processes are a number of *cognitive processes*. Further, just as there are different types of discourse ranging along the unplanned/planned continuum, so too there are different discourse and cognitive processes responsible for the discourse types. For convenience sake the various discourse and cognitive processes will be divided into two sets. The first set are *primary processes*, so called because they help create discourse at the unplanned end of the continuum, which, as has been previously argued, is both chronologically and socially primary. The second set are *secondary processes*. They are used in the construction of planned discourse. Thus communicative data occur when primary processes are invoked and modelled data when secondary processes are used.

Primary processes

Some of the most important primary discourse and cognitive processes are listed in Table 12. It is hypothesised that these processes are developmental. That is their prominence in SLD will coincide with the order in which they are listed. Each process is responsible for one of the types of linguistic product listed in the previous section. However, language users do not lose the ability to operate the earlier processes as they master the use of the later ones in L2 discourse. Semantic simplification, for instance, can reoccur at a late stage whenever the learner lacks the lexis he needs to encode a proposition.[7] Similarly, vertical construction continues to serve as a means of extending the complexity of utterances. Also, all the discourse processes can be observed in native-speaker speech.

The initial problem for the learner is how to express propositions with minimal L2 resources and also how to ease the burden placed on his processing mechanisms by the need for 'controlled' rather than 'automatic' processing. To solve this problem the learner augments his L2 knowledge with his world knowledge. This knowledge includes (1) knowledge of the conceptual schema which can be used to segment physical events (i.e. amodal categories such as those reflected in case grammar), (2) knowledge of the communicative functions which language can serve, (3) knowledge of how to exploit the situational features of the context to supplement what is verbally encoded and (4) knowledge of how language is organised in terms of an attitudinal (i.e. modality) and a propositional component. The basis of early SLD is

TABLE 12.
Primary Processes in SLD

Discourse processes	Cognitive processes
1 Imitate a part of the whole of the previous utterance.	1 Match the incoming verbal signals with the available phonetic representations and memorise them.
2(a) Express interpersonal meanings by means of single lexical items and formulaic utterances. (b) Make use of discourse routines even if this means switching the topic.	2(a) Memorise frequently occurring and communicatively important lexical items and classify in terms of their interpersonal use. (b) Memorise a small number of 'scripts'.
3(a) Simplify the semantic structure of a message by omitting meaning elements that are redundant or that can be realised by a non-verbal device (e.g. mime).	3(a) Construct an underlying conceptual structure of a message. (b) Compare this structure with the frame of reference shared with the interlocutor. (c) Eliminate redundant elements and elements for which no lexical item is available.
4 Extend a message vertically by: (a) Imitating (part of) another speaker's utterance and adding to it (b) Building on your own previous utterance (c) Juxtaposing two formulaic utterances.	4 Hold just-mentioned items in short-term memory in order to work on them by addition, insertion or substitution.
5 Reduce reliance on shared knowledge and non-verbal devices by distinguishing various functional meanings linguistically	5(a) Establish form–function correlates by attending closely to external input (This may require a reorganisation of categories to match TL categories.) (b) Analyse into separate elements previously memorised chunks of speech and relate these to specific meanings

the exploitation of this world knowledge in terms of existing L2 knowledge (mainly lexis) and the particular contexts of interaction the learner finds himself required to operate in. This exploitation takes the form of semantic simplification. The learner simplifies the propositional content of messages in accordance with those elements of meaning he considers most informative and the lexis he has available to him. Semantic simplification is likely to be supported by other processes such as the use of mime and lexical substitution. Its principal contribution to SLD is to enable the learner to automatise existing lexis and to internalise new lexis together with some modality markers, although at this stage these will have no clearly defined functional distribution (i.e. they will be used more or less in free variation—see Wagner Gough, 1975).

One of the principal ways by which the learner extends his ability to share meanings is through the extension of messages vertically. It is this process that probably accounts for early negation and interrogation. Vertical extension produces utterances such as:

No/like ice cream (= 'I don't like ice cream')
What/you want? (= 'What do you want?)

Vertical extension is also the process by which two formulas are juxtaposed:

That one/I don't know

Later, as the process becomes more sophisticated the learner is able to operate on such strings as those above by substituting lexical elements. Vertical extension is a very powerful device. It helps the learner produce utterances that are less propositionally reduced and also to internalise new patterns for combining utterance constituents.

Truly grammatical utterances occur when the learner is ready to reduce his reliance on shared knowledge and non-verbal devices. This is achieved cognitively by attending to morphological features of the input and perhaps also by analysing formulas into their constituent parts. It is likely that at this stage of development the learner will seek out more challenging topics entailing reference to displaced activity.

The learner will perceive and internalise morphological features, storing them in such a way that they are coded for the specific meanings which they can realise. Features which earlier were used in free variation are now sorted out into increasingly tighter form-function relationships.

Secondary processes

There are probably a great variety of secondary processes which the learner can use to help him plan discourse and which are responsible for modelled data. However, two key secondary processes can be identified; these are *monitoring* and *borrowing*.

Monitoring is a supplementary strategy. When the learner has the chance to plan discourse he can first use those processes associated with unplanned discourse, and then improve his performance by monitoring. The improvement involves an extensive search of L2 knowledge in order to locate the best available resources for expressing the intended message. It can take a number of forms including the filling out of propositional slots which had been left unencoded as a result of semantic simplification and the addition of various morphological features. Monitoring is likely to involve the use of L2 knowledge that is less automatic and more analytic than the L2 knowledge involved in unplanned discourse. It is, therefore, not restricted to Monitoring in the Krashen sense, but covers both editing with metalinguistic knowledge and editing by 'feel'. Monitoring is a means of maximising L2 knowledge in order to produce the best possible utterance.

Borrowing is a replacement strategy. Corder (1978b) uses the term to describe the deliberate use of the L1 in the construction of L2 utterances. The learner bypasses the primary processes by initiating an utterance in his L1. He then searches his L2 knowledge in order to make the best possible translation. If the search reveals gaps in L2 knowledge, the learner may adjust his initial L1 utterance to enable him to use the L2 knowledge which he has been able to locate. Borrowing can result in a series of initiations and searches before the learner is satisfied and produces the utterance.

The role of processes in SLD

Before the role of primary and secondary processes in SLD can be considered it is necessary to decide precisely what is meant by 'SLD'. I shall take it to mean the learner output which occurs in communicative speech and which is responsible for the 'natural' order of development. Primary processes contribute *directly* to the knowledge which the learner draws on when taking part in unplanned discourse. Secondary processes only contribute *indirectly* to this knowledge.

The primary processes serve as the principal means of (1) automatising existing non-analytic knowledge; (2) acquiring new non-analytic knowledge. They are the means by which the learner spontaneously produces simple structures in an informal style. Because the primary processes are developmentally ordered a fairly well-defined order of development, which is 'natural', will arise. It is hypothesised that in order to participate in unplanned discourse the learner is obliged to make use of primary discourse processes and the L2 knowledge which is tied to them. Only in exceptional circumstances will L2 knowledge that is not natural to the use of these processes be available for use in unplanned discourse.

The secondary processes contribute directly to analytic L2 knowledge. They serve both to automatise existing analytic knowledge and also to add to it. In this respect, therefore, the knowledge which they help to develop is not available for use in unplanned discourse. However, secondary processes can facilitate 'natural' development in two ways. In certain circumstances they can lead to the overlearning of specific L2 forms with the result that these are available for use with primary processes. However, this is rare and only occurs when the forms are constantly practised in modelled speech. The second way is more important. Secondary processes store up a body of L2 knowledge, which, although not immediately accessible in unplanned discourse eventually becomes so when the learner reaches a stage of development involving primary processes which are capable of utilising this knowledge. It is in this sense that analytic L2 knowledge 'sensitises' the learner to language forms, which can then, when the time is ripe, be more readily exploited in communicative speech. However, this knowledge will not appear in unplanned discourse until it has been activated for use by the appropriate primary processes.

The role of processes in SLD can be displayed in the form of a model:

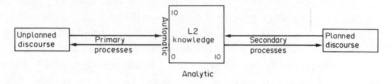

FIG. 13. The role of processes in SLD.

It needs to be emphasised that in many cases the learner will not be using purely primary or purely secondary processes. On many occasions the learner will oscillate between the two types of processes, sometimes using primary ones and sometimes secondary ones. Even individual utterances may be formed through their joint application. Which processes are used will be a function of situational factors involving who talks to whom, when, where and about what. In this sense, therefore, secondary processes are of central importance for SLD and, as will be argued in the next chapter, it would be a mistake to neglect them entirely in classroom teaching. Learners need to be able to engage in a variety of discourse types from the unplanned to the planned end of the continuum.

This explanation of the learner's output emphasises the role of processes, both internal and external. These account for the *order* of development. They can also help to explain variation in the *rate* of development which is evident in individual learners.

Explaining the rate of development

Learners vary greatly in the rate at which they acquire grammatical competence in a L2. On the one hand there are learners who acquire considerable fluency and accuracy within twelve months and on the other there are learners who learn almost nothing in a much longer period of time. In order to account for these individual differences it is necessary to consider two sets of factors: (1) various affective factors which control the extent to which the learner engages in L2 discourse; and (2) interactional factors to do with the type of discourse the learner takes part in. Both sets of factors are relevant to SLD in a natural and classroom setting. They constitute the factors which initiate and sustain SLD.

Affective factors

Affective factors which influence how much interaction in the L2 the learner participates in include motivation and personality. There is considerable evidence to indicate that motivation contributes to rapid and successful SLD. The work of Gardner and Lambert (1972) indicates that SLD can be supported by both an integrative motivation (i.e. when the learner wishes to identify with the culture of the L2 group) and by an instrumental motivation (i.e. when the learner's goals are functional) and which is the more powerful may be the result of the overall learning situation. Where the L2 is being learnt as a foreign language (e.g. French in the USA) integrative motivation seems more powerful, but where it is learnt as a second language (e.g. English in the Philippines) instrumental motivation predicts greater success.[8] Irrespective of the learner's overall motivation, his attitude to specific learning tasks (what Brown, 1981, calls 'task motivation') will also influence how quickly he learns the L2. Personality has not been shown to be so consistently related to rate of development as motivation, but this may be because of the difficulties of reliably measuring personality variables. Strong (1983) has suggested that personality traits control the quality of rather than the quantity of interaction. He found that the fast learners in his study were more 'talkative' and 'responsive' than the slow learners.

Affective variables control the rate of SLD by regulating both the quantity and quality of interaction the learner engages in. The highly motivated, talkative and responsive learner is likely to take part in more interaction involving the L2. In Seliger's (1977) terms he will be a 'high input generator'. It would also seem likely that this kind of learner will also engage in more unplanned discourse and will therefore have the opportunity to exercise primary processes on a more regular basis. The poorly motivated learner generates little discourse of any type. The more introverted learner may prefer to participate in planned discourse and as a result may initially lack fluency in communicative speech. However, it is important to emphasise that according to the model of SLD which has been proposed, affective factors do not relate directly to L2 knowledge, but to the types of interaction that govern the way in which knowledge is acquired.

Interactional factors

In contrast to Krashen's Monitor Model the theory of SLD advanced in this chapter emphasises the importance of both listening and speaking. Krashen talks of 'comprehensible input'. The variable-competence model of SLD emphasises *interaction*. It is argued that SLD results not only from attending to the language that is addressed to the learner but also by actively helping to construct discourse using whatever resources are available. Rapid development is the result of using the L2 to construct unplanned discourse.

A number of discourse features considered likely to facilitate rapid SLD were listed at the end of Chapter 5. The key factor was the opportunity afforded the learner to *negotiate* meaning with an inter-locutor, preferably one who has more linguistic resources than the learner and who is adept at 'foreigner/teacher talk'. It is through negotiation that the learner is able to make use of the various primary processes responsible for unplanned discourse. Negotiation requires that the focus is on meaning rather than form. In the classroom this is more likely in interactions which have social or framework goals than in those with medium-centred goals. The latter type of inter-actions are more likely to involve planned discourse, which, it has been hypothesised, only contribute indirectly to SLD and only when later opportunities arise for activating analytic knowledge in unplanned discourse. If, then, SLD is equated with communicative speech and the 'natural' order of development, it will be principally facilitated when the learner has the chance to operate primary processes in the nego-tiation of unplanned discourse.

The two sets of factors—affective and interactional—are inter-related. Rapid SLD is the product of the quantity and quality of the interactions the learner is involved in. In this sense it is the interactional factors which are crucial. However, the affective factors influence both how much and which kind of discourse the learner contributes to. In this sense it is the affective factors which initiate and sustain SLD.

Summary

This chapter began by outlining two problems with a dual-competence model such as that proposed by Krashen. The Monitor Model cannot adequately account for language-learner variability, which can best be described in terms of a continuum from 'communicative' to 'modelled' language use. Also the Monitor Model is theological in insisting that 'acquired' and 'learnt' knowledge are separate and entirely unrelated.

A variable-competence model avoids these problems. The theory that has been proposed has the following features:

(1) SLD is characterised by both vertical and horizontal variability. At any single point of development the learner will have access to alternative rules. The learner progresses through a series of developmental stages involving formulaic speech, proposition-ally-reduced speech, syntactic utterances, morphologically marked utterances and complex utterances. This development is characteristic of the communicative speech which occurs in unplanned discourse. A different pattern of development will be apparent in modelled speech occurring in planned discourse.

(2) Both vertical and horizontal variability can be explained by the kinds of discourse and related cognitive processes involved in the construction of unplanned/planned discourse. Vertical vari-ability occurs because the learner has access to different pro-cesses depending on the type of discourse. Horizontal variability occurs as a product of using these discourse processes. Primary processes consisting of semantic simplification and vertical extension among others are responsible for the 'natural' order of development. Secondary processes such as monitoring and borrowing are responsible for modelled speech. Primary pro-cesses activate and augment non-analytic knowledge. Secondary

processes activate and augment analytic knowledge. Learning to use one set of processes does not aid the use of the other set. Thus, if the goal is unplanned discourse, taking part in planned discourse will not directly help, although it will make available L2 knowledge which can be activated later on by the primary processes.

(3) The rate of SLD is governed by the quantity and quality of the interactions involving the learner. Rapid development along the 'natural' route occurs when the learner has the chance to negotiate meaning in unplanned discourse. Various affective factors such as personality and motivation influence the learner's preparedness to take the necessary risks involved in contributing to unplanned discourse.

The variable competence model emphasises the dynamic nature of SLD. It does so by recognising the inherent variability of the learner's knowledge system and by focusing on language *use* as the mechanism by which development takes place.

Notes

1. Krashen and Seliger (1976) make much the same point. They argue that the classroom constitutes both a formal linguistic environment for developing 'learning' and a source of primary linguistic data for 'acquisition'.
2. The problem of Krashen's insistence on the separateness of 'acquired' and 'learnt' knowledge has already been discussed in the previous chapter when the non-interface hypothesis was considered.
3. There have been several studies of variability in interlanguage, notably those by the Dickersons (e.g. Dickerson, 1975). Tarone (1983) reviews a number of these studies.
4. This is certainly true of FLD. It is not necessarily the case in SLD, however. When the L2 is learnt for certain special purposes to do with restricted codes or with formal discourse, it is possible that the mastery of planned discourse will become primary.
5. It may be useful to distinguish between the 'order' and the 'sequence' of development. The term 'sequence' could be used to describe the series of overlapping stages outlined in (1) to (5). The term 'order' would then be used to refer to the ordering of grammatical development in morphology and syntax. It could then be claimed that the 'sequence' of development is 'natural' and universal, while acknowledging that some differences in the 'order' of development can take place as a function of the learner's L1.

6. This process of overlearning leading to use in 'communicative' speech followed by eventual disappearance is precisely that reported for '-ing' by Lightbown (1983)—see Chapter 2.
7. Semantic simplification is also one of the processes that can be invoked in the use of simplified registers such as foreigner/teacher talk.
8. Krashen (1981b) argues that integrative motivation is more likely to lead to more successful acquisition, as instrumental motivation may lead to acquisition ceasing once the learner has developed sufficient L2 resources to satisfy his functional needs. This, however, assumes that learners either have an integrative or an instrumental motivation. In fact, it is likely that many learners have *both* (see Burstall, 1978).

Chapter 8

Applications for Teaching a Second Language

THERE has been a marked reluctance to apply the results of SLD research to language teaching. Tarone *et al.* (1976) argue there are no reliable guidelines to be got from research and give seven reasons why this is so. SLD research is restricted in linguistic scope, it has only just begun to investigate the cognitive processes and learning strategies of SLD, the contribution of individual variables such as personality and motivation has not been evaluated, the methodology for both the collection and analysis of L2 data is still developmental and few studies have been replicated. These authors also point out that teaching practice and research practice are very different, for whereas teachers operate according to the immediacy of the need in the language classroom, researchers follow a slow, bit-by-bit approach.

There are some sound reasons, however, why the gulf between research and language teaching should not continue. Pedagogic practice cannot wait until SLD researchers are satisfied they possess a theory that can withstand any empirical test any more than it could wait until linguists had devised a grammar that met fully the criteria of descriptive and explanatory adequacy. It is not reasonable to argue for delay when the knowledge that SLD research is capable of providing, incomplete as it is, is knowledge that teachers do not have. Providing the applications are sensible (i.e. are not entirely revolutionary and are flexible) they are justified. This has been increasingly realised in the last few years. Many SLD researchers now spell out what they think should happen in a language classroom. For example,

Burt and Dulay (1981) feel confident enough about their view of SLD to make a number of positive applications. They emphasise the need to subordinate linguistic form to subject content by teaching the L2 through subjects such as science and arts and crafts. A further reason why delay is unnecessary is that much of the advice coming from SLD researchers points in the same direction that language teaching is heading for other reasons i.e. one that can be loosely called 'communicative'. It is unlikely, therefore, that there will be any major conflict between what SLD research recommends and what other linguistic forms of enquiry have to suggest.

Foremost among those researchers ready to advise language teachers has been Krashen. His basic position is that language teaching should try to foster 'acquisition'. Krashen (1982b) outlines in some detail how this is to be achieved. The classroom must provide 'optimal input' by: (1) ensuring that the input is comprehensible to the learners; (2) making it relevant and interesting; (3) making no attempt to sequence it grammatically; (4) offering it in sufficient quantity; (5) keeping the learners' filter[1] levels low so that they are open to it; and (6) providing tools for conversational management. There is a limited role for 'learning', which should be restricted (1) to rules that are learnable, portable and not yet acquired and (2) to certain situations where there is sufficient time and the focus on form is appropriate. Krashen uses these parameters to evaluate a number of methodologies. He concludes that Asher's (1977) Total Physical Response and Terrell's (1977) Natural Method are likely to succeed because they meet the conditions for 'optimal input' and appropriate 'learning', whereas Audiolingualism and Cognitive Code are likely to be less successful because they do not meet these conditions. Krashen's insistence on only a minor role for 'learning' and the battery of techniques that have been traditionally used to foster this is a direct application of his theory. However, his proposal is a revolutionary one,[2] it seeks to challenge and reject the traditions that language teaching has developed over several centuries. It is only tenable if the theory from which it derives is proof against the limitations described by Tarone *et al.* A number of reasons have already been put forward why this is not so.

It is one thing to apply research based on naturalistic SLD to classroom teaching and quite another to apply research based on classroom SLD itself. This is a point that is recognised by Tarone *et al.* (1976)

> Given that speech does vary in different social situations, and given that most data on ILs have been collected *outside* the classroom situation, we must assume that little of the current research on second language learning can be directly applied to the classroom. (p. 26)

The lack of research treating classroom SLD as a distinct acquisitional type has motivated the writing of this book. If classroom SLD is different to naturalistic SLD, then, there is no basis for applying the research findings. If it is similar, a basis exists. The position that has been outlined in Chapter 7 is that SLD is not a unitary phenomenon but a varied one according to whether it occurs via primary or secondary processes. In many classrooms the secondary processes will predominate as a result of the planned discourse which takes place there. The communicative skills that result will only be applicable to certain kinds of formal language use. However, classrooms also offer the opportunity for unplanned discourse through exposure to the TL in more conversation-like interactions. This will foster development via the primary processes and aid communicative skills for taking part in more informal language use. If the aim of language teaching is to develop fluency in conversations (and perhaps also writing of some kinds), then classroom SLD is likely to resemble naturalistic SLD because the same processes will need to be activated. If the aim of language teaching is to develop the ability to do well in examinations or to produce carefully planned and monitored written work, then classroom SLD is not likely to resemble naturalistic SLD. The availability of a theory that addresses itself specifically to classroom SLD (although it is, of course, applicable to other types of SLD) enables applications to language teaching to be made with greater conviction.

The applications proposed in this chapter will not be revolutionary. The limitations of current SLD research are recognised. The applications are offered, however, without apology in the hope that they give some coherence, some way of organising attitudes into a systematic theory of second language teaching at a time when divergence and variety are often recommended for their own sake.

The components of language teaching

What exactly is 'language teaching'? It is possible to identify a number of components (Fig. 14). The focal point is the classroom because this is where contact between the teacher, the learner and the materials occurs. Here the participants interact in the variety of ways described in Chapter 5. The model is helpful because it isolates, somewhat artificially, the different components that directly or indirectly contribute to and shape classroom interaction.

(1) *Policy*

This refers to the underlying rationale for providing a course of language teaching. The rationale may derive from a national language policy regarding the roles that the L2 is to play in the community or from an educational policy regarding the aims of the school curriculum. The policy can be clearly articulated so that teachers and learners are aware of what it states or it can be implicit with no conscious awareness by teachers and learners of what it is.

(2) *Approach*

Strevens (1977) defines approach as 'a commitment to particular specified points of view—to an ideology, one might say—about language teaching' (p. 23). Thus the approach determines whether or not there is a syllabus and what kind of syllabus there should be. Directly or indirectly the approach influences how classroom interaction is organised as a result of the general attitudes to the nature of the teaching–learning task adopted by teacher and learners.

(3) *Syllabus*

There are different views of what a syllabus consists of. Minimally, it can consist of just a list of items to be learnt. Generally, however,

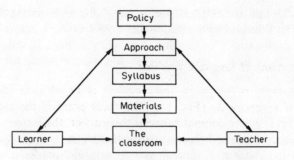

FIG. 14. The components of language teaching.

syllabus design involves the twin procedures of selection and grading. The list so constructed is ordered, either hierarchically or chronologically. It can be used either as a teaching list or as a check list.

Not all approaches lead to a formally-constituted syllabus, as described above. Many teachers operate only with a number of general aims and decide on the content of individual lessons on a day-by-day basis. The 'syllabus' that results is not an explicit one; it is derived from 'concurrent' analysis rather than a 'pre-course' analysis of what the learners need. It is, however, arguably still a syllabus.

(4) *Materials*

A syllabus may be implemented in more than one way by preparing alternative materials to reflect its content. Materials include texts books, audio-visual aids and any other realia the treacher uses. In terms of the distinction between 'core' and 'framework' goals described in Chapter 5, materials are the means for achieving the 'core' goals.

(5) *The classroom*

No matter how organised the treacher is, no matter how committed to any one approach, what takes place in the classroom will always remain, to some extent at least, unpredictable. One reason for this is that all interaction, even the most planned, will require some degree of negotiation which can only occur *in situ*. Another reason is that 'framework' and 'social' goals will always arise and cannot easily be planned for. What occurs in the language classroom, therefore, cannot be constrained entirely by the choice of policy, approach, syllabus and materials. It is likely, however, that the *degree* of choice will be determined by these other components.

(6) *The teacher*

The teacher brings to the classroom more than a lesson plan and teaching materials; he also brings his personal opinions of what constitutes appropriate behaviour for the teacher and pupil in language classrooms, his personality, his communicative skills, his prior knowledge of the pupils (and/or pupils similar to them), his knowledge of the TL and in some cases of the students' mother tongues and he may also possess some knowledge of theoretical and applied linguistics.

(7) *The pupil*

The pupil also brings a host of purely individual factors to the classroom—his personality, his knowledge of what language is and does, his world knowledge, his knowledge of his mother tongue, a set of attitudes and motivation for learning the TL, an aptitude for learning, a cognitive style and maybe some notion of what is the best way to learn a second language (see Pickett, 1978).

The aim of this final chapter is to examine the applications of the variable competence theory expounded in Chapter 7 for the seven components of 'language teaching'.

Policy

Policy is placed at the top of the model of language teaching in Fig. 14 because in many cases it determines the nature of all the other components. It is national policy that determines *what* language is taught, for instance. In many multilingual nations there is often a choice of more than one L2 as the lingua franca—in South Africa, for example, there is a choice among English, Afrikaans and various black African languages. A national language policy, however, is only likely to succeed if it is in accord with the socio-economic aspirations of the learners—in South Africa the policy of using Africaans as the medium of instruction in black upper primary and secondary schools failed. Where national policy does not dictate *what* languages are to be taught (as is the case in Britain), educational policy may well influence both *what* is taught and *how* it is taught. Thus in Britain there has been an educational decision, often taken by schools themselves, to teach French, German or Spanish as 'foreign' languages rather than Urdu or Bengali, despite the fact that there are substantial numbers of indigenous British people who speak these latter languages as mother tongues. The manner in which 'foreign' languages are taught in Britain is also strongly influenced by educational policy—the format of public examinations emphasises the importance of correctness of usage and not surprisingly leads to an approach which practises planned discourse and consequently secondary learning processes.

Policy, then, is likely to determine what kind of competence the learners achieve. If the L2 is a favoured language, motivation to learn it will be strong enough for the required processes to operate. But if the kind of performance that is rewarded by the educational system is different from that socially required there is likely to be a conflict in learner attitudes that results in either slow and insubstantial development or the acquisition of a type of competence which is not appropriate for the kinds of interactions in which the learner will have to take part in in real life. It is, for instance, difficult to fool students that what they should develop are skills for participating in unplanned discourse if the kind of skills demanded by the examination they are studying for are those relating to planned discourse.

Approach

It is at the level of approach that the variable-competence model of SLD has the clearest applications. Whereas linguistic theory has been able to make substantial contributions to language teaching practice by suggesting specific techniques (e.g. discourse analysis is currently being pedagogically exploited through the use of exercises based on 'discourse plans'; see Candlin, 1981), this has not been the case, nor will be, where theories of language development are concerned. These theories, however, may well provide a sounder basis for orienting language teaching ideologically than linguistic theory.

There are a welter of methods of language teaching but relatively few approaches. Roberts (1982) identifies two current approaches—what he calls the 'communicative' approach, which is targeted towards helping the student develop the competence to perform in real life by helping him to perform speech acts fluently, correctly and appropriately, and the 'humanistic/psychological' approach which emphasises the primacy of affective factors in language learning and advocates taking a 'whole person' approach. These fashionable approaches exist side-by side with the 'traditional method' approach, which is structure-dominated and teacher-centred. Other language teaching theorists have made similar distinctions. Stern (1981) distinguishes the '*L*' approach, which is linguistic, analytic and formal and the '*P*' approach, which is experiential, psychological and pedagogic; he discusses the Council of Europe systems-learning project as an example of the former and the 'humanistic' methods (e.g. Silent Way and Community Language Learning) as examples of the latter. Language teaching according to Stern, is faced with a 'code-communication dilemma'. It has to decide to what extent language teaching should be a formal study or involve natural communication. Ellis (1982c) also sees two current approaches, which he labels 'formal communicative' and 'informal communicative'. These are contrasted with the more traditional 'non-communicative' approach. Brumfit (1980) makes a distinction between approaches which emphasise 'accuracy' and those that emphasise 'fluency'. The correlation between these various descriptive terms is shown in Table 12. Obviously all attempts to reduce the myriad of approaches to one or two specific types requires a high level of abstraction and is potentially dangerous. It might be better to do as Littlewood (1981) does and treat the distinction in Table 13 as non-categorical; the basic distinction between what is 'communicative' and what is not should reflect a continuum and not a dichotomy.

The variable competence model suggests that in order to evaluate the contribution made by these different approaches it is necessary to separate out two sets of aims. The first set relates to the *L2 knowledge* that is to be developed and the second to the *type of discourse* in which the learner is to participate.

TABLE 13.
Approaches to Second Language Teaching

	I	II	III
Roberts (1982)	traditional method	communicative	humanistic/ psychological
Stern (1981)		'*L*' approach	'*P*' approach
Ellis (1982)	non- communicative	formal communicative	informal communicative
Brumfit (1980)		accuracy	fluency

If L2 knowledge can be accrued both as a result of participating in unplanned and planned discourse by operating both primary and secondary discourse processes, then it does not matter whether the approach is a formal one based on accuracy or an informal one based on fluency. TL knowledge will result from the kinds of interactions typical of both approaches. If the internalisation of L2 knowledge is considered separately from its use—and it is arguable whether this is possible—no clear case can be made out for advocating an informal as opposed to a formal approach or vice-versa. Such a case can only be made out if different types of knowledge are distinguished—for instance, 'acquired' and 'learnt' knowledge—and claims made regarding their non-transfer. The variable competence theory makes no such claims. It posits a *single* knowledge store. Thus although a formal approach is likely to result in analysed knowledge and an informal approach in non-analysed knowledge there is no clear demarcation between them, and, given the right conditions of use, the one can be converted into the other. According to the socio-cognitive theory there is no 'code-communication dilemma' where *L2 knowledge* is concerned. Any decision regarding which approach to adopt, therefore, should be based only on individual factors such as the age of the student (young children will have difficulty with planned discourse) and personality (introverted learners may feel threatened if asked to participate in unplanned discourse right away).

There are three possible routes to L2 knowledge:

(1) *By using primary processes in unplanned discourse*

This is the route that will occur in 'naturalistic SLD'. It can also occur in a classroom providing the right kind of interactions take place. It results in knowledge of the non-analysed type. According to some theorists (e.g. Sharwood-Smith, 1981) it has the disadvantage of being a slow process. According to other theorists it is not possible in the early stages of SLD because the relevant processes can only operate when they have some material to work on. A third criticism is that it can lead to 'pidginised' speech. All three criticisms are disputable, however—it may not be a slow process if use as well as acquisition of knowledge is considered, there are plenty of successful 'street' learners who make it all the way from beginning to end by the 'primary' processes, and 'pidginised speech' is probably the result of communicative need rather than of instructional opportunities.

(2) *By using secondary processes in planned discourse*

This is the route that is likely to occur in classrooms where formal instruction based on consciousness-raising and practice dominates. It results in knowledge of the analysed type. The most common criticism of this approach is that this knowledge cannot be used in spontaneous conversation. This can be countered, however, by maintaining—as the variable competence theory does—that analysed knowledge can evolve into non-analysed knowledge fairly rapidly when the need to communicate in real conversations arises.

(3) *By an integrated approach involving both primary and secondary processes*

This is the route advocated by Brumfit (1980); the teacher alternates between concentrating on formal presentations of new language items (i.e. accuracy) and communicative discussions (i.e. fluency). It is likely to result in both analysed and non-analysed knowledge and may help one to evolve into the other, thereby speeding up the rate of development. This approach can only be attacked by maintaining a non-interface position (see Chapter 6). It is the 'middle way' recommended not only by Brumfit but by a host of other theorists including Stevick (1982).

The evaluation of the different approaches, however, requires a consideration of the *type of discourse* which is the language teaching goal. Ultimately, because L2 knowledge can be acquired via primary or secondary processes, what is important is not so much the knowledge as the *use* to which this knowledge is to be put. The variable competence theory hypothesises that knowledge that arises from planned discourse will not be available for immediate use in unplanned discourse because different processes are involved. What are the applications of such a hypothesis for language teaching? The answer depends on the kind of learner.

Imagine an adult learner who intends visiting Britain soon and wants to develop sufficient competence to engage in natural conversation with British people. It is evident that what he requires is a course which will stimulate him to use primary processes in unplanned discourse. He must learn how to negotiate meaning using whatever resources he possesses and in so doing will build up non-analysed knowledge characterised by the developmental stages described in Figure 12. The approach that is most likely to satisfy his requirements is an 'informal communicative' one that emphasises fluency rather than accuracy. It might be argued, of course, that a 'formal communicative' approach (i.e. one that taught pragmatic competence explicitly) would be useful to this learner as he would have the opportunity to activate the analysed knowledge which he acquired once he arrived in Britain and started to take part in unplanned discourse. It seems unnecessary, however, to follow such an indirect route to the kind of competence this learner needs, when the direct route could be chosen. Also not all learners are able to switch from secondary to primary processes when occasion demands; they may clam up and try to avoid taking part in unplanned discourse.

Consider now another adult learner whose main purpose for taking a language course is also to participate in natural conversation with other speakers of English but who already lives in Britain. The main difference between this learner and the first is that he has the chance to activate any analysed knowledge he acquires in the classroom by taking part in ordinary conversations in the 'street'.[3] It is less imperative, therefore, that the classroom affords the opportunity to experience unplanned discourse, although some time spent using primary processes by communicating with whatever resources are available would still seem desirable. This learner might be expected to gain from either a formal or informal communicative approach or from one that integrated both.

It is not hard to think of learners who could benefit most from a formal approach—communicative or non-communicative. An adult learner who has many years of successful language learning behind him and who has progressed to the final stage of the primary processes (i.e. has begun to distinguish functional meanings linguistically) would seem well-suited to a course that attempts to provide advanced analysed knowledge through consciousness-raising. Such a learner may well be the typical ESP learner that courses such as the 'Focus' series (Allen and Widdowson, 1975–80) are designed for. According to Widdowson (1978), though, the type of knowledge that the ESP learner needs is not 'usage' but 'use'. He becomes a better communicator by learning rules of use and practising how to apply these in monitoring activities that are cognitively challenging (Ellis, 1982c). Whether the target is 'use' or 'usage', however, the kind of approach envisaged is one that trains those procedures for engaging in planned discourse.

Children (i.e. those under 12 years) will in most cases not find it easy to use secondary processes. Both monitoring and borrowing come more easily after Formal Operations have been reached. Here, then, an 'informal communicative' approach, in particular one that stresses learning through activity, seems most suitable. However, if one of the aims was the development of conventional writing skills, some ability to monitor would be desirable. While it is possible to 'compose' in writing using primary processes, 'transcribing' by means of the conventions of the written medium require an ability to search into the corners of the L2 knowledge store in order to edit what is spontaneously produced (see Smith, 1982, for an interesting account of the writing process which follows these lines).

Although there will be some learners who do not need to monitor, most will. Formal teaching—communicative or non-communicative—should have as one of its major aims the development of monitoring skills, in particular the ability to use this process selectively and appropriately. The goals of a formal approach should include the provision of analysed knowledge and practice in monitoring.

The purpose of this discussion of why it is important to consider *types of discourse* in evaluating approaches to language teaching has been to emphasise that different learners will require different kinds of teaching according to whether they wish to participate in unplanned or planned discourse or both. It is not possible to evaluate the various approaches in absolute terms, only in relative ones. A 'bad' approach is one that offers formal interactions when informal ones are required and vice-versa; a 'good' approach is one that offers interactions of the type the learner expects to take part in in real life. If an 'informal communicative' approach is given primacy, this will only be because of the importance that is attached to unplanned discourse in language use.

Syllabus

It has already been noted that a syllabus can involve either 'pre-course' or 'concurrent' selection of items. Most of the following discussion, however, will be concerned with the former as it is this which has come to be thought of as the 'syllabus' in British teaching circles at least. The basis of selecting and organising the teaching content has dominated second language teaching in Britain over the last decade, starting with the work of the Council of Europe (e.g. Van Ek, 1976; Wilkins, 1976) and continuing into the '80s (e.g. Johnson, 1982). In general, the debate has paid scant regard to SLD theory, preferring to assume that language learning is like all other types of learning in that it is facilitated by a systematic exposure to the target knowledge. The debate has been about how best to systematise the exposure.

A number of different positions will be identified and then considered in the light of the variable competence theory of SLD. The positions are:

(1) The syllabus should list and sequence the items of *linguistic knowledge* that are to be learnt.
(2) The syllabus should list and possibly sequence the *language functions and notions* (together with their linguistic exponents) that are to be mastered.
(3) The syllabus should list the *discourse processes* that the learner needs to employ in order to participate in interpersonal interaction.
(4) The syllabus should list and sequence the *communicative activities* in which the learners will be asked to participate.

Each of these positions is tenable both in terms of a teaching syllabus and a checklist. It is also possible to design a hybrid syllabus by combining two or more of these approaches. Brumfit's (1980) suggestions regarding a 'spiral syllabus', which feeds-in functions and notions around a grammatical core, constitute an example of such a syllabus.

From the point of view of the variable competence theory any syllabus that seeks to specify the teaching content linguistically, either directly as in (1) or indirectly as in (2), implies a formal approach which will practise secondary processes in planned discourse. In contrast, any syllabus that does not select and sequence the language items to be learnt but instead indicates the kinds of activities which the learner will participate in implies an informal approach which will practise primary processes in discourse that is more or less unplanned. A broad distinction corresponding to this 'formal/informal' dichotomy is that between 'content/procedural' syllabuses. A 'content' syllabus states in one way or another the target knowledge as a *product*; a 'procedural' syllabus seeks to describe the kind of behaviours which the learner will have to undertake in order to develop L2 knowledge and as such is concerned with the *process* of development.

An interesting possibility regarding 'content' syllabuses is that they should be sequenced to reflect the universal order of SLD. It could be argued that because this takes account of the natural sequence evident in 'unplanned' discourse it would provide a basis for 'informal' teaching. However, what is important from the learner's point of view is not the knowledge of the TL but the procedures of language use. Providing the learner is afforded the opportunity to use the primary processes in unplanned discourse, the 'natural order' will automatically occur; there is, therefore, no need to organise the presentation of material in accordance with it. Indeed, if the syllabus were so organised and materials developed to practise specific items of knowledge the result would be planned discourse and an encouragement to the learner to use secondary processes to cope with it. The teaching that would result would still be formal. The case for ordering the linguistic content in accordance with the order of acquisition in unplanned discourse, is, however, still a strong one, providing that it is recognised that this will not in itself facilitate the learner's ability to take part in everyday conversations. To this end more information is required about the order of acquisition of different grammatical systems and, also, where (2) is concerned of the order in which various communicative functions are 'naturally' mastered.

A 'content' syllabus is usually framed in terms of the 'rules' that are to be learnt. Where unplanned discourse is concerned, the evidence suggests that instruction based on importing 'rules' is not likely to succeed (see Chapters 2 and 5). There is, however, some evidence to suggest that instruction based on 'formulas' is more likely to be successful (see Chapter 4), perhaps because this does not require any abstract representation of the language form. An analysis of learner needs may be able to furnish information regarding those language functions that are communicatively important and frequently needed by the learner. These functions can then be taught to the learner in formal ways. In other words, the notional–functional syllabus, while unlikely to lead to 'rules' that can be used in unplanned discourse, may be admirably suited to providing the learner with useful formulas, which he will be able to use in spontaneous speech. The disadvantage that has often been levelled at notional–functional syllabuses—that it leads to 'language-like behaviour' rather than to knowledge of the generative system—becomes in this new light its strength. Second language development begins with 'language-like behaviour' so it might make sense to devise the content of the syllabus accordingly for at least the early stages.

In general, however, where the target is competency in unplanned discourse the most appropriate type of syllabus is the 'procedural' one. One possibility for such a syllabus is (3) i.e. a list of discourse processes. This, however, may be of limited value. In the first place, it is difficult to see how a list such as that provided in Table 11 can be converted into practice materials, but more importantly simply listing the processes fails to recognise the centrality of negotiation in the construction of discourse i.e. the relevant discourse processes are not only the learner's but also the teacher's. However, some interesting suggestions along the lines of (3) have been made by Hatch (1978b) and as Krashen (1982) notes, one of the main aims of the classroom must be to equip the learner with the tools for managing conversations. It may well prove possible to teach some of the procedures required, particularly, if it can be shown that 'communication strategies' are developmentally ordered, as some preliminary work (e.g. Chesterfield and Chesterfield, 1983) indicates they might be.

From the perspective of an 'informal' approach the syllabus with the greatest potential is (4). A syllabus that specifies only the activities the learner will participate in has the overriding advantage of allowing the learner to select his own inputs and outputs. This type of 'procedural' syllabus recognises the importance of negotiation, through which linguistic data appropriate to the learner's level can be made available and practised.

The most substantial attempt at a 'procedural' syllabus based on activities that is currently available is that used in the experimental 'Bangalore Project'. This is based on schools in Bangalore and Madras. There is little published literature dealing with it, but useful accounts can be found in Prabhu (1980) and in Johnson (1982). Prabhu, the project's director, adopts a very similar position regarding the classroom learning of a second language as that propounded by Newmark (1966), who argued that students should not be formally instructed but left to work out the language system for themselves in much the same way as young children acquire their mother tongue. Because Prabhu believes that L2 knowledge is best learnt when the learner is attending to meaning, he dismisses the idea of any kind of linguistic syllabus and also of formal teaching procedures such as drilling and error correction. The syllabus that has been designed consists of lists of graded activities; for each activity, which is designed to cover a lesson, there is a specific task which poses some kind of cognitive challenge to the learners. The content of the activities reflects the everyday topics which the students might engage in both inside and outside school (e.g. school timetables; maps and plans; simple calculations). Prabhu argues (see Johnson, 1982) that there is no danger of failing to ensure coverage of the language because the grammatical system is bound to be covered in the 'teacher–learner talk' that accompanies the variety of tasks. Initial reports suggest that the students did succeed in learning and using 'new' structures. It is, however, too early to make any conclusive evaluation of the project.

One of the major difficulties in the design of a 'procedural' syllabus such as that used in the 'Bangalore Project' concerns the selection and sequencing of activities. The Project adopted as one of its principles that the activities should be ordered in such a way that the later ones could assume and exploit the problem-solving strategies developed in the earlier ones. This did not obviate the need for initial 'rehearsal' as a preparation for the main task of a lesson and it would appear that this could take the form of direct instruction, at least in vocabulary (e.g. concepts like 'north-east' were taught prior to a map reading activity). Obviously the less successful the grading of activities, the greater the need for 'rehearsal'. At the moment what principles should be followed to ensure an adequate grading is not clear, although the following are likely to be important:

—language-perception distance; tasks can be ranged in complexity according to what the relationship is between contiguous events and the language used.[4]
—the quantity and quality of the non-linguistic features of the task; Littlewood (1981) writes, 'The general level of difficulty of the task is determined largely by how numerous, how obvious and how easily discernible the distinguishing features are'. (p. 24)
—the nature of the operations to be performed in the activity; e.g. Littlewood distinguishes 'sharing' information and 'processing' information and suggests the latter is more difficult.
—the complexity of the language required to perform the activity.

The general aim of each activity must be to set the learner the right level of challenge by providing a task which allows the use of previous knowledge and experience and at the same time requires 'new' language and strategies.

There are two further points worth making about a 'procedural' syllabus based on activities. The first is that there is nothing to stop some aspect of language form or use constituting one of the activities. Krashen (1981b) pointed out that when he was a student in a French lesson, he experienced useful input when the teacher tried but failed to explain a point of grammar; with some learners linguistics is just as suitable a topic as anything else. Johnson (1982) notes that notional syllabuses can also be used as carriers of language if they are treated as specifications of means rather than ends. In other words it is not so much the syllabus *per se* that determines what kind of learning takes place as the pedagogic use that is made of the syllabus. The second point is that a 'procedural' syllabus can be used in conjunction with a linguistic or functional check list, which will serve the double purpose of enabling a record of the progress students make to be kept and of helping to identify the language and strategies required in subsequent activities.

Ultimately the type of syllabus that is chosen must depend on the type of learning that is required. Just as a 'content' syllabus is not likely to lead to interactions that foster primary processes, so a 'procedural' syllabus will not encourage secondary processes. The choice is a relative one.

Materials

The materials that are required for an 'informal' approach aimed at promoting primary processes in unplanned discourse will be very different from those used to promote a 'formal' approach based on a structural or functional syllabus. The criteria below are suggested as guidelines for determining suitable materials for 'fluency' work:

(1) There must be a *communicative purpose* (i.e. *not* merely a pedagogic one). The test of whether there is or is not a communicative purpose is how successful completion of a task is judged; if the task is evaluated in terms of the behavioural outcome rather than its manner of performance, it is communicative.

(2) There must be a focus on the *message* rather than on the channel; i.e. the interactants must be concerned with what they have to say rather than how they are going to say it.

(3) There must be an *information-gap* i.e. one speaker must not know what the other speaker is going to say, although he may often be able to predict it.

(4) The communication stimulated by the task must be *negotiated* rather than predetermined. This means that the task must not exert rigid control over the language to be used but must allow the speakers to make adaptations in content and expression in the light of feedback they receive. There is likely, therefore, to be considerable variety of forms used.

(5) The speakers must be allowed to use whatever *resources*—verbal and non-verbal—they possess, irrespective of whether these conform to normal native speaker behaviour or not. There must be no pedagogic intervention from the teacher, but this does not preclude, of course, the use of various topic-incorporation devices[5] that characterise 'natural' communication such as that occurring between mother and child.

These criteria are based on similar criteria proposed by Ellis (1982c) and Harmer (1982). Underlying all of them is the necessity of a *desire to communicate*. This, however, is not so much a characteristic of the materials themselves as the result of the learner's attitude to learning the L2 and to the tasks he is given.[6] The criteria have been framed with speech in mind, but they can be easily adapted to writing when the aim is 'composition' rather than 'transcription' (Smith, 1982).

Published materials often make claims to be 'communicative', although often without specifying precisely what is meant by this. Materials designed to instruct the student in the correct forms required by a 'rule' or to realise a language function or notion are not likely to satisfy the five criteria listed above. Such materials derive from a 'formal communicative' rather than an 'informal communicative' approach and will practise planned rather than unplanned discourse. In general, materials that practise the latter will be found in 'resource' rather than 'course' books. There are now a large number of resource materials available (see Lake and Stokes, 1983).

It would be a mistake, however, to think of materials as being either informally or formally communicative. Different materials will meet none, some or all of the specifications. The level of formality/informality is to be measured in degrees in much the same way as the level of planning in discourse construction; the distinction belongs to a continuum, not a dichotomy. Table 14 describes a number of different language activities in terms of the five criteria. It is clear that some activities such as substitution tables or fully scripted dialogues are entirely 'formal' while other activities such as symbol-drawing and reconstructing story-sequences are entirely 'informal'. Still other activities such as cued dialogues or twenty-questions are partly 'formal' and partly 'informal'. It should be pointed out, however, that often it is not so much the materials that determine what kind of discourse is practised as the manner in which the materials are exploited by the classroom interactants. For example, substitution tables could become the basis for an 'informal' activity if the students were asked to expand a skeleton table using their own examples and worked cooperatively in pairs or groups; the task-talk that this would stimulate would belong to unplanned discourse.

TABLE 14.
A Description of Language Teaching Activities

Activity	Example	1	2	3	4	5
1. Substitution tables	Stevick (1982; p. 99)	×	×	×	×	×
2. Scripted dialogues	Revell (1979; p. 33)	×	×	×	×	×
3. Cued dialogues	Revell (1979; p. 50)	√	×	√	×	√
4. Twenty Questions		√	√	√	×	×
5. Reconstructing story sequences	Byrne and Rixon (1979; p. 25)	√	√	√	√	√
6. Symbol drawing	Wight *et al.* (1972)	√	√	√	√	√

From the point of view of the variable competence theory of SLD it is not important to select activities related to situations in which the learner is likely to need to use the L2. What is important is that the processes required for participating in the type of discourse required by the learner are activated. In the case of unplanned discourse this will depend on the extent to which the activities meet the five criteria of informality and not on the situational content. It is likely, however, that the learner's *desire to communicate* will be greater when there is situational relevancy.

Brumfit (1978) has pointed out that fluency-activities have always had a place in language teaching. The use of discussion based on multiple choice questions following a comprehension passage is a good example. This activity meets all five criteria. Informal communicative materials are not new. What is new is the proposal that they might be necessary and sufficient for taking part in unplanned discourse and that formal materials (i.e. those that do not meet the five criteria) are neither necessary nor sufficient.

Resource books containing informal communicative activities frequently adopt the point of view that these materials are best used as a means of consolidating TL knowledge that has been learnt from more formal exercises. The informal activities are slotted into the 'communicative practice' stage of the traditional presentation–practice lesson format. To this end, the materials-writers often try to predict the language forms that will be required to perform the various activities. This approach to the use of informal activities may well help to make analysed knowledge more rapidly available for use in unplanned discourse, but there is a danger that, because the approach is essentially still a formal one, the teacher will fail to realise that activation can only occur when the focus is on meaning and the learner has the chance to use the primary processes. If he treats the utterances the learner produces as samples of the L2 by formally correcting errors rather than as communication, the result will be pedagogic discourse and the learner will be encouraged to continue using secondary processes. A safer approach might be to treat informal activities as entirely self-contained and so to make no attempt to integrate them with more formal work. Such an approach is entirely compatible with the variable competence theory which maintains that SLD can take place entirely on the basis of unplanned discourse.

If materials designed to practise unplanned discourse are to be entirely self-contained, the problem about what to do with the complete beginner again arises. How can activities be devised to encourage the use of primary processes when the learner possesses no L2 resources? There are two possible solutions to this problem. The first is Asher's Total Physical Response method (see Asher, 1977). This is based on an initial 'silent period', when the only responses the student is required to make are non-verbal ones. The teacher presents a number of instructions, which in the initial stage relate entirely to objects present in the situational context, and the students carry these out. Although the instructions are ordered according to a structural syllabus, Asher emphasises that the content of the lessons is flexible and 'can be shifted around without negative consequences' (p. 42). As there is no planned 'consciousness-raising' the input that is conveyed through the instructions is primarily that which occurs in 'unplanned' discourse. Asher, in fact, emphasises that, with the exception of pronunciation, the 'biological wiring' responsible for FLD also operates in SLD. An alternative to Total Physical Response is to select activities for early SLD that do not require very much productive language from the students e.g. art and handicraft activities. These will involve the teacher giving simple explanations and instructions which have an immediate locus of reference. The need to communicate will ensure that the teacher makes the necessary adaptations to facilitate the primary processes. These kinds of materials are part and parcel of everyday teaching in British primary schools, which in many ways provide an ideal environment for learning through unplanned discourse.

There is no need to discuss in detail the range of formal language-learning activities which are the stock in trade of textbook writers. It is, however, worth commenting on the importance of activities that can be used to practise and develop the learner's monitoring skills. Such activities might be very simple in the first place (e.g. copying sentences or underlining errors in sentences) and much more complex later on (e.g. selecting rhetorically appropriate utterances from a set of options provided). Thus, monitoring exercises can be mechanical or cognitively challenging. It is important, however, that due regard is paid to appropriate use of monitoring. The often recommended practice of audio-recording fluency practice and then playing back to the students to allow them to self-correct would seem a clear example of inappropriate use, as it confuses planned and unplanned discourse. The provision of varied and appropriate materials for practising monitoring is an aspect of language teaching that has been neglected and that requires attention.

The teacher, the students and the classroom

The final components of language teaching will be discussed together in terms of the patterns of interaction which can occur in the classroom context. Purely individual factors relating to learning and teaching style will not be considered, not because they are not important but because they fall outside the compass of the variable competence theory. The aim is to collate and summarise the observations made about classroom interaction and SLD in Chapter 5.

A competency for participating in informal interaction is more likely to develop from what has been called 'exposure' than from 'instruction'. Precisely what form this 'exposure' should take has been discussed in detail in Chapter 5, where it was suggested that the issue of central importance is the choice of interactive goals. Activity-centred, framework and social goals are more likely to aid the development of primary processes than message-oriented goals. The selection of activity-centred goals is effected by decisions taken at the level of approach, which in turn influences the type of syllabus and materials that are used. By opting for an informal approach, a procedural syllabus and materials that meet the five criteria of informal communicativeness proposed in the previous section, activity-centred goals can be ensured. The choice of approach also influences framework and social goals. If a general decision is taken to insist on the use of the L2 for *all* interactions occurring in the classroom and not just pedagogic ones (as will be obligatory in classrooms where the pupils speak different L1s which the teacher is not familiar with) then L2 interactions with framework and social goals will occur. The importance of this for facilitating a competency for unplanned discourse cannot be overstated. Social and framework goals, however, do not require an informal approach; they can also occur in a formal approach as part of general classroom management. As Chapter 6 pointed out, all *instruction* involves *exposure*.

CSL–I*

Whereas the type of interaction goals can be determined largely by decisions taken at the level of approach, the type of address system— the other dimension which Chapter 5 suggested was important for SLD—cannot. The address systems that occur are likely to be the result of decisions taken on a moment-by-moment basis as the interaction unfolds. It is for this reason that Johnson (1982) and Brumfit (1978), among others, have argued that 'communicative' language teaching involves far more than syllabus design; it involves the whole question of methodology. Language teaching materials are not in themselves 'communicative'. They become 'communicative' as a result of the types of address that arise from the way the materials are exploited by the teacher and student in the classroom. The comments made about how the chosen type of address affects the opportunities for SLD, which were made in Chapter 5, can be reviewed here in terms of two related aspects of classroom behaviour; interactive roles and feedback.

(1) *The allocation and distribution of roles in the classroom*

It is the roles that student and teacher adopt that control the nature of the linguistic environment in the classroom. If the teacher adopts the traditional role of 'knower' and assigns the student the role of 'information seeker' (see Corder, 1977) it is doubtful whether the resulting discourse will afford opportunities for using the primary processes. If the teacher is not to act as 'knower' what other roles are open to him? There are two principal choices; those of onlooker and partner.

When the teacher takes on the role of 'onlooker' emphasis is placed on symmetrical role-relationships. The teacher withdraws from the scene in favour of student–student activity. The facilitative nature of this type of discourse has been illustrated in Chapter 5. Student–student interaction is likely to be characterised by a quantitative intake, a felt need to communicate, student control over the propositional content, adherence to the 'here-and-now' principle, the performance of a range of speech acts. In this way the opportunity for negotiation is secured as the students are able to determine the relevance of their own utterances to the interaction. Of course, not all student–student interactions will achieve this, but negotiation is more likely to occur in these interactions than in teacher–class interaction. Also, certain kinds of activities will prove more successful in stimulating facilitative interaction than others; informal activities such as symbol drawing and reconstruction of story sequences can be most effectively implemented in student–student interaction.

There are disadvantages. One is that the students will not receive an input sufficiently rich in those L2 features they are ready to develop. Because they are exposed to the restricted language of other students, their interlanguage may pidginise. This is more likely in classrooms where the learners are homogeneous in ability and TL knowledge. However, Krashen (1981b) argues that the language that learners address to each other may come quite close to meeting input-requirements because it is 'more natural and more usually understood' (p. 105). Even students who are considered homogeneous are likely to have a different lexical knowledge of the TL which can be shared in interaction with other students. Another possible disadvantage of student–student interaction is that the teacher may feel his own security in the classroom is reduced because his control over what pupils say and do is diminished. An insecure teacher will pass on his own lack of confidence to the students who will be less likely to learn as a consequence. This, however, need not be the case. The teacher will still be called upon to play a major role in organising and managing activities. As Strevens (1978) points out a learner-centred approach to language teaching places greater rather than smaller demands on the teacher.

The partner role involves the teacher providing only samples of the L2 and guidance without rules; it constitutes what Allwright (1979) calls 'a minimal model of language teaching'. In many classrooms it may not be feasible for the teacher to take on the kind of partner role that the mother adopts with the young child—class size alone may preclude it. What is important, however, is that the teacher allows the students to take the lead and then adjusts his own discourse contributions to provide an appropriate level of input. The difficulties of achieving this, while at the same time maintaining order in the classroom interaction, are considerable, however. For this reason, 'partnership' will work best in teacher–student and teacher–group rather than teacher–class interaction.

Acting as 'partner' rather than 'knower' is not an abdication of responsibility. It is an acceptance of the necessity of sharing management activities in the classroom (Allwright, 1978). Whereas learner–centredness is fairly well-defined at the level of approach, its meaning is much less certain at the level of methodology. Allwright suggests twelve different management activities involving choice of task, adoption of standards and distribution of work and lists the major risks of teacher-centred classrooms i.e. frustration, confusion spoon-feeding, time-wasting, demoralisation and dependence breeding. More important than any of these, however, is the danger of 'instruction' monopolising interaction and so preventing 'exposure'. The most effective way of avoiding this danger is for the teacher to accept the role of 'partner'.

The effects of role choice and distribution are potentially of far greater importance than approach, syllabus design or materials. Different methods can result in very similar roles for students and teacher and consequently very similar types of interaction. Approaches that have concerned themselves with the humanistic side of the learner (see Stevick, 1976, 1980 and 1982) have recognised the need for reciprocity of roles in classroom communication most clearly. The success reported for Community Language Learning (e.g. LaForge, 1979) is predictable from and explicable by the variable competence model. CLL places a premium on the teacher as onlooker and partner.

(2) *The provision of feedback in the classroom*

Role choice is closely related to the provision of feedback. The teacher as 'knower' will probably conceive of feedback in terms of the identification and correction of learner errors and the positive reinforcement of correct utterances. The resulting focus will be on the channel rather than on the message. There are both practical and theoretical reasons why such feedback may not be helpful for developing a competency in unplanned discourse. Allwright (1975) argues that teachers fail to operate clearly-defined correction procedures and so are often inconsistent. Theoretically, learners do not progress by being corrected but by helping to construct discourse. However, despite inconsistencies in practice and reservations about the overall effectiveness of correction procedures, error detection/correction has been found to be one of only two characteristics common to all language teaching methods (Krashen and Seliger, 1975).

Correction need not be conceived of as *formal* correction; it can be thought of as a *procedural* device. By checking, requesting clarification, requesting confirmation, pointing out substantive inaccuracies and suggesting alternatives through such processes as repetition, prodding, and modelling (Gaies, 1977), the teacher can provide feedback within a framework of discourse negotiation. If correction is seen as a procedural device the focus will be on the maintenance of intersubjectivity rather than either the grammaticality or appropriateness of an utterance. The teacher will draw attention to a breakdown in communication but not to formal errors. Obviously, which view of correction is adopted depends on what the pedagogic goal is; if it is competency for unplanned discourse, then correction should take the form of a procedural device, but if it is competency for planned discourse, formal correction is needed.

Opinions about the value of error-correction vary greatly. Holley and King (1975) noted that trainee teachers often overcorrect and recommended that they should only correct obviously incorrect answers and that they should avoid immediately filling student pauses. In contrast, Hendrickson (1978) concludes that error correction can help adult learners to discover the functions and limitations of L2 lexical and grammatical forms. The nature of the feedback to be provided and the manner of its provision are areas where there is little current agreement in language teaching. The way to a clearer policy is to be found once again in the distinction between primary and secondary processes of language use. Where the focus is on SLD by means of primary processes, correction must be part of the overall process of negotiation, but where the focus is on monitoring, the kinds of procedures envisaged by Hendrickson are valid.

Conclusions

This chapter has set out to suggest how the variable competence theory can be applied to the practice and theory of language teaching.

This theory of SLD was based on what is known about the nature of classroom second language learning. It represents, however, only an initial statement. It would be premature to use it as the basis for drawing up hard and fast principles of language teaching. The applications that have been proposed should be treated as speculative, although they require no excuse, as they are better informed than many *ad hoc* decisions taken by teachers and course designers day by day.

The main proposal has been that a clear distinction needs to be drawn between approaches, syllabuses, materials and methodologies that are suitable for developing primary processes of language use and those that are suitable for developing secondary processes. In general, language teaching has given greater emphasis to the latter with the result that countless learners develop a knowledge of the TL without being able to use it in unplanned discourse. The current vogue for 'communication activities' has done something to redress the balance, although it is probably true to say that in the vast majority of language classrooms around the world there is little in the way of unplanned discourse still. Also, there is a continuing reluctance by teachers to accept that SLD can take place very successfully simply by the learners taking part in spontaneous interaction, even in the beginning stages. If this chapter has emphasised the importance of an 'informal' approach and reciprocal classroom roles for students and the teacher, this is not because these are the only ways to ensure successful learning but because ordinary conversation is in many ways the most natural type of discourse and because there has been so little of it in classrooms. The pendulum should not swing too far, however, for 'formal' language teaching based on planned discourse will continue to be of great importance for many language learners.

Notes

1. Krashen uses the term 'filter' to refer to the mechanism the language learner uses to screen the input he receives. If the filter is 'high' little input gets through to the processing mechanisms responsible for 'acquisition'.
2. Krashen and Terrel (1983) argue that the 'natural' approach is not revolutionary but traditional in the sense that it is a return to the recognition that successful SLD occurs when the learner has the chance to experience the natural uses of language in communication. However, most language teachers today would see a rejection of grammar teaching in one form or another as revolutionary.

3. However, not all L2 learners who live in Britain will in fact experience regular contact with native-speakers. Many learners will be socially and psychologically distanced with the result that their principal source of interaction will be the classroom. Such learners will also require the opportunity to use primary processes in unplanned discourse.

4. The term 'language-perception distance' is used by Blank *et al.* (1978). The underlying premise is that language that relates to the immediate context is easier to use and learn than language which relates to displaced activity.

5. Examples of topic-incorporation devices are expansions, paraphrase, repetition and requests for clarification. It has been hypothesised that these are important for language development because they help to sustain discourse.

6. Because it is the learner's attitude to L2 learning that is so important, it follows that materials aimed at fostering appropriate attitudes are needed. In other words, 'learner materials' as well as 'teaching materials' are required. There are in fact a number of 'learner guides' available (see Toney (1983) for a review).

Bibliography

ADAMS, M. (1978) Methodology for examining second language acquisition. In Hatch, E. (ed.).

ALEXANDER, L. and DUGAS, A. (1972–3) *Look, listen and learn, Bks I and II,* Centre Educatif et Culturel and Longman Canada Ltd.

ALLEN, P. and WIDDOWSON, H. (eds.) (1975–80) *English in Focus Series,* Oxford University Press.

ALLWRIGHT, R. (1975) Problems in the study of the language teacher's treatment of learner error. In Burt, M. and Dulay, H. (eds.), *On TESOL '75,* Teachers of English as a Second Language.

ALLWRIGHT, R. (1977) Turns, topics and tasks: patterns of participation in language learning and teaching. Paper given at TESOL National Convention, Miami. Also in Larsen-Freeman, D. (ed.).

ALLWRIGHT, R. (1978) Abdication and responsibility in language teaching. Paper given at the 1978 Berne Colloquium on Applied Linguistics.

ALLWRIGHT, R. (1979) Language learning through communication practice. In Brumfit, C. and Johnson, K. (eds.), *The Communicative Approach to Language Teaching,* Oxford University Press.

ALTMAN, H. (1980) Foreign language teaching: focus on the learner. In Altman, H. and Vaughan-James, C. (eds.), *Foreign Language Teaching: Meeting Individual Needs,* Pergamon Press, Oxford.

ARTHUR, B. *et al.* (1980) The register of impersonal discourse of foreigners: verbal adjustments to foreign accent. In Larsen-Freeman, D. (ed.).

ASHER, J. (1977) *Learning Another Language through Actions: The Complete Teacher's Guidebook,* Sky Oaks Productions.

ATKIN, J. (1978) Talk in the infant classroom. *English in Education,* **12,** 10–14.

BAILEY, N., MADDEN, C. and KRASHEN, S. (1974) Is there a 'natural sequence' in adult second language learning? *Language Learning,* **24,** 235–44.

BARNES, D. (1969) Language in the secondary classroom. In Barnes, D, Britton, J. and Rosen, H. *Language, the Learner and the School,* Penguin.

BARNES, D. (1976) *From communication to curriculum,* Penguin.

BATES, E. (1976) *Language and Context,* Academic Press.

BIALYSTOK, E. (1981) Some evidence for the integrity and interaction of two knowledge sources. In Andersen, R. (ed.), *New Dimensions in Second Language Acquisition Research,* Newbury House.

BIALYSTOK, E. (1982) On the relationship between knowing and using forms. *Applied Linguistics,* **3,** 3, 181–206.

BIALYSTOK, E. and FRÖHLICH, M. (1977) Aspects of second language learning in classroom settings. *Working Papers on Bilingualism,* **13,** 2–26.

BLACK, C. and BUTZKRAMM, W. (1978) Classroom language: materials for communicative language teaching, *ELT Journal,* **XXXII,** 4, 270–4.

BLANK, M., ROSE, S. and BERLIN, L. (1978) *The Language of Learning: the Preschool Years.* Grune & Stratton.

BLOOM, L. (1970) *Language Development: Form and Function in Emerging Grammars.* Research Monograph 59, MIT Press.

BRIÈRE, E. (1978) Variables affecting native Mexican children's learning Spanish as a second Language, *Language Learning*, **28**, 1, 159–74.

BROOK, V., SCHLUE, K. and CAMPBELL, C. (1980) Discourse and second language acquisition of yes/no questions. In Larsen-Freeman, D. (ed.)

BROOKS, N. (1960) *Language and Language Learning*, Harcourt Brace and World.

BROWN, H. (1980) The optimal distance model of second language acquisition. *TESOL Quarterly*, **14**, 2, 157–64.

BROWN, H. (1981) Affective factors in second language learning. In Alatis, J., Altman, H. and Alatis, P. (eds.), *The Second Language Classroom*, Oxford University Press.

BROWN, R. (1968) The development of WH questions in child speech. *Journal of Verbal Learning and Verbal Behaviour*, **7**, 279–90.

BROWN, R. (1973) *A First Language: The Early Stages*, Harvard University Press.

BRUMFIT, C. (1978) 'Communicative' language teaching: an assessment. In Strevens, P. (ed.), *In Honour of AS Hornby*, Oxford University Press.

BRUMFIT, C. (1980) From defining to designing: communicative specifications versus communicative methodology in foreign language teaching, mimeograph, University of London Institute of Education.

BURMEISTER, H. and UFERT, D. (1980) Strategy switching? In Felix, S. (ed.).

BURSTALL, C. (1978) Factors affecting foreign-language learning: a consideration of some recent research findings. In Kinsella, V. (ed.) *Language Teaching and Linguistic Surveys*, Cambridge University Press.

BURT, M. and DULAY, H. (1980) On acquisition orders. In Felix, S. (ed.).

BURT, M. and DULAY, H. (1981) Optimal language learning environments. In Alatis, J., Altman, H. and Alatis, P. (eds.), *The Second Language Teaching Classroom*, Oxford University Press.

BUTTERWORTH, G. and HATCH, E. (1978) A Spanish-speaking adolescent's acquisition of English syntax. In Hatch, E. (ed.).

BUTZKAMM, W. (1980) Verbal play and pattern practice. In Felix, S. (ed.).

BUTZKAMM, W. and DODSON, C. (1980) The teaching of communication: from theory to practice. *IRAL*, **XVIII**, 4, 289–309.

BYRNE, D. and RIXON, S. (1979) *ELT guide 1: Communicative Games*, NFER.

CANCINO, H., ROSANSKY, E. and SCHUMANN, J. (1978) The acquisition of English negatives and interrogatives by native Spanish speakers. In Hatch, E. (ed.).

CANDLIN, C. (ed. & trans.). (1981) *The Communicative Teaching of English*, Longman.

CARROLL, J. (1967) Foreign language proficiency levels attained by language majors near graduation from college, *Foreign Language Annals*, **1**, 131–51.

CAZDEN, C., CANCINO, H., ROSANSKY, E. and SCHUMANN, J. (1975) *Second Language Acquisition Sequences in Children, Adolescents and Adults*, Final Report, United States Department of Health, Education and Welfare.

CHAUDRON, C. (1983) Foreigner talk in the clasroom—an aid to learning? In Seliger, H. and Long, M. (eds.).

CHESTERFIELD, R. and CHESTERFIELD, K. (1983) Natural order in children's use of second language learning strategies, mimeograph paper.

CHIHARA, T. and OLLER, J. (1978) Attitudes and attained proficiency in EFL: a sociolinguistic study of adult Japanese speakers. *Language Learning*, **28**, 1, 55–68.

CHOMSKY, N. (1959) Review of 'Verbal Behaviour' by B. F. Skinner. *Language*, **35**, 26–58.

CHOMSKY, N. (1965) *Aspects of the Theory of Syntax*, MIT Press.

CHUN, J. (1979) The importance of the language-learning situation: is 'immersion' the same as the 'sink-or-swim method'? *Working Papers on Bilingualism*, **18**, 136–61.

CLARK, R. (1974) Performing without competence. *Journal of Child Language*, **1**, 1–10.

COHEN, A. and SWAIN, M. (1976) Bilingual education: the 'immersion' model in the North American Context. *TESOL Quarterly*, **10**, 1.

COOK, V. (1981/2) Second language acquisition from an interactionist viewpoint. *Interlanguage Studies Bulletin*, **6**, 1, 93–111.

CORDER, S. (1967) The significance of learners' errors. *IRAL*, **5**, 161–9.

CORDER, S. (1974) Error analysis. In Allen, J. and Corder, S. (eds.), *The Edinburgh Course in Applied Linguistics*, Vol 3, Oxford University Press.

CORDER, S. (1976) The study of interlanguage. In *Proceedings of the Fourth International Congress in Applied Linguistics*, Hochschulverlag.

CORDER, S. (1977) Language teaching and learning: a social encounter. In Brown, D., Yorio, C. and Crymes, R. (eds.), *On TESOL '77*, Teachers of English to Speakers of Other Languages.

CORDER, S. (1978a) Strategies of communication. In *AFinla*, **23**.

CORDER, S. (1978b) Language distance and the magnitude of the language learning task. *Studies in Second Language Acquisition*, **II**, 1.

CORDER, S. (1981) Formal simplicity and functional simplification in second language acquisition. In Andersen, R. (ed.), *New Dimensions in Second Language Acquisition Research*, Newbury House.

CROSS, T. (1977) Mothers' speech adjustments: the contribution of selected child listener variables. In Snow, C. and Ferguson, C. (eds.), *Talking to Children*, Cambridge University Press.

CUMMINS, J. (1981) The role of primary language development in promoting educational success for language minority students. In *Schooling and Language Minority Students: a Theoretical Framework and Evaluation*, pp. 3–49, Evaluation, Dissemination and Assessment Center, California State University.

DICKERSON, L. (1975) The learner's interlanguage as a system of variable rules. *TESOL Quarterly*, **9**, 4, 401–7.

DICKSON, W. (1982) Creating communication-rich classrooms: insights from the sociolinguistic and referential traditions. In Wilkinson, L. (ed.), *Communicating in the Classroom*, Academic Press.

DULAY, H. and BURT, M. (1973) Should we teach children syntax? *Language Learning*, **23**, 245–58.

DULAY, H. and BURT, M. (1974) Natural sequences in child second language acquisition. *Language Learning*, **24**, 37–53.

DULAY, H. and BURT, M. (1978) Some remarks on creativity in language acquisition. In Ritchie, W. (ed.), *Second Language Acquisition Research*, Academic Press.

DULAY, H., BURT, M. and KRASHEN, S. (1982) *Language Two*, Oxford University Press.

EDWARDS, A. and FURLONG, V. (1978) *The Language of Teaching*, Heinemann Educational.

ELLIS, R. (1980) Classroom interaction and its relation to second language learning. *RELC Journal*, **11**, 2, 29–48.

ELLIS, R. (1981) The role of input in language acquisition: some implications for second language teaching. *Applied Linguistics*, **2**, 1, 70–82.

ELLIS, R. (1982a) The origins of interlanguage. *Applied Linguistics*, **3**, 3, 207–23.

ELLIS, R. (1982b) Discourse processes in classroom second language development. Unpublished doctoral thesis, University of London.

ELLIS, R. (1982c) Informal and formal approaches to communicative language teaching, *ELT Journal*, **36**, 2, 73–81.

ELLIS, R. (1984) Can syntax be taught?: a study of the effects of formal instruction on the acquisition of WH questions by children, *Applied Linguistics*, **5**, 2.

ELLIS, R. and TOMLINSON, B. (1980) *Teaching Secondary English: a Guide to the Teaching of English as a Second Language*, Longman.

ELLIS, R. and WELLS, G. (1980) Enabling factors in adult–child discourse. *First Language*, **1**, 46–82.

FAERCH, C. and Kaspar, G. (1980) Processes in foreign language learning and communication. *Interlanguage Studies Bulletin*, **5**, 1, 47–118.

FATHMAN, A. (1975) The relationship between age and second language productive ability, *Language Learning*, **25**, 2, 245–53.

FATHMAN, A. (1976) Variables affecting the successful learning of English as a second language. *TESOL Quarterly*, **10**, 4, 433–41.

FELIX, S. (1977) Kreative and reproduktive Kompetenz in Zweitsprachenwerb. In Huntfield, H. (ed.), *Neue Perspectiven der Fremdsprachendidaktik*, Kronberg.

FELIX, S. (1978) Some differences between first and second language acquisition. In Waterson, N. and Snow, C. (eds.), *The Development of Communication*, Wiley.

FELIX, S. (1980) Cognition and development: a German child's acquisition of question words. In Nehls, D. (ed.), *Studies in Language Acquisition*, Julius Groos Verlag.

FELIX, S. (ed.) (1980) *Second Language Development*, Gunter Narr Verlag.

FELIX, S. (1981) The effect of formal instruction on second language acquisition, *Language Learning*, **31**, 1, 87–112.

FERGUSON, C. (1971) Absence of copula and the notion of simplicity. In Hymes, D. (ed.) *Pidginization and Creolization of Languages*, Cambridge University Press.

FERGUSON, C. and DEBOSE, C. (1977) Simplified registers, broken languages and pidginization. In Valdman, A. (ed.), *Pidgin and Creole*, Indiana University Press.

FERRIER, L. (1978) Some observations of error in context. In Waterson, N. and Snow, C. (eds.), *The Development of Communication*, Wiley & Sons.

FILLMORE, C. (1968) The case for case. In Bach, E. and Harms, R. (eds.), *Universals of Linguistic Theory*, Holt Rinehart & Winston.

FILLMORE, W. (1976) The second time around: cognitive and social strategies in second language acquisition, unpublished doctoral thesis, University of Stanford.

FILLMORE, W. (1979) Individual differences in second language acquisition. In Fillmore, C., Kempler, D. and Wang, W. (eds.), *Individual Differences in Language Ability and Behaviour*, Academic Press.

FILLMORE, W. (1982) Instructional language as linguistic input: second-language learning in classrooms. In Wilkinson, L. (ed.), *Communicating in the Classroom*, Academic Press.

FREED, B. (1980) Talking to foreigners versus talking to children; similarities and differences. In Scarcella, R. and Krashen, S. (eds.), *Research in Second Language Acquisition*, Newbury House.

FURROW, D., NELSON, K. and BENEDICT, H. (1979) Mothers' speech to children and syntactic development: some simple relationships. *Journal of Child Language*, **6**, 423–42.

GAIES, S. (1977) The nature of linguistic input in formal second language learning: linguistic and communicative strategies. In Brown, H., Yorio, C. and Crymes, R. (eds.), *On TESOL '77*, Teachers of English to Speakers of Other Languages.

GAIES, S. (1979) Linguistic input in first and second language learning. In Eckman, F. and Hastings, A. (eds.), *Studies in First and Second Language Acquisition*, Newbury House.

GARDNER, R. (1980) On the validity of affective variables in second language acquisition: conceptual, contextual and statistical considerations. *Language Learning*, **30**, 2, 255–70.

GARDNER, R. and LAMBERT, W. (1972) *Attitudes and Motivation in Second Language Learning*, Newbury House.

GARVEY, C. (1977) Play with language and speech. In Ervin-Tripp, S. and Mitchell-Kernan, C. (eds.), *Child Discourse*, Academic Press.

GENESEE, F. (1982) Experimental neuropsychological research on second language processing, *TESOL Quarterly*, **16**, 3, 315–24.

GREENFIELD, P. and DENT, C. (1980) A developmental study of the communication of meaning: the role of uncertainty and information. In Nelson, K. (ed.), *Children's Language*, *Vol.* 2, Gardner's Press.

GREENFIELD, P. and SMITH, J. (1976) *The Structure of Communication*, Academic Press.

GREMMO, M., HOLEC, H. and RILEY, P. (1977) *Interactional Structure: the Role of Role*, Melanges Pedagogiques, CRAPEL.

GREMMO, M., HOLEC, H. and RILEY, P. (1978) *Taking the Initiative: Some Pedagogical Applications of Discourse Analysis*, Melanges Pedagogiques, CRAPEL.

GUILLAME, P. (1973) First stages of sentence formation in children's speech, translated from French by Clark, E. In Ferguson, C. and Slobin, D. (eds.), *Studies of Child Language Development*, Holt Rinehart & Winston.

GUMPERZ, J. and HERAMSIMCHUK, E. (1972) The conversational analysis of social meaning: a study of classroom interaction. In Shuy, R. (ed.), *Sociolinguistics: Current Trends and Perspectives*, Georgetown Monographs in Language and Linguistics.

HAKUTA, K. (1974) A preliminary report of the development of grammatical morphemes in a Japanese girl learning English as a second language. *Working Papers on Bilingualism*, **3**, 18–43.

HALE, T. and BUDAR, E. (1970) Are TESOL classes the only answer? *Modern Language Journal*, **54**, 487–92.

HALLIDAY, M. (1980) Language as code and language as behaviour: a systemic-functional interpretation of the nature and ontogenesis of dialogue. In Lamb, S. and Makkai, A. (eds.), *Semiotics of Culture and Language*, Twin Willows.

HARMER, J. (1982) What is communicative? *ELT Journal*, **36**, 3, 164–8.

HATCH, E. (ed.) (1978a) *Second Language Acquisition*, Newbury House.

HATCH, E. (1978b) Discourse analysis and second language acquisition. In Hatch, E. (ed.).

HATCH, E. (1978c) Discourse analysis, speech acts and second language acquisition. In Ritchie, W. (ed.), *Second Language Acquisition Research*, Academic Press.

HATCH, E., PECK, S. and WAGNER-GOUGH, J. (1979) A look at process in child second-language acquisition. In Ochs, E. and Schieffelin, B. (eds.), *Developmental Pragmatics*, Academic Press.

HENDRICKSON, J. (1978) Error correction in foreign language teaching: recent theory, research and practice. *Modern Language Journal*, **LXII**, 8, 387–98.

HENZL, V. (1979) Foreigner talk in the classroom. *IRAL*, **XVII**, 2, 159–65.

HERNANDÉZ-CHAVÉZ, E. (1977) The development of semantic relations in child second language acquisition. In Burt, M., Dulay, H. and Finocchiaro, M. (eds.), *Viewpoints on English as a Second Language*, Regents.

HOLLEY, F. and KING, J. (1975) Imitation and correction in foreign language learning. In Schumann, J. and Stenson, N. (eds.), *New Frontiers in Second Language Learning*, Newbury House.

HOSENFELD, C. (1976) Learning about language: discovering our students' strategies. *Foreign Language Annals*, **9**, 2, 117–29.

HUANG, J. and HATCH, E. (1978) A Chinese child's acquisition of English. In Hatch, E. (ed.).

JAMES, J. (1980) Learner variation: the monitor model and language learning strategies. *Interlanguage Studies Bulletin*, **2**, 2, 99–111.

JOHNSON, K. (1982) *Communicative Syllabus Design and Methodology*, Pergamon.

KEENAN, E. and SCHIEFFELIN, B. (1976) Topic as a discourse notion: a study of topic in the conversations of children and adults. In Li C. (ed.), *Subject and Topic*, Academic Press.

KLIMA, E. and BELLUGI, V. (1966) Syntactic regularities in the speech of children. In Lyons, J. and Wales, R. (eds.), *Psycholinguistic Papers*, Edinburgh University Press.

KRASHEN, S. (1977) Some issues relating to the monitor model. In Brown, H., Yorio, C. and Crymes, R. (eds.), *On TESOL '77*, Teachers of English as a Second Language.

KRASHEN, S. (1978) Individual variation in the use of the monitor. In Ritchie, W. (ed.), *Second Language Acquisition Research*, Academic Press.

KRASHEN, S. (1981a) Bilingual education, acquiring English and the case of Richard Rodriquez, mimeograph, University of Southern California (also CABE Newsletter).

KRASHEN, S. (1981b) *Second Language Acquisition and Second Language Learning*, Pergamon Press, Oxford.

KRASHEN, S. (1981c) Consciousness raising and the second language acquirer: a response to Sharwood-Smith, mimeograph, University of Southern California.

KRASHEN, S. (1982) *Principles and Practice in Second Language Acquisition*, Pergamon Press, Oxford.

KRASHEN, S. and SCARCELLA, R. (1978) On routines and patterns in language acquisition and performance. *Language Learning*, **28**, 283–300.

KRASHEN, S. and SELIGER, H. (1975) The essential characteristics of formal instruction. *TESOL Quarterly*, **9**, 173–83.

KRASHEN, S. and SELIGER, H. (1976) The role of formal and informal linguistic environments in adult second language learning. *International Journal of Psycholinguistics*, **3–4**(5), 15–20.

KRASHEN, S. and TERREL, T. (1983) *The Natural Approach: Language Acquisition in the Classroom*, Pergamon Press, Oxford.

KRASHEN, S., BUTLER, J., BIRNBAUM, R. and ROBERTSON, J. (1978) Two studies in language acquisition and language learning. *ITL: Review of Applied Linguistics*, **39–40**, 73–92.

KRASHEN, S., JONES, C., ZELINKSI, S. and USPRICH, C. (1978) How important is instruction? *ELT Journal*, **XXXII**, 4, 257–61.

KRASHEN, S., SELIGER, H. and HARTNETT, D. (1974) Two studies in adult second language learning. *Kritikon Litterarum*, **3**, 220–8.

LABOV, W. (1970) The study of language in its social context, *Studium Generale*, **23**, 30–87.

LADO, R. (1964) *Language Teaching*, McGraw Hill.

LaFORGE, P. (1979) Reflection in the context of community language learning, *ELT Journal*, **33**.

LAKE, S. and STOKES, J. (1983) Survey review: information gap materials. *ELT Journal*, **37**, 1, 89–94.

LARSEN-FREEMAN, D. (1976) An explanation for the morpheme accuracy order of learners of English as a second language. *Language Learning*, **26**, 1, 125–35.

LARSEN-FREEMAN, D. (1978) Evidence of the need for a second language acquisition index of development. In Ritchie, W. (ed.), *Second Language Acquisition Research*, Academic Press.

LARSEN-FREEMAN, D. (ed.) (1980) *Discourse Analysis in Second Language Acquisition Research*, Newbury House.

LENNEBERG, E. (1967) *Biological Foundations of Language*, Wiley & Sons.

LEOPOLD, W. (1949) *Speech Development of a Bilingual Child: a Linguist's Record, Vol. 3 Grammar and General Problems in the First Two Years*, Northwestern University Press.

LEOPOLD, W. (1954) A child's learning of two languages, *Georgetown University Round Table on Languages and Linguistics*, 7, 19–30, Georgetown University Press.

LIGHTBOWN, P. (1983) Exploring relationships between developmental and instructional sequences in L2 acquisition. In Seliger, H. and Long, M. (eds.).

LIGHTBOWN, P., SPADA, N. and WALLACE, R. (1980) Some effects of instruction on child and adolescent ESL learners. In Scarcella, R. and Krashen, S. (eds.), *Research in Second Language Acquisition*, Newbury House.

LITTLEWOOD, W. (1981) *Communicative Language Teaching*, Cambridge University Press.

LOCOCO, V. (1976) A comparison of three methods for the collection of L2 data: free composition, translation and picture description, *Working Papers on Bilingualism*, **8**, 59–86.

LONG, M. (1977) Teacher feedback on learner error: mapping cognitions. In Brown, H., Yorio, C. and Crymes, R. (eds.), *On TESOL '77*, Teachers of English to Speakers of Other Languages.

LONG, M. (1980) Inside the 'black box': methodological issues in classroom research on language learning. *Language Learning*, **30**, 1, 135–7.

LONG, M. (1981a) Input, interaction and second language acquisition, Paper presented at the New York Academy of Sciences Conference on Native and Foreign Language Acquisition.

LONG, M. (1981b) Questions in foreigner talk discourse. *Language Learning*, **31**, 1, 135–57.

LONG, M. (1983a) Does second language instruction make a difference? A review of the research, *TESOL Quarterly*, **17**, 3, 359–82.

LONG, M. (1983b) Native speaker/non-native speaker conversation and the negotiation of comprehensible input, *Applied Linguistics*, **4**, 2, 126–41.

LONG, M. and SATO, C. (1983) Classroom foreigner talk discourse: forms and functions of teachers' questions. In Seliger, H. and Long, M. (eds.).

LOVEDAY, L. (1982) *The Sociolinguistics of Learning and Using a Non-native Language*, Pergamon Press, Oxford.

LYONS, J. (1969) *Introduction to Theoretical Linguistics*, Cambridge University Press.

McDONOUGH, S. (1981) *Psychology in Foreign Language Teaching*, Allen & Unwin.

McLAUGHLIN, B. (1978) The monitor model: some methodological considerations. *Language Learning*, **28**, 2, 309–32.

MacNamara, (1973) Nurseries, streets and classrooms: some comparisons and deductions. *Modern Language Journal*, **57**, 250–4.

McTear, M. (1975) Structure and categories of foreign language teaching sequences. In Allwright, R. (ed.), *Working Papers: Language Teaching Classroom Research*, University of Essex, Department of Language and Linguistics.

Martin, G. (1980) English language acquisition: the effects of living with an American family. *TESOL Quarterly*, **14**, 3, 388–90.

Mason, C. (1971) The revelance of intensive training in English as a foreign language for university students. *Language Learning*, **21**, 2, 197–204.

Milon, J. (1974) The development of negation in English by a second language learner. *TESOL Quarterly*, **8**, 2, 137–43.

Nelson, K. and Gruendel, J. (1979) At morning it's lunchtime: a scriptal view of children's dialogues. *Discourse Processes*, **2**, 73–94.

Newmark, L. (1966) How not to interfere with language learning. *International Journal of American Linguistics*, **32**, 1, II, 77–83.

Newport, E., Gleitman, H. and Gleitman, L. (1977) Mother I'd rather do it myself: some effects and non-effects of maternal speech styles. In Snow, C. and Ferguson, C. (eds.), *Talking to Children*, Cambridge University Press.

Ochs, E. (1979) Planned and unplanned discourse. In Givon, T. (ed.), *Syntax and Semantics, Vol 12 Discourse and Semantics*, Academic Press.

Perkins, K. and Larsen-Freeman, D. (1975) The effect of formal language instruction on the order of morpheme acquisition. *Language Learning*, **25**, 2, 237–43.

Phillips, S. (1972) Participant structures and communicative competence: Warm Springs children in community and classroom. In Cazden, C., John, V. and Hymes, D. (eds.), *Functions of Language in the Classroom*, Teachers College Press.

Pickett, G. (1978) *The Foreign Language Learning Process*, British Council.

Pienemann, M. (1980) The second language acquisition of immigrant children. In Felix, S. (ed.).

Politzer, R. (1980) Requesting in elementary school classrooms. *TESOL Quarterly*, **14**, 2, 165–74.

Politzer, R. and Weiss, L. (undated), *Improving achievement in foreign language*, The Center for Curriculum Development.

Politzer, R., Ramirez, A. and Lewis, S. (1981) Teaching standard English in the third grade: classroom functions of language. *Language Learning*, **31**, 1, 171–93.

Prabhu, N. (1981) 'Bangalore Project' 1980, mimeographed report, Institute of Education, University of London.

Ravem, R. (1968) Language acquisition in a second language environment. *IRAL*, **6**, 2, 175–85.

Ravem, R. (1974) The development of WH questions in first and second language learners. In Richards, J. (ed.).

Revell, J. (1979) *Teaching Techniques for Communicative English*, MacMillan.

Richards, J. (ed.) *Error Analysis*, Longman.

Richards, J. (1974) A non-contrastive approach to error analysis. In Richards, J. (ed.).

Rivers, W. (1964) *The Psychologist and the Foreign Language Teacher*, University of Chicago.

Rivers, W. and Temperley, M. (1978) *A Practical Guide to the Teaching of English*, Oxford University Press.

Roberts, J. (1982) Recent developments in ELT—Part 1. *Language Teaching*, **15**, 2, 94–105.

ROSANSKY, E. (1975) The critical period for the acquisition of language: some cognitive development considerations. *Working Papers on Bilingualism*, **6**, 92–102.

ROSANSKY, E. (1976) Methods and morphemes in second language acquisition research. *Language Learning*, **26**, 2, 409–25.

SCARCELLA, R. and HIGA, C. (1981) Input, negotiation and age differences in second language acquisition. *Language Learning*, **31**, 2, 409–37.

SCHATZ, M. (1978) On the development of communicative understandings: an early strategy for interpreting and responding to messages. *Journal of Cognitive Psychology*, **10**, 271–301.

SCHERER, A. and WERTHEIMER, M. (1964) *A Psycholinguistic Experiment in Foreign Language Teaching*, McGraw-Hill.

SCHOUTEN, M. (1979) The missing data in second language learning research. *Interlanguage Studies Bulletin*, **4**, 3–14.

SCHUMANN, J. (1976) Second language acquisition research: getting a more global look at the learner. In Brown, H. (ed.), *Papers in Second Language Acquisition*, Language Learning Special Issue, 4.

SCHUMANN, J. (1978) *The Pidginization Process: a Model for Second Language Acquisition*, Newbury House.

SCHUMANN, J. (1980) The acquisition of English relative clauses by second language learners. In Scarcella, R. and Krashen, S. (eds.), *Research in Second Language Acquisition*, Newbury House.

SCOLLON, R. (1976) *Conversations with a One Year Old*, University of Hawaii.

SELIGER, H. (1977) Does practice make perfect?: a study of interaction patterns and L2 competence. *Language Learning*, **27**, 2, 263–75.

SELIGER, H. (1979) On the nature and function of language rules in language teaching. *TESOL Quarterly*, **13**, 3, 359–69.

SELIGER, H. (1982) On the possible role of the right hemisphere in second language acquisition. *TESOL Quarterly*, **16**, 2, 307–14.

SELIGER, H. and LONG, M. (eds.), (1983) *Classroom Oriented Research in Second Language Acquisition*, Newbury House.

SELINKER, L. (1972) Interlanguage. *IRAL*, **10**, 3, 209–30.

SHAPIRA, R. (1978) The non-learning of English: a case study of an adult. In Hatch, E. (ed.).

SHARWOOD-SMITH, M. (1981) Consciousness-raising and the second language learner. *Applied Linguistics*, **11**, 2, 159–69.

SINCLAIR-DE-ZWART, H. (1973) Language acquisition and cognitive development. In Moore, T. (ed.), *Cognitive Development and the Acquisition of Language*, Academic Press.

SINCLAIR, J. and BRAZIL, D. (1982) *Teacher Talk*, Oxford University Press.

SINCLAIR, J. and COULTHARD, M. (1975) *Towards an Analysis of Discourse*, Oxford University Press.

SLOBIN, D. (1977) Language change in childhood and in history. In MacNamara, J. (ed.), *Language Learning and Thought*, Academic Press.

SMITH, F. (1982) *Writing and the Writer*, Heinemann.

SMITH, P. Jr. (1970) *A comparison of the cognitive and audiolingual approaches to foreign language instruction, The Pennsylvania foreign language project*, The Center for Curriculum Development.

SNOW, C. (1976) The language of mother-child relationship. In Rogers, S. (ed.), *They Don't Speak our Language*, Arnold.

SNOW, C. and HOEFNAGEL-HÖHLE, M. (1978) Age differences in second language acquisition. In Hatch, E. (ed.).

STEINBERG, D. (1982) *Psycholinguistics: Language, Mind and World*, Longman.

STERN, H. (1981) Communicative language teaching and learning: toward a synthesis. In Alatis, J., Altman, H. and Alatis, P. (eds.), *The Second Language Classroom*, Oxford University Press.

STEVICK, E. (1976) *Memory, Meaning and Method*, Newbury House.

STEVICK, E. (1980) *Teaching Languages: a Way and Ways*, Newbury House.

STEVICK, E. (1982) *Teaching and Learning Languages*, Cambridge University Press.

STREVENS, P. (1977) A theoretical model of the language learning/teaching process. In Strevens, P., *New Orientations in the Teaching of English*, Oxford University Press.

STREVENS, P. (1978) Special purpose language learning: a perspective. In Kinsella, V. (ed.), *Language Teaching and Linguistics: Surveys*, Cambridge University Press.

STRONG, M. (1983) Social styles and second language acquisition of Spanish speaking kindergartners. *TESOL Quarterly*, **17**, 2, 241–58.

STUBBS, M. (1976) Keeping in touch; some functions of teacher talk. In Stubbs, M. and Delamont, S. (eds.), *Explorations in Classroom Observation*, Wiley and Sons.

SVARTVIK, J. (ed.) (1973) *Errata: Papers in Error Analysis*, Gleerup.

SWAIN, M. (1981) Target use in the wider environment as a factor in its acquisition. In Andersen, R. (ed.), *New Dimensions in Second Language Acquisition Research*, Newbury House.

TARONE, E. (1982) Systematicity and attention in interlanguage. *Language Learning*, **32**, 1, 69–82.

TARONE, E. (1983) On the variability of interlanguage systems. *Applied Linguistics*, **4**, 2, 142–63.

TARONE, E., COHEN, A. and DUMAS, G. (1976) A closer look at some interlanguage terminology: a framework for communication strategies. *Working Papers on Bilingualism*, **9**, 76–90.

TARONE, E., SWAIN, M. and FATHMAN, A. (1976) Some limitations to the classroom applications of current second language acquisition research. *TESOL Quarterly*, **10**, 1, 19–31.

TERREL, T. (1977) A natural approach to second language acquisition and learning. *Modern Language Journal*, **6**, 325–37.

TERREL, T., GOMEZ, E. and MARISCAL, J. (1980) Can acquisition take place in the language classroom? In Scarcella, R. and Krashen. S. (eds.), *Research in Second Language Acquisition*, Newbury House.

TONEY, T. (1983) Survey review: guides for language learners. *ELT Journal*, **37**, 4, 352–8.

TURNER, D. (1978) The effect of instruction on second language learning and second language acquisition. Paper presented at 12th annual TESOL convention, Mexico City.

UPSHUR, J. (1968) Four experiments on the relation between foreign language teaching and learning. *Language Learning*, **18**, 1 and 2, 111–24.

VAN EK, J. (1976) *The Threshold Level for Modern Language Learning in Schools*, Longman.

VARADI, T. (1973) Strategies of target language learner communication: message adjustment, Paper presented at VI Conference of the Romanian–English Linguistic Project in Timisoara.

VYGOTSKY, L. (1962) *Thought and Language*. MIT Press.

WAGNER-GOUGH, J. (1975) Comparative studies in second language learning. *CAL-ERIC/CLL Series on Languages and Linguistics*, **26**.

WARDHAUGH, R. (1970) The contrastive analysis hypothesis. *TESOL Quarterly*, **4**, 122–30.

WELLS, G. (1974) Learning to code experience through language. *Journal of Child Language*, **1**, 243–69.

WELLS, G. (1979) Adjustments in adult–child conversation: some effects of interaction. In Giles, H., Robinson, W. and Smith, P. (eds.), *Language: Social Psychological Perspectives*, Pergamon Press, Oxford.

WELLS, G. (1981) Becoming a communicator. In Wells, G. *et al.*, *Learning Through Interaction*, Cambridge University Press.

WELLS, G. and MONTGOMERY, M. (1981) Adult–child interaction at home and at school. In French, P. and MacLure, M. (eds.) *Adult–child Conversation*, Croom Helm.

WELLS, G. and ROBINSON, W. (1982) The role of adult speech in language development. In Fraser, C. and Scherer, K. (eds.), *Advances in the Social Psychology of Language*, Cambridge University Press.

WELLS, G., BARNES, S., GUTFREUND, M. and SATTERLY, D. (forthcoming) Characteristics of adult speech which predict children's language development, to appear in *Journal of Child Language*.

WELLS, G., MONTGOMERY, M. and MACLURE, M. (1979) The development of discourse: a report on work in progress, *Journal of Pragmatics*, **3**, 337–80.

WESCHE, W. and READY, D. (1983) Foreigner-talk discourse in the university classroom, Paper given at the University of Michigan Conference on Applied Linguistics.

WIDDOWSON, H. (1975) The significance of simplification. In *Studies in Second Language Acquisition*, 11, 1, University of Indiana Linguistic Club. Also in Widdowson, H. (1979), *Explorations in Applied Linguistics*, Oxford University Press.

WIDDOWSON, H. (1978) *Teaching Language as Communication*, Oxford University Press.

WIDDOWSON, H. (1979a) Approaches to discourse. In Widdowson, H., *Explorations in Applied Linguistics*, Oxford University Press.

WIDDOWSON, H. (1979b) Rules and procedures in discourse analysis. In Myers, T. (ed.), *The Development of Conversation and Discourse*, Edinburgh University Press.

WIGHT, J., NORRIS, R. and WORSLEY, F. (1972) *Concept 7–9 Unit 3: Communication*, E. J. Arnold.

WILKINS, D. (1976) *Notional Syllabuses*, Oxford University Press.

WODE, H. (1976) Developmental sequences in naturalistic L2 acquisition. *Working Papers on Bilingualism*, **11**, 1–31.

WODE, H. (1978) The L1 vs L2 acquisition of English interrogation. *Working Papers on Bilingualism*, **15**, 37–57.

WODE, H. (1980a) Operating principles and 'universals' in L1, L2 and FLT. In Nehls, D. (ed.), *Studies in Language Acquisition*, Julius Groos Verlag.

WODE, H. (1980b) *Learning a Second Language 1. An Integrated View of Language Acquisition*, Gunter Narr Verlag.

WOLL, B., FERRIER, L. and WELLS, G. (1975) Children and their parents—who starts the talking, why and when, Paper presented at the Conference on Language and the Social Context, Stirling University.

YORIO, C. (1980) Conventionalized language forms and the development of communicative competence. *TESOL Quarterly*, **XIV**, 4, 433–42.

Appendix A

Notational Conventions for Transcripts

---

1. The teacher's or researcher's utterances are given on the left-hand side of the page.
2. The pupils' utterances are given on the right-hand side of the page.
3. The teacher's utterances are labelled 'T', the researcher's utterances are labelled 'R' and the pupils' utterances, if identified are labelled by their initials, and, if not, by 'P'.
4. Each 'utterance' is numbered for ease of reference in the discussion of the transcripts. An 'utterance' consists of a single tone unit except where two tone units are syntactically joined by means of a subordinator or other linking word or contrastive stress has been used to make what would 'normally' be a single tone unit into more than one.
5. Pauses are indicated in brackets:
   (.) indicates a pause of a second or shorter;
   (.3.) indicates a pause of 3 seconds, etc.
6. XXX is used to indicate speech that could not be deciphered.
7. Phonetic transcription (IPA) is used when the pupils' pronunciation is markedly different from the teacher's pronunciation and also when it was not possible to identify the English word the pupils were using.
8. ... indicates that the speaker did not complete an utterance, i.e. that his speech 'tailed off'.
9. Words are underlined in order to show
   overlapping speech between two speakers;
   very heavily stressed words.
10. A limited amount of contextual information is given, where appropriate in brackets.

Index

(Numbers in brackets refer to notes)
